The Flight and Fall of the Eagle

A History of Medieval Germany 800-1648

John R. Sommerfeldt

Hamilton Books

An Imprint of
Rowman & Littlefield
Lanham • Boulder • New York • Toronto • Plymouth, UK

Copyright © 2017 by Hamilton Books
4501 Forbes Boulevard, Suite 200, Lanham, Maryland 20706
Hamilton Books Acquisitions Department (301) 459-3366

Unit A, Whitacre Mews, 26-34 Stannary Street,
London SE11 4AB, United Kingdom

All rights reserved
Printed in the United States of America
British Library Cataloguing in Publication Information Available

Library of Congress Control Number: 2016948978
ISBN: 978-0-7618-6838-5 (pbk : alk. paper)—ISBN: 978-0-7618-6839-2 (electronic)

∞™ The paper used in this publication meets the minimum requirements of American National Standard for Information Sciences Permanence of Paper for Printed Library Materials, ANSI/NISO Z39.48-1992.

This book is dedicated to my dear wife,
Gail N. Lord,
and to the readers of its many versions,
readers who became my collaborators

Marsha Dutton
Ohio University

E. Rozanne Elder
Western Michigan University

Kelly Gibson
University of Dallas

Daniel M. La Corte
Saint Ambrose University

John R. Sommerfeldt, Jr.
Marietta, Georgia

Thomas J. Sommerfeldt
Elk Rapids, Michigan

Francis R. Swietek
University of Dallas

Kaitlyn M. Willy
University of North Texas

Contents

Preface	ix
Map: The Empire in the Eleventh and Twelfth Centuries	xi
1 The Eagle Is Born	1
2 Restoring the Roman Empire	5
A. Prelude to Empire	5
B. The Carolingians Replaced	7
C. Protecting the Homeland	10
D. Creating a State	12
E. Enlisting Leaders of the Church	13
F. Administering the Kingdom	14
G. Italy and Empire	16
H. The Ottonian Renaissance	17
J. Hrotswitha of Gandersheim	19
K. The End of the Old Warrior's Campaign	20
3 Growing Peace and Prosperity	23
A. The Agricultural Revolution	23
B. Otto II: Advances and Setbacks	26
C. Sources of Strength	29
D. A Flourishing Culture	29
4 A Vision of Christendom	31
A. The Early Years of Otto III	31
B. Pope Sylvester II	32
C. Adelbert of Prague, Boleslav the Bold, and Stephen of Hungary	33
D. Church Reform and Roman Restoration	34
E. Intellectual Life under Otto III	35

	F. The End of the Reign	36
5	Reform and Imperial Theocracy	37
	A. The King and Emperor	37
	B. Episcopal and Monastic Reform	38
	C. Imperial Theocracy	39
	D. The Making of the Theocrat	40
	E. The Governance of the Empire	41
	F. Universality and Regionalism	42
6	The Construction of a State	45
	A. Choosing the King	45
	B. The Governance of the Realm	46
	C. The Triumphant Warrior and Diplomat	49
	D. Conrad and the Church	51
	E. Death and Legacy	52
7	Apogee of Empire	55
	A. The Accession of Henry III	55
	B. The Governance of the Realm	56
	C. Dealing with Dukes and Kings	57
	D. Defending Frontiers	58
	E. The Benevolent Theocrat	58
	F. The Reform Captures Rome	59
8	The Investiture Conflict	63
	A. Reform: The Second Phase	63
	B. Henry IV	64
	C. The Battle Is Joined	66
	D. The Roots of the Struggle	69
9	The Great Settlement	71
	A. Henry V Ascends the Throne	71
	B. Pursuing a Compromise	74
	C. The Resolution	76
10	Kings, Cistercians, and Crusades	79
	A. Lothar the Saxon	79
	B. Cistercians and the Third Stage of the Reform	80
	C. The Schism of 1130	82
	D. The Reign of Conrad III	83
	E. Calling a New Crusade	83
	F. The Journey to the East	85
	G. The Other Crusades	86
11	Three Gifted Germans	89
	A. Anselm of Havelberg and the Idea of Progress	89
	B. Hildegard of Bingen: The Sibyl of the Rhine	91

	C. Otto of Freising Offers a Mirror for Princes	93
12	The Red-Bearded Ruler	97
	A. The Long Reign Begins	97
	B. Building a Power Base	98
	C. Capturing the Church	99
	D. Taming the Most Powerful	100
	E. The First Italian Expedition and the Diet of Besançon	100
	F. The Second Italian Expedition and the Diet of Roncaglia	102
	G. The Third and Fourth Expeditions	104
	H. The Fifth and Sixth Expeditions	105
	J. The Defiance of Henry the Lion	107
	K. The Third Crusade	108
	L. The Legacy	109
	M. Assessments	112
13	The Flowering of Medieval German Literature	113
14	The Turning Point	119
	A. Henry VI, an Ambitious Emperor	119
	B. Pope Innocent III	121
	C. The Much-disputed Succession	122
	D. The End of the Ottonian Empire	123
15	Political Reconstitution	127
	A. The Failure of Imperial Rule	127
	B. The Golden Bull	130
	C. Continuing Decentralization	132
	D. Territorialism	135
16	The Late Medieval Laity	139
	A. The Governing and Military Classes	139
	B. Merchants, Manufacturers, and Tradesmen	140
	C. The Farmers' Life	142
	D. Pandemic and Persecution	143
17	Thirteenth-Century Friars and Holy Women	145
	A. Blackfriars	146
	B. Holy Women	149
18	Fourteenth-Century Spiritual Leaders	157
	A. Meister Eckhart	157
	B. John Tauler	159
	C. Henry Suso	160
	D. John Ruusbroec	162
	E. Gert Groote and the Devotio Moderna	163
19	The Failure of the Institutional Church	165
	A. The Late Medieval Papacy	165

B. The Babylonian Captivity	165
C. The German Church: The Bishops	168
D. The German Church: Parish Life	168
E. Popular Piety	169
F. Indulgences	171

20 The Cusanus — 173
- A. Youth and Education — 173
- B. The Council of Basel — 174
- C. The Mission to Constantinople — 175
- D. The Papal Legate — 175
- E. The Reforming Cardinal — 176
- F. The Bishop of Brixen — 176
- G. The Wide Range of Intellectual Concerns — 177
- H. The Last Days — 178

21 The Death of the Eagle — 179
- A. Two German Reformers — 179
- B. The Indulgence Controversy — 180
- C. Biblical Editions and Translations — 181
- D. Grace and Free Choice — 182
- E. The Churches Split — 183
- F. The Thirty Years' War — 183

Genealogical Tables	187
The Saxon and Salian Kings of Germany	188
The Hohenstaufen and Their Rivals	189
The Luxemburg, Hapsburg, and Wittelsbach Rulers	190
Index I: Most Important Persons	191
Index II: Lands, Peoples, and Their Languages	195
Index III: Major Cities and Towns	197

Preface

I was but a lad when my father, Hans Sommerfeldt, would lecture the family, after Sunday dinner, on issues such as: "Why Helmut von Moltke was more important than Otto von Bismarck in the unification of Germany." All those gathered at the table were on the verge of sleep, though not so much as to attract Father's attention. I alone listened eagerly, and my fascination with German history has continued to this day–but only as a hobby.

Nevertheless, my father insisted to his dying day that the center of my academic interests was medieval German history. This book then is in some small way a verification of his claim, despite the fact that all of my other books have centered on intellectual history, especially that of the twelfth century.

Old men should have a hobby, I think, and I am an old man of eighty plus years. So, in writing this book I have returned to my old hobby: the history of Germany in the middle ages.

I have been hindered in teaching courses on this topic by the fact that there is no suitable text book in the English language. To be sure, there are books in English about the history of medieval Germany, but none of them address the full chronological range of the topic.

Another difficulty is that the books suitable for use as texts concentrate almost exclusively on political history. Politics were, of course, an essential part of the medieval German experience, but my own interests, and surely those of a wide audience, extend to other aspects of human culture–to economics, social experiences and structures, and the life of the mind. Given the wide range of topics addressed in this volume, I trust that it will be useful as a text book. I hope that it responds to the complaint of a colleague at another university who bemoaned the absence of a suitable text for her course on medieval Germany.

Like my last book, *Christianity in Culture,* this book was written for a wide audience, for anyone with intelligence and curiosity but no special training in historical scholarship. To this end I have called on a wide range of readers–housewives, engineers, public school teachers, and business executives–whose comments have assured me that the book is suitable for a lay audience. To keep my story accurate, I have also asked a number of scholars in many fields to read and comment on the early drafts of this book.

One example may suffice. When Daniel La Corte, a former student and now a professor of history, read my few lines in Chapter XVI on the origin of the Black Death, he wrote me a cautionary note. It seems that a new theory on the origin of that disease was being circulated. He sent me several articles from medical and scientific journals that supported the new interpretation. I then spoke of this to my well-read internist, Robert W. Israel, Jr., M.D., who sent me several additional articles on the subject. Finally, I brought up the subject at a family gathering. My wife's daughter and son-in-law, both pathologists, were celebrating with us and she provided a convincing explanation. The result of Dr. Robin Amirkhan's analysis, confirmed by her husband Dr. Nelson Amirkhan, is but a few lines in Chapter XVI, but a few lines in which I have considerable confidence. This is but one example of the generous assistance I have received in the writing of this book.

Assistance of another kind I received from my brother Tom, a mechanical engineer, and my son John, a manager in a major telecommunications firm. Both quickly returned their comments on each chapter. Their responses kept me from writing a book intelligible only to professional historians. Rozanne Elder, my very first and most brilliant graduate student, has now retired from highly valuable service to the scholarly world. She helped immensely, but in a quite different way. Rozanne has a splendid command of the English language, which served her well as editor of the hundreds of translations and studies brought forth by Cistercian Publications. Rozanne kindly read and revised–sometimes extensively–each chapter of this book. It is by far the better for her suggestions, almost all of which were incorporated into my text.

My deepest gratitude goes to my wife, Gail Lord, whose eagle eye caught many errors and whose tireless fingers typed the manuscript in its many successive forms. I am also grateful to Dean Hunter, her son and my friend, for creating the computer format for this book. My daughter and son, Kathy and John, are responsible for many contributions to this book.

John R. Sommerfeldt
University of Dallas

Map

The Empire in the Eleventh and Twelfth Centuries

The Empire in the Eleventh and Twelfth Centuries

Chapter One

The Eagle Is Born

On Christmas Day in the year 800, Pope Leo III anointed and crowned Charles, the king of the Franks, as Roman Emperor. Ever afterwards, from his day to ours, scholars and school children have referred to him as Charles the Great–or Charlemagne if they are French, Karl der Grosse if they are German. Although Charles' empire, comprising most of western Europe, was eventually split into countries we know as France and Germany, Italy, Belgium, and the Netherlands, his legacy lived one–especially in German speaking lands. He became the model for royal and imperial rule in Germany in the centuries that followed his death in 814. His popularity among Germans is shown by the enduring legend that he is still resting in a mountain lair and will come to life some day to restore the glories of his empire.

Charles was the model ruler, as we are told by his biographer Einhard. Charles, Einhard tells us, displayed the virtues that subsequent emperors sought to emulate: the Germanic warrior code, the tradition of classical scholarship, and the faith traditions of Christianity.

The education of medieval rulers largely followed Charles' practice and his program for his own sons, who, "as soon as their age permitted, had to learn to ride like true Franks and practice the arts of war and the chase." Charles and his medieval successors also followed another ancient Germanic educational practice: "During meals there was either singing or a reader to whom he could listen. Histories and the great deeds of men of old were read." Indeed, he "had all these old rough songs that celebrate the deeds and wars of ancient kings written out for transmission to posterity." Charles even "began a grammar of his native [Germanic] language."

Such aspirations to scholarship may seem strange in a Germanic warrior chief, but this was only the beginning of Charles' academic interests. Einhard relates that "the plan he adopted for his children's education was to have both boys and girls instructed in the liberal arts." In this his children were following in their father's footsteps, for Charles "was such a master of Latin that he could speak it as well as his native tongue." He was less fluent in Greek, though he could understand it well. Charles would often employ his spare time practicing the writing of Greek, but the moments he could devote to that pursuit were too rare to let him achieve great success.

In initiating a renewal of classical scholarship, a "Carolingian Renaissance," Charles was motivated both by his appreciation of the knowledge of antiquity and by practical considerations. His empire and its tributaries, which included much of western and central Europe, required educated administrators. There was no other or better way to educate them than by the liberal arts curriculum that had been devised in ancient times for the express purpose of preparing public officials.

Long before Charles' educational revival, the Church had adopted classical studies, finding them indispensable for learning, understanding, and teaching the Christian religion and thus serving as the educational prerequisite to leadership positions in the Church. Charles was eager to raise the level of competence of both civil and ecclesiastical officials throughout his empire. Consequently he mandated that all cathedrals and monasteries should establish schools or reform existing ones, so that talented lads–even from humble families–could prepare themselves for careers as counts, bishops, abbots, or scholars.

Einhard tells us that "Charles cherished the Christian religion with the greatest fervor and devotion." We learn that "he was a constant worshiper, attending church each morning and evening, and even after nightfall–in addition to attending daily Mass." His children went with him whenever possible, thus imbibing both Christian doctrine and practice. In addition to the Germanic sagas, Charles had selections from Scripture and the Church Fathers read at meals–his favorite source was the *City of God* of Saint Augustine of Hippo (354-430).

The result of Charles' efforts was a growing body of leaders who, like the emperor himself, exhibited or at least valued the best qualities of three cultures: Germanic, Christian, and classical. Like many other geniuses–Pericles the Athenian, the Roman Emperor Octavian Augustus, Saint Bernard of Clairvaux, and the reformer Martin Luther–Charles was not only a leader of society but also a sort of incarnation of the cultural forces that characterized his age. Charles exhibited in his life and thought the characteristics of something new: western European culture, the synthesis of Germanic, Christian, and classical traditions.

A synthesis is not merely a mixture of elements but a combination that produces something new. If we combine oxygen and hydrogen, the result is a simple mixture of gases. But if we throw a lighted match into that mixture, the result will be not only an explosion, but also water–a compound very different from the elements of which it is composed. Ancient elements, when combined, exploded in a strikingly similar way and yielded something entirely new: western culture.

Nothing new, however, is born without labor pains. There are, indeed, tensions in the synthesis that is western culture, some of which were already apparent even in Charles' day. A continuing problem in Christian culture is apparent from an examination of Charles' sex life. Einhard tells us, with some embarrassment, that his church-going hero married,

> a daughter of Desiderius, king of the Lombards, in response to his mother's bidding, but he repudiated her at the end of a year. He then married Hildegard, a woman of high birth and fathered three sons by her–Charles, Pepin, and Louis–and as many daughters–Hruodrud and Bertha and Gisela. He had three other daughters besides these–Theoderada, Hiltrud, and Ruodhaid–two by his third wife Fastrada and the third by a concubine whose name has escaped my memory. At the death of Fastrada he married Liutgard, who bore him no children. After her death he had three concubines: Gersuinda, by whom he had Adaltrud; Regina, who was the mother of Drogo and Hugo; and Ethelind, by whom he had Theodorich.

It does seem as if Charles kept a woman behind every curtain in the palace. And there is obviously some tension between this sort of behavior and the scriptural texts he had heard read aloud. Yet Charles, all his embarrassed contemporaries admitted, was a sincere, even an exemplary Christian. This schizoid sort of behavior has not disappeared from our own culture. We all know of people who attend church regularly on Sunday, but have no scruples about cheating their customers on Monday. Christianity delineates a rigorous standard of behavior which some people, even those sincerely professing that religion, find it difficult to maintain.

Another persistent tension in western culture has been the relationship of Church and state. One of Charles' favorite books, as we have seen, was Augustine's *City of God*. It would be quite fair to say that Charles saw his empire as the realization of the City of God on earth and that he considered himself its mayor. After all, the bishop of Rome, the patriarch of the West, had anointed him Roman emperor. He was surely God's agent on earth, chosen, like David of old, to rule God's people. And, indeed, Charles' nickname in the colloquies in his palace school was "David."

Charles appointed learned bishops, built churches, reformed monastic and cathedral schools, sponsored Christian missionaries, and sent alms to churches everywhere–notably those in Rome and the Holy Land. He also determined how church services were to be held and even made an unsuccessful stab at determining church doctrine by supporting a revival of a form of Arianism.

It is not that Charles denied the legitimate and traditional functions of the Church. It is simply that he thought himself the divinely appointed head of the Church–at least of its temporal affairs. But what of the sphere of competence of the clergy who preached and administered the sacraments? In a letter of 796 to Bishop Leo III of Rome, Charles declared: "It is our part, with the help of divine holiness, to defend, by armed strength everywhere, the holy Church of Christ from the outward onslaught of pagans and the ravages of infidels, to strengthen within the Church the knowledge of the Catholic faith." What was left to the bishops? Prayer–and that prayer surely included intercession for Charles and his armies.

The obvious difficulty with this sort of Church-state relationship, called Caesaropapism, is that religious goals can be ignored in the interest of the state. A good example is the forced baptism of Charles' enemies, the Saxons. He conquered them, lined them up at a river, and gave them a choice between emerging as Christians or not at all. Such forced conversions typified Charles' self-defined role as leader of Christianity. Nevertheless, many contemporary churchmen were appalled; they knew it took more than submersion to make a Christian. They also realized that this sort of identification of Christianity with submission to a conqueror would make the Saxons hate both. Caesaropapism would continue to plague western culture, as we shall see.

Chapter Two

Restoring the Roman Empire

A. PRELUDE TO EMPIRE

The Germanic peoples of the fourth and fifth centuries had entered the Roman Empire in search of new homes, greater security, and the benefits of late Roman civilization. In contrast, the barbarian invaders of the ninth century–the Vikings, Saracens, and Magyars–came to plunder, rape, enslave, and destroy. This wave of invasions would precipitate profound, indeed drastic, changes in western culture and civilization.

The annals of many a monastery allow us to reconstruct the terror and confusion caused by Viking raids from the North. In the late eighth and throughout the ninth centuries, fierce Northmen sailed out each spring from their homes in Norway, Denmark, and Sweden. They occupied much of England and Ireland and, able to reach virtually all of Europe through its waterways, wreaked havoc in France, Spain, and Italy. They also ventured into eastern Europe, establishing the new state of Rus at Kiev. These swashbuckling seafarers were ready to row and sail small shallow-draft boats across the rough Atlantic even as far as North America.

From the South, across the Mediterranean, sailed the Saracen warriors of North Africa. They too were great seamen and notorious pirates, but soon piracy failed to satisfy them. They conquered Sardinia (809), Corsica (810), and finally Sicily (899), and they established bases on the Italian mainland from which to plunder and terrorize the whole peninsula. Nor did southern France escape their devastating raids.

From the East, somewhat later than the other barbarians, came the Magyars. They swept out of central Asia, across the steppes of southern Russia and up the Danube, arriving in German lands at the end of the ninth century.

For over fifty years the German people suffered from the surprise attacks of these fierce horsemen.

In this time of dire need, the people of western Europe naturally turned to their governments for protection. That help did not usually come. Charles the Great's grandsons and their successors recklessly spent their energy and resources in virtually constant fraternal battles over territory and rarely came to the defense of their people. Even when willing to resist, these Carolingian rulers found it increasingly difficult to counter the highly mobile invaders. By the time an army could be assembled and ride to the relief of a city besieged by Vikings, the boats of their Nordic attackers had disappeared with their loot and captives back down the river on which they had come up from the sea, already heading up another river to plunder other towns and monasteries. As a result of these invasions and the incompetence of their rulers, the people of Europe suffered terribly.

The response to these crises differed radically from country to country, from region to region. In France and Italy the crises led to feudalism–a sort of do-it-yourself government established by private contract. Bishops, counts, abbots of monasteries–or anyone else willing and able to supply military and administrative leadership–were looked to by the people for protection and justice. Thus, the powers of government were either assumed by these people or conferred on them by a still greater authority.

Feudalism did not come to Germany at this time except along its western frontier. Instead, Germany became the center of a new revival of the Roman Empire. The reasons for this are several. For one thing, Germany was spared the attacks of the Saracens, who had found the Alps too formidable an obstacle to cross. Although the Vikings did sail up German rivers to plunder and destroy, few German people–even those living immediately to the south of Nordic lands–suffered extensively at their hands. Instructive is an entry for the year 883 made by a monk of Fulda in the annals of his abbey: "The Northmen, sailing up the Rhine, plundered and burned many villages. But Liutbert, the archbishop of Mainz, with a small band of troops, attacked those Vikings and, after killing many of them, recovered much of the treasure they had taken." The troops which the archbishop led likely included a large number of farmers. Unlike the society of France, where farmers were no longer trained to fight, German social classes were as yet mostly undifferentiated by occupation. In this largely tribal culture every man and boy was trained in the use of arms.

A story like that of Liutbert's response recurs in the Fulda annals for the year 885. In this case others joined the formidable archbishop:

> The Northmen entered the territory around Liège, looting all sorts of provisions to support their intended wintering there. But Liutbert, the archbishop of Mainz, and Count Heimrith, as well as others, fell suddenly upon the invaders,

killed many of them, and drove the others into a small stronghold. The Germans then recovered the provisions that the Northmen had collected. The Northmen, after enduring a long siege during which they suffered greatly from hunger, finally fled from their stronghold during the night.

The Vikings found it much more profitable to plunder the wealth of France than the less affluent and more competently defended areas in the eastern part of what had been Charles the Great's lands.

Against the Magyars, however, German warriors fought with little success. The German farmer had remained an infantryman. He could not stand alone against the tactics of a mounted adversary who appeared suddenly from nowhere, struck swiftly, and used his arrows to deadly effect. A monk of an abbey at Trier supplies some grim data:

> In 907, the Bavarians were defeated with great bloodshed by the Magyars. Duke Arnulf was killed in this battle. In 908, the Magyars again crossed our borders and again devastated Saxony and Thuringia. In 909, the Magyars forced their way into Swabia. In 910, the Franconians fought on their frontier with Bavaria against the Magyars, were miserably defeated, and were put to flight.

So the sorry tale continues. No part of the German lands was unaffected; few German people were spared.

B. THE CAROLINGIANS REPLACED

During these critical years, the last–in Germany–of the sadly inept Carolingians, Louis the Child, died. A chronicler wrote: "King Louis, the son of the Emperor Arnulf, died in 911, and since the royal line was now extinct, he was succeeded by Conrad, duke of Franconia." This succession constituted an innovation, for it replaced inheritance with election as the chief means of selecting the German ruler. It is true, however, that inheritance would influence, sometimes decisively, the choice made by those electing a new king or emperor.

An election requires electors. Just who were they? The poet and historian Wipo tells us: "Some of the leaders came together." Those "leaders" who assembled at Forchheim in Bavaria surely included several bishops, the most important of them Hatto, the archbishop of Mainz and the leading proponent of Conrad's election. Duke Otto of Saxony, the most powerful of the German leaders, refused election on grounds of advanced age and counseled his peers to choose Conrad, duke of Franconia.

Among the lay leaders at Forchheim were surely many counts. Charles the Great had created counts in the eighth century to serve as local administrators, combining judicial and law enforcement powers within their counties. During the disintegration of the Carolingian empire under Charles's successors, the more enterprising of these counts assumed independent status and pronounced themselves military leaders and judges. The still more enterprising among them asserted their power over whole regions and were addressed as duke, a word taken from the Latin *dux*, meaning leader. These duchies were Saxony, in the north; Frisia, in the northwest; Lotharingia, in the west; Swabia, in the southwest; Bavaria, in the southeast; and Franconia in the middle. Thuringia, located between Saxony and Franconia, was sometimes independent and sometimes a territory ruled by Saxony. The "Franks, Saxons, Swabians, and Bavarians" elected Conrad I, reported the *Annals of Swabia*, thus reviving the old Germanic practice of electing leaders by popular consent. Undoubtedly this acclamation by the people, another ancient Germanic practice, was a part of the coronation ceremony.

The conferring of a crown carried less weight than the consecration of the new ruler. This ceremony had a still more ancient origin. The prophet Samuel anointed David as king of Israel, to mark the choice of God himself. Charles the Great had received anointing with oil at the hands of the pope in Rome at a ceremony on Christmas Day in the year 800, symbolizing and affirming God's choice of him as Roman emperor. In the same way, King Conrad I's anointing showed him as the choice of both God and the people.

Conrad, however, proved inadequate to the task for which he had been chosen. He proved incapable of organizing resistance to the repeated incursions of the Magyars. The monk of Trier's *Chronicle* records the devastation still being wrought by these Asiatic invaders:

> In the year 916 of the Incarnation, without opposition, the Magyars devastated Franconia and Thuringia. In 913, they wasted the fields of the Swabians. In 915, they wasted all of Swabia with fire and sword, and they harried all of Thuringia and Saxony. In 917, the Magyars drove through Swabia into Alsace up to the borders of Lotharingia.

Conrad's failure to protect his new kingdom led the duke of Lotharingia to refuse to recognize Conrad's authority and instead to swear allegiance to the king of France. The other dukes and the leading churchmen of the realm established themselves still more firmly as regional powers, winning the allegiance of their people by offering what Conrad could not. Despite his sincere intentions, Conrad had failed to give his people the service that is the first duty of all governments: protection.

Conrad, however, had little time left on the throne. Happily, he prepared better for his people's life through his choice of a successor than he had through the years during which he reigned. The Chronicler of Trier noted:

> In the year 919 of the Incarnation, King Conrad died. He was in all respects a man of insight, gentle, and a friend of divine learning. As he perceived that the

day of his death was near, he summoned his brothers and other relatives–the great men among the Franconians. He exhorted them as a father that there should be no discord in the realm over the choice of his successor as king. He commanded them to choose Henry, the duke of Saxony, a man of energy and a strong friend of peace. Moreover, he sent to Henry the scepter and the crown with the admonition that he should shield and protect the realm.

Conrad's choice was not the only factor in the accession of Henry I, however. The Chronicler of Trier recorded: "In 920, Duke Henry was unanimously chosen king by the Franconians, Swabians, Bavarians, Thuringians, and Saxons."

Henry proved to be a forceful king, "beginning his reign by strictly enforcing the peace." He led an expedition into Bohemia with the intent of protecting Germany's eastern frontier. He won over to Christianity Slavic peoples to the East and Danes to the North. He brought back the duchy of Lotharingia into the kingdom. Most importantly, in 931 Henry hurled back yet another Magyar invasion by defeating the enemy at the Battle of the Unstrut.

Moreover, Henry devised a plan of national defense that would block all future incursions into his realm. In his *Deeds of the Saxons*, Widukind of Corvey records Henry's grand plan: "From the free farmers subject to military service he chose one out of every nine and ordered those elected to move into forts and in them to build houses for all the people of the area. He saw to it that one third of all the produce of the region was to be stored up in these forts." When the Magyars came riding and raiding on their swift ponies, the people could withdraw into these forts, or burgs, and there they could be safe.

In the year 935, Henry I suffered a stroke, and a year later he "reached his life's end," apparently due to the effects of that stroke. Widukind wrote: "On the death of Henry, the father of his country and the greatest and best of kings, the entire Frankish and Saxon people chose as their leader his son Otto, who had already been designated as king by his father." Both popular election and inheritance were involved in Otto I's accession. But perhaps most influential in Otto's selection was an assembly of the "dukes and leading governors [probably counts]" held at the Cathedral of Saint Mary built by Charles the Great in Aachen. According to Widukind, "They placed their new leader on a throne and made him king by placing their hands in his, vowing loyalty and promising him aid against his enemies."

These elaborate procedures were not enough to establish Otto firmly on the throne. Hildebert, the archbishop of Mainz, declared Otto "chosen by God" and, picking up a sword from the altar, said: "Receive this sword, with which you shall drive away all the enemies of Christ by the divine authority given to you." That sword, Hildebert declared, was meant "to establish a most enduring peace among all Christians." After being anointed with oil,

Otto was led to the throne of Charles the Great and formally installed. A celebration of the Mass followed, invoking God's aid for the newly consecrated king.

C. PROTECTING THE HOMELAND

Archbishop Hildebert's conferral of the ceremonial sword was not an empty ritual. Otto was pledged to "drive away all enemies," and of these there were many. The German people were menaced by forces on both eastern and western fronts.

The threat to Lotharingia from West Frankland was led by the French king, Louis IV (936-954). Angry at the recapture of Lotharingia by Otto's father, Louis invaded that land in 938, responding to the request of its duke, Giselbert. In 940, Otto invaded in turn, virtually without opposition, and set up his camp overlooking the banks of the Seine on the road to Paris. Otto did not pursue Louis, but instead met with him and arranged a reconciliation. Faced with a rebellion at home, Louis appealed for help to Otto, who joined his erstwhile enemy in defeating the rebels at Rheims. It was on German soil, however, at Ingelheim, that a church council met in 948 to settle the matter. Pope Agapetus' legate, Bishop Marinus of Bomarzo, presided. The two kings, Otto and Louis, appeared together, and the council excommunicated the leader of the French rebellion, who reluctantly submitted to the council's mandate. Otto had taken up the sword in defense of his people, and in so doing he secured the westernmost part of the German lands from invasion.

Otto also wielded his sword, though most often not in person, against a threat from the East, the many groups, tribes, and nations of Slavs. The most unified of these Slavic peoples were the Bohemians, whose lands lay east of the mountains forming a barrier thrusting westward into lands being settled by Germans. In 929, Otto's friend, Duke Wenceslaus of Bohemia, was murdered by his brother Boleslav, who coveted his authority. Boleslav then cut off the annual contribution to the German treasury which had sealed the Bohemian-German alliance. Otto punished the murderers and restored cordial relations with Bohemia.

Other Slavs who lived along the Elbe River also refused to pay tribute to Otto. He slowly but surely pacified one tribe, the Abodrites, primarily by employing Saxon forces living adjacent to them. Otto created frontier super-counties called marches to defend the eastern borders and placed the most effective of the Saxon leaders in charge of them. Widukind writes: "Hermann Billung and Count Gero were the two men who, throughout Otto's reign, not only kept the Slavic Wends in check by their untiring efforts but firmly established German authority in the marches between the Elbe and the Oder." Otto also continued his father's policy of building frontier forts to defend the local populace. So effective were these forts in providing and preserving peace that Slavic peoples who had once threatened the Saxon frontier often moved into them and intermarried with their German neighbors.

A far greater danger to the realm than either the French or the Slavs was still the Magyars. Against them too Otto continued his father's policy of building frontier forts, and these increasingly became centers from which local leaders could launch counterattacks. However, more was needed. Otto amassed a huge army composed of Franconians (East Franks), Bavarians, Swabians, and Bohemians that met the Magyars in 955, just south of Augsburg on the banks of the Lech river. The Magyar light cavalry relied almost exclusively on the showers of arrows their bowman let loose. Speed, not hand-to-hand combat, was their forte, whereas the German knights were heavily armed and armored and mounted on chargers.

To overcome the Magyars, the Germans employed the weight of their cavalry charge and the force of their superior ability at individual combat. The Magyars employed tactics well suited to their speed, including an encircling attack on the Bohemians guarding the wagon trains in the German rear. Widukind of Corvey relates the story: "The King saw that the battle was going in favor of the enemy. So he spoke to his comrades, exhorting them in this way: 'We need stout hearts in straits like this. God is our hope and defense. It is better to die gloriously in battle than drag out our lives in slavery.'" Otto led with more than rousing words, as Widukind reports: "Seizing his sword and shield and brandishing the lance [that, it was believed, had pierced Christ's side], Otto was the first to turn his horse toward the enemy. He showed himself a truly gallant soldier and a splendid commander. The enemy turned and ran, stunned by the charge. Those who were overtaken by our men were slain."

The German forces then captured the Magyar camps and freed the prisoners held there. The surviving Magyars fled to their homeland on the middle Danube, to what is now Hungary, and settled down to farm the rich soil of that broad valley. Within a hundred years they had been converted to Christianity and would soon become the bulwark of Western Europe against future invasions from the East.

Otto's victory provided his people with their first and basic need: security from external enemies. Widukind records the people's response:

> The king was glorified in his splendid triumph. He was acclaimed by the army as father of his country and highest commander [*imperator*]. He then decreed that fitting honor and praise be offered to God on high in all the churches. The victor returned to the Saxons amid both solemn ceremony and great popular rejoicing. He was welcomed with great good will, for no king had won such a victory for two hundred years.

Having provided his grateful subjects with peace, Otto now faced the task of seeing to their other great need: the domestic order that stems from justice.

D. CREATING A STATE

Protecting the people from invasion was not all that was needed to bring about the birth of the medieval German state. All people need a means of adjudicating disputes fairly, and thus attaining justice. A legal code, created specifically to ensure justice, was in fact available to Otto's people. Prohibitions of murder, theft, adultery, and like crimes were enshrined in the collective memories of the people. If two farmers had a boundary dispute, for example, they would take the issue to their village council, which would ascertain the relevant evidence by questioning those who had been present when the plot of land in question was purchased from or granted by the original landholder. The disputant who brought forth the most credible witnesses won his or her suit.

The same procedure, on a grander scale, was followed when the litigants were highly placed in the political, social, and economic structure of society. Members of the upper class took their disputes to their overlord, perhaps to their count, who consulted the great and wise men of his court. But if that court's decision were appealed, who held the appellate authority? Whoever claimed to have this authority had to possess the power to enforce his decisions, and, in the tenth century, that power meant military might. Did the territorial leader, the duke, hold the most coercive force in his land? Or was it the king who held supreme military and judicial power?

Understandably, Otto claimed supreme military power in his kingdom. However, the governance of the many and extensive lands of Germany required assistants or delegates, and the traditional and obvious answer was to recognize the power already adhering in the dukes and make them the agents of the crown.

This was not easily done. The dukes jealously guarded their power and independence. One example of ducal infidelity may suffice to demonstrate this point. In the year 937, Arnulf, the duke of Bavaria, died. Otto then recognized Arnulf's brother Berthold as duke, but Berthold too died, and Otto appointed his own brother Henry as duke. Both appointments met the stubborn resistance of Arnulf's son, Eberhard. Eberhard sought to strengthen his hand against Otto by joining in a coalition with Gilbert, duke of Lotharingia, and Otto's brother Henry. The new duke, Henry, was not satisfied with Bavaria and had greater ambitions that included the royal crown. Otto crushed this coalition, but he faced the need for supportive dukes in Bavaria, Lotharingia, and, as it turned out, the other duchies.

Despite Henry's actions, Otto's initial solution was to appoint family members–his brothers, sons, and sons-in-law–to ducal rank and power. Like Henry, these relatives grew increasingly more attached to the local interests of their new domains and to their own regal ambitions to be effective and obedient agents of the crown. Rebellions led by relatives, even in Otto's own duchy of Saxony, became endemic. By 939 Otto had wrested ducal power from his relatives, although he left them their own lands. However, Otto still faced the need for subsidiary agents with power, for no monarch can govern his realm by himself.

E. ENLISTING LEADERS OF THE CHURCH

Otto's effective solution to this problem saved Germany from being reduced to a collection of small, independent, and warring territories characteristic of contemporary France and Italy. Otto granted to the bishops responsible for the spiritual welfare of the people in their dioceses an additional and weighty task. He bestowed on them immunity from the temporal power of the local count and gave them the right to administer justice in areas formerly governed by counts. By this means Otto gave bishops the same status as counts in their own separate territories, and he augmented those territories and powers with generous gifts. These acts reduced the territorial power base of both dukes and counts, rendering them less capable of effective rebellion. His action also provided each area with a clerical watchdog to assure that the lay aristocracy continued to serve the interests of the king.

This solution worked well, for the king could command the loyalty of bishops far more easily than he could that of lay lords. When a duke or count died, his son ordinarily took over his office. That son owed his position to his birth, not to the king, and was apt to adopt an independent stance. A bishop, on the other hand, could leave no legitimate heirs, and the king could, and did, nominate a successor loyal to himself. This system worked well for a century and a half. It made Germany the most effective state on the continent–until the twelfth century.

Otto's system had additional advantages and some disadvantages. As territorial lords, the bishops had the political power and economic resources to provide the king with troops–indeed episcopal forces came to form the backbone of the royal army. On the other hand, it is clear that bishops, already heavily burdened with spiritual duties and the care of their flocks, were now faced with administrative duties as extensive as those of a count. This burden was largely relieved by the appointment of a lay advocate, *Vogt*, as the administrator of the bishop's temporal responsibilities–presiding over courts and providing troops, for example.

The most perplexing issue that resulted from the Church's dual roles in the temporal and spiritual spheres was the selection of bishops. Since the earliest days of the Church, bishops had been elected by the local clergy and people. Clearly the king needed to have a role in the selection of his chief administrators, the bishops.

The Ottonian practice was for the king to nominate a cleric to the bishopric; then the clergy of the diocese–usually represented by the clergy attached to the cathedral–would elect that nominee, and the people would acclaim the bishop elect. The king's range of choices was limited, however. A growing number of reformers in the tenth century insisted that the clergy be both virtuous and learned, the clerical leadership qualifications of the early Church. This insistence was not to be a problem for another century, as the Ottonians and their successors down to 1056 supported the reform and generally nominated bishops with high spiritual and intellectual qualifications. The bishops whom the king chose were not mere political puppets. They were among his chief advisors and sometimes opposed his policies.

Among the bishops nominated by Otto were some of his relatives. He chose his natural half-brother William to be the archbishop of Mainz, who was the primate or presiding prelate of the German Church. Otto's cousin Henry he nominated to the powerful archbishopric of Trier. Most importantly, Otto nominated his youngest brother, Bruno, to the archbishopric of Cologne.

F. ADMINISTERING THE KINGDOM

Otto's kingdom was extensive, including all of what is now Germany and Austria. Otto's authority also extended over roughly the northeastern quarter of what is now France. The kingdom included lands now in western Poland and all of the present-day Czech Republic. Even before Otto's expeditions to Italy, his rule extended over lands now in Slovenia, parts of Croatia, and a significant section of northwestern Italy. Only the western and southeastern parts of Otto's realm had been part of the Roman Empire of antiquity and consequently retained roads still capable of carrying significant traffic. For the rest, Otto and his contemporaries had to rely on horses and boats.

Yet it was necessary for Otto to be constantly on the move from ducal fortress to bishopric, from count's seat to monastery, from one of the royal estates to another. Otto's rule was not based on the supervision of a central bureaucracy over local representatives. His was a personal rule, and he and his entourage had to be seen and his justice felt. His royal power was enhanced by attendance and his crowned appearances at church festivals and religious ceremonies. At each of the stops on the royal itinerary, the king expected–and received–hospitality for himself and his court, for both men and horses. Traveling with the king were bishops and counts of the region, along with his and their servants, and the royal chaplains who also served collectively as the royal chancellery. Wherever the king was, petitioners of high and low estate came from near and far to have their cases considered by the king himself. This entourage was surely a grave financial burden on the cathedral, monastery, or estate at which the court stayed.

When the issue facing the king was sufficiently important, the court might draw representatives from an entire duchy or sometimes even the whole realm. This assembly–as yet only loosely organized–was the forerunner of the later German Diet or parliament. Since both bishops and the lay aristocracy were present, the assembly sometimes addressed religious issues and thus became a church synod or regional council. The acts of these assemblies/councils were written down, with little distinction between religious and temporal legislation.

Perhaps the best example of how the religious and temporal powers worked in harmony–strengthening both, it was thought–is the establishment of the archbishopric of Magdeburg, situated on the Elbe River in what was the easternmost part of Saxony. Magdeburg's territory abutted the marches, the super counties established by Otto to protect German settlers and assimilate the Slavic population.

The Abbey of Saint Maurice at Magdeburg, a monastery founded and richly endowed by Otto, was a daughter house of the Abbey of Saint Maximinus at Trier, a leading proponent of the reform movement. Magdeburg and its monastery thus represented the ideal site for the solemn celebration of Otto's sacral kingship when he was traveling in the northeastern part of his realm.

Otto conceived the idea of a new archbishopric at Magdeburg that would supervise the German settlements to the East through its spiritual authority over the newly established marches and bishoprics. During an expedition to Italy, Otto obtained the support of Pope John XII for his initiative and, in 962, the pope sent northward the necessary letter of authorization.

As its first archbishop, Otto chose Adelbert, formerly abbot of Saint Maximinus at Trier, then abbot of Weissenberg in Alsace, and thus familiar with the western German duchies of Lotharingia and Swabia. Adelbert had also accumulated a store of information about the whole kingdom, having earlier served as a notary in the royal chancery. Fluent in the Slavic language, he had been sent in 964 to the court at Kiev with the aim of converting the inhabitants of Rus to Christianity. Though Olga, the duchess of Kiev, had requested this missionary journey, the death of her husband, Duke Igor, prevented its success. Even so, Adelbert's knowledge of both German and Slavic intellectual and institutional culture made him the ideal imperial cleric to promote Otto's political and religious goals.

G. ITALY AND EMPIRE

Italy in Otto's day was a hotbed of contesting rivalries. In the south the Byzantine Greeks held the toe and heel of the peninsula. The Saracens ruled Sicily. Central Italy was dominated by the States of the Church–the Roman Church–and hence also referred to as the Patrimony of Peter. Control of Rome itself was contested by the powerful families of the city and surrounding area. Northern Italy suffered from a struggle over its kingship.

The Italian crown had been held by Rudolf II of Burgundy, a territory roughly encompassing the southwest quarter of present-day France. But the real power in the Burgundian kingdom was Count Hugh of Arles. Hugh also controlled most of the petty princes in Italy, with the notable exception of Alberic II of Spoleto, who controlled Rome and the papacy. Hugh died in 948, and Berengar of Ivrea, who had enjoyed Otto's protection, was elected king. Many of the local rulers and many of the Italian bishops–including the pope–refused to recognize Berengar and rallied around Adelheide, the widow of Hugh's son Lothar.

Into this boiling caldron of political enmity, Otto inserted himself in 951. He proclaimed himself king of Italy at Pavia, its capital, and married Adelheide. It is quite likely that Otto intended to forestall similar territorial ambitions by the dukes of Bavaria and Swabia, Italy's transalpine neighbors. Otto was not to stay long in Italy however; another ducal revolt demanded his attention at home.

At this time Rome was seething with armed conflict. The feudal lord of Rome and its dependent central Italian patrimony was the pope. The vassals of the pope coveted the papal office and its political power, with the result that intrigue, treachery, and murder had come to surround the See of Peter. From 896 to 904, there had been, on the average, one pope a year. The tenth century saw worse: for several decades Rome was controlled by an infamous "lady senator," Marozia. The contemporary chronicler Benedict of Sant' Andrea wrote: "The pope [Stephan VIII] having died, Marozia ordained her son John to the most sacred seat. And he is called John XI. Rome was ruled by the power of a woman."

Marozia was also the mother of Alberic II, who deposed her and succeeded to her power. Benedict of Sant' Andrea reports that "his yoke grew heavy upon the Romans and upon the holy apostolic see. The pope dared not to do anything without the commands of Prince Alberic." In 955, Alberic placed his son Octavian on the chair of Peter and as pope Octavian was called John XII. Benedict reports that "he led a life so licentious and so openly wicked that he might as well have been a heathen. He hunted constantly, behaving not like a pope but like a wild man. He was given over to debauchery and surrounded himself with a crowd of evil women."

Faced with an Italian coalition determined to take over Rome, John XII called on Otto to retrace his steps and come to his aid. So, in 961, as the chronicler Benedict of Saint' Andrea reports, "Otto the king came into Italy with a great multitude of people." In February of 962, having pacified both northern Italy and the Papal States, "Otto was extolled with high praise and was called Augustus. The king and the queen were crowned emperor and empress in the Church of the Chief of the Apostles."

Otto had twice sworn, in 961 and 962, to uphold the pope's claim to rule over the lands of central Italy. But it was clear that the newly crowned emperor had no intention of surrendering any part of his imperial power to the pope, any more than he would surrender ultimate authority to the other great lords in the peninsula. This resistance led Pope John to rebellion. Otto responded by deposing John and selecting a new pope. As soon as Otto started for home, John led an army into Rome and reassumed the papacy. Otto returned once more to the city, deposed John again, and selected a new pope who took the name Leo VIII.

Leo recognized political reality and issued the following decree:

> In the council held at Rome in the Church of the Holy Savior, I, Bishop Leo, servant of the servants of God, with all the clergy and people of Rome, by our apostolic authority bestowed on the lord Otto, king of the Germans–and on his successors in the kingdom of Italy forever–the right of choosing the successor to the pope. Likewise, he shall have the right to ordain the pope, the archbishops, and the bishops, so that they shall receive their investiture with the symbols of their office and their consecration from him.

In much of Italy, as in Germany, Otto ruled largely through his bishops, who kept the lay lords in line. Because Otto and his successors (until at least 1056) were genuinely interested in the welfare of the Church, they insisted on restoring the traditional qualifications of virtue and learning for high office in that Church. Thus reform of the Church necessitated a renaissance of classical culture.

H. THE OTTONIAN RENAISSANCE

Perhaps the most instructive life of the many bishops known from Otto's time is that of his youngest brother, Bruno. Bruno was born in 925, and he was a precocious child, as his biographer Ruotger tells us:

> When this noble child was four years old, he was sent [by his father, King Henry I] to Utrecht to be instructed by the venerable Bishop Balderic in the classics of ancient thought. Under his tutor's guidance he began by reading the poet Prudentius. This poet is Catholic in faith and aspiration, excellent in both

> eloquence and in truth, pleasing in meter and rich in meaning. His verses delighted the boy's heart.

Both classical learning and Christian virtue were to remain Bruno's great loves throughout his life. At Trier he added Greek to his educational repertoire under the tutelage of Israel, a bishop from Brittany. "As time went on," Ruotger wrote, "his eager mind grasped all the branches of liberal studies within the range of Greek and Latin eloquence."

When Bruno's elder brother Otto ascended the German throne, the new king called Bruno to attend him at court. Since that court was itinerant, Bruno "took his library with him everywhere" and, furthermore, collected "many sources and materials for his studies." Bruno was not only a devoted scholar who "occupied himself tirelessly with reading and thinking," he also exhibited the same zeal for religious practices: "He allowed himself no luxuries. He refused over and over again to wear fine and soft clothing in the king's palace. Among servants clad in royal purple and knights gleaming with gold he wore the simple garb and sheepskins of a farmer." Contemporaries saw Bruno's virtue reflected in his clothing; they also experienced that virtue in his pastoral care, so that "many people profited by his words and yet more by his example." That example shone forth in Bruno's humility: "By his behavior he showed himself as one who would avoid human praise." In short, Bruno exhibited the leadership qualifications of the early Church, the qualifications being revived by the tenth-century reform movement.

It is little wonder that when Wiefrid, the aged archbishop of Cologne, died in 953, Bruno was the unanimous choice of the clergy and laity of the archdiocese, of course with the accord of the king. Cologne was located within the duchy of Lotharingia, where a rebellion by the duke had been recently quashed. Otto decided that there was no better replacement possible than Bruno. Otto gave Bruno control of the huge duchy on the western frontier. Bruno took pains to fulfill his functions as administrator of Lotharingia, acting, for example, as the go-between in a controversy between Otto and the French king. However, Bruno was first and foremost a pastor, seeing to it that virtuous and learned bishops were appointed everywhere in Lotharingia. He encouraged monastic reformers, supported the hermits who often served as roving preachers, and undertook a program of church building. His authority was cheerfully received because of the deeply spiritual life that informed his pastoral manner and style.

Although Bruno died at the early age of forty, his influence lived on, above all in the lives and works of his episcopal recruits in Lotharingia. Sigebert of Gembloux, author of the life of Bishop Theoderich of Metz, remembered the golden days of Otto and Bruno's time: "I rightly recall the times of Otto as fortunate, when the government and society were reformed by renowned prelates, when wise men restored peace to the churches and integrity to religion. One could then see and indeed experience the truth of the philosopher's saying: 'Happy the state where rulers are philosophers and where philosophers rule.'" Contemporaries saw the Ottonian Renaissance as a revival of the virtues taught in apostolic times and of the classical learning thought to provide convincing support for those values.

J. HROTSWITHA OF GANDERSHEIM

In the midst of the great plain that sweeps across all of north Germany, stands a range of heavily wooded mountains, the Harz. This remote location was the site of one of the most important cultural centers in tenth-century Germany. The community of religious women who lived at Gandersheim were canonesses, following the Rule of Saint Augustine. The precepts of that rule aimed at love of God and the community and were expressed in shared possessions, humility, and obedience to the superior, the abbess, who was chosen by her community. They prayed together and served each other, especially their physically or spiritually fragile sisters. And they studied the literary and philosophical classics of antiquity.

Foremost among the scholars at Gandersheim was Hrotswitha. Apparently she was not of noble birth, unlike her abbess Gerberga, who was a niece of the Emperor Otto. No information survives of Hrotswitha's schooling–only that she was a scholar, poet, dramatist, and historian. She was well versed in the ancient Latin works of Horace, Ovid, and Virgil, and she wrote plays in imitation of Terence. Hrotswitha's style meticulously followed that of her ancient models, but the content of her works was unabashedly Christian, promoting virtue through learning.

It is hard to imagine some of Hrotswitha's plays being staged by the sisters. In her play *Paphnutius*, for example, the dialogue seems more appropriate to the classroom than to the stage. The subject is music, not the music played or sung, but the scientific basis of sound, the branch of physics called acoustics. The disciple asks: "What is music, teacher?" Paphnutius responds: "One of the branches of philosophy, my son. Arithmetic, geometry, music, and astronomy form the quadrivium." The professor distinguishes three kinds of music: the celestial, the human, and the instrumental. The celestial, he explains, is produced by the "seven planets and the celestial globe." The music these produce "is so pleasant and sweet that, if it were heard, all people from East to West would follow the sounds." But, we learn, "our Creator" foreknew and prevented our hearing it. Even in the unheard music of the spheres, Hroswitha believed, rational discourse can discover God's activity.

Much more obviously Christian is Hrotswitha's play *Dulcitius*, dealing with the martyrdom of three saintly maidens, Agape, Chionia, and

Irene—Love, Purity, and Peace. Dulcitius is a Roman governor who lusts after the girls and locks them in a washhouse. He comes to claim them during the night, but darkness leads him to embrace various cauldrons and boilers, covering himself with soot. In a scene reminiscent of a slapstick comedy, he frightens off his guard of soldiers, dismays the doorkeeper, and leads his wife to think him mad. *Dulcitius* must have been much more fun to produce than *Paphnutius*, but the goals of the two plays were ultimately the same: to portray God's workings in the world and respond in the language of classical thought. Both Bruno and Hrotswitha saw virtue and learning as necessary to the Christian communities they served. Both saw renaissance and reform as two sides of the same coin.

It was also in the Emperor's interest to promote both virtue and learning in his clergy. Otto's itinerant court required learned scribes for his chancery, able to compose, issue, and copy decrees and legal decisions. Indeed, that chancery served as an institution of higher education for the brightest of the youngsters who had already shown themselves advanced in their mastery of classical prose, poetry, philosophy, and science. Those who excelled in the duties of the royal chancery were sometimes sent out as ambassadors—one, John of Gorze, to the court at Cordova of Caliph Abd er-Rhamen III. It was from Otto's cadre of officials that the emperor most often chose his nominees to bishoprics and other high church offices, in which those well-educated officials served as both pastors and governors. As a result, Germany and the Empire was the best governed and shepherded state in tenth- and early eleventh-century Europe.

K. THE END OF THE OLD WARRIOR'S CAMPAIGN

Otto died at Memleben, a little town in the Harz Mountains, on May 7, 973, in his sixty-first year. His body was buried at Magdeburg, the archbishopric he had founded. His heart was interred in a fortress in his beloved Harz Mountains. Those who attended his funeral included delegates from Russia, Hungary, Bulgaria, and Byzantium. Also appearing were Danes and Poles, and the son of Duke Boleslav II of Bohemia represented his father.

The historian Widukind reported the response of the German people to Otto's death:

> The people gave voice to his praise, recalling that he had ruled his subjects with paternal piety. They remembered how he had liberated them from their enemies by conquering by force of arms the proud Magyars, Saracens, Danes, and Slavs. He had brought Italy under his sway. He had destroyed the temples of his heathen neighbors and set up churches and priests in their place.

And Widukind added his own assessment: "The world was fortunate while Otto held the scepter." Thietmar of Merseburg remembered Otto's reign as "an age of gold." Otto's contribution to his country is perhaps best summed up by the legend struck on one of his coins: *renovatio imperii Romanorum*, "the restoration of the Empire of the Romans."

Chapter Three

Growing Peace and Prosperity

A. THE AGRICULTURAL REVOLUTION

The warrior and governing class of medieval Germany–together with the clergy–probably never included more than five percent of the people who lived there during the ninth through the twelfth centuries. The other ninety-five percent supported themselves, their governors and protectors, and their spiritual guides through their agricultural labor.

Except in the far northern areas bordering the sea–sparsely populated at first because the soil was sandy and less fertile–medieval German farmers lived on manors. These were large, virtually self-sufficient farms on which some thirty or forty families lived in a village, a collection of modest dwellings centering on a church and a nearby house for the manorial lord. The lord, a mounted warrior or knight, was granted the manor by his lord in return for military service. The overlord was typically a count, a margrave (the count of a large frontier area called a march), or duke. Manorial lords and farmers lived in a symbiotic relationship. The manorial lord provided the farmer with protection, justice, and plots of land. The farmers, in return, worked their share of the land and provided the lord with a portion of the manor's produce, thus freeing the lord for the exercise of his military duties.

Though each family possessed its own portion of land, the farmers found it efficient to work the land together. Plowing, harrowing, fertilizing, weeding, and harvesting together made community consultation and decisions mandatory. The village council gradually evolved from this need, taking on the functions of local government not reserved for the lord. Each season and each major farming activity were marked on the manor with appropriate festivals celebrated by the entire community. The villagers were deeply involved in each other's concerns and cares, and accepted collective responsibility for each other's health and welfare.

Villagers also shared some lands in common. Each village possessed a woodland that was a source of building material and fuel. The wood was a source of food as well, for the villagers let their pigs run loose there, feeding on acorns and whatever else nature provided. The villagers selected one of their number to be a swineherd, whose responsibility it was to look after the pigs and prevent their straying too far, often with the help of one of the local lads. The village devoted some of its land to a common. On this commonly held land, individual families pastured their cattle, again delegating one of the manor's men to be a cowherd, and assigning at least one of the village's boys to assist him. Other specialized workers were the smith, the leather worker, and the miller. All the other men and boys–and when necessary the women and girls–devoted themselves to raising the food that was necessary for themselves and the whole society.

The arable land of the manor was jointly cultivated by the villagers. Land plots held by each family were scattered throughout the fields to ensure that each received its share of the good, bad, and middling soil. Since their ox-drawn (later horse-drawn) plows needed room to turn at the end of each furrow, it was obvious that this unplowed space could be kept to a minimum if each family's land were arranged in long, narrow strips. The lord's holdings were interspersed in strips along with those of the farmers.

During the tenth century, the peace, law, and order provided by Otto I and his successors made farming life more secure and less burdensome than it had been before their dynasty's rule. Still more instrumental to this progress was a series of inventions that culminated in an agricultural revolution.

The first of these technological innovations was a new sort of plow. The farmers of antiquity had used a "stick plow" with which they scratched the earth's surface. This plow worked well enough in light, less fertile soils but required at least two plowings done at right angles. The new plow, designed for heavy soil, weighed far more and needed to be wheeled. These innovations prevented the tool from rising out of the rich, heavy soils of much of northern Europe. A mold board integral to this plow turned the soil over, thus aerating and enriching it with the rotting weeds now turned under. This radically new invention was the ancestor of the plows still used today, and made it possible for the first time to exploit fully the soil of the rich river valleys of northern Europe.

To pull this heavy plow, farmers required four yoke of oxen (eight animals). As very few farmers indeed could afford eight oxen, this provided additional incentive toward communal agriculture. Oxen can pull heavy loads, but they are slow moving animals, so early medieval people turned to the more efficient horse to provide locomotive power. This innovation was made possible by two brilliant inventions. The first was a new, heavy, iron horse-shoe which protected horses' hooves from injury. In the moist climates north of the Alps, wet soil caused hooves to soften, to rot, and to crack when the horse stepped on stones. Forging horse-shoes required a smith and a supply of iron. The smith gained his skill through apprenticeship, and the iron ore with which he worked was fortunately plentiful in German lands.

The second invention, the horse collar, made the horse a really effective farm animal. Ancient horse harnesses consisted of straps around the animal's neck. These reduced not only the horse's intake of air but also its blood supply to the brain when the animal pulled heavy loads. With the invention of the horse collar, the animal could push with its whole strength against a pad resting on its shoulders–a pad that would not interfere with its breathing or circulation.

Properly shod and harnessed, a horse was able to exert about fifty percent more pulling power than an ox, and the horse's greater endurance made it possible for farmers to work an additional hour or two each day. The clear gain resulted in a corresponding increase in production. Since horses move much more swiftly than oxen, the benefits of using them to provide cheaper and more rapid transportation by road were also significant. Furthermore, the horse's greater speed made it possible to cultivate lands farther from the village. Increased production made growing, harvesting, and transporting foodstuff less subject to climactic fluctuation. Villages increased in size, resulting in greater security and increasing numbers of people gaining access to the amenities of community life.

Another of the agricultural innovations that greatly improved food production north of the Alps was three-field crop rotation. Ancient agriculture had employed a two-field system that meant that only half the land was producing crops at a given time. The other half of the land had to lie fallow to prevent it becoming exhausted. The new system divided the same amount of land into three fields, only one of which lay fallow. Crops from the two that were planted increased the productive portion to two-thirds of the available land. Staggering planting between fall and spring and farming four (or more) fields increased yields still further. Thus, with the same number of plowmen and draft animals, more acreage could be kept under cultivation. The tangible results of this great gain in labor productivity paid off in the tenth, eleventh, and twelfth centuries when the extra manpower was devoted to the clearing of forests. Swamps were drained and land reclaimed with the help of another new device, the windmill. Streams were dammed and the force of the spill was used to drive yet another new tool, the water mill, that employed still another new invention, the rotary grindstone, in the production of flour.

These were not the only benefits of the three-field system. By making possible a greatly improved rotation of crops, it allowed farmers to replenish the fertility of the soil by planting nitrogen–adding legumes like peas, lentils, or beans as an early crop. These legumes added valuable proteins to the average family's diet, and this benefit was reflected in a greater capacity for work, increased resistance to illness and disease, a lower infant mortality rate, and longer life expectancy. All these factors, as well as a warming of the climate, contributed to a steady growth in population. In the regions of old settlement–generally speaking in the western parts of the Empire–there was much energy devoted to clearing of forests and the establishment of new villages and towns to house the increasingly dense population. The growing population also led to a great migration, the *Drang nach Osten* that drove German settlement ever farther to the East.

The expanded production of northern European farmers made possible the accumulation of economic surpluses that were necessary not only to support a larger population but also to encourage the increasing specialization of functions necessary for the process of urbanization. Freeing some workers from fields provided the population necessary to establish towns whose townsfolk could draw food and raw materials from the surrounding countryside. Villagers became rich enough not only to spare some of their output but also to purchase the manufactured goods and professional services of the townsfolk. Surpluses were, and still are, absolutely necessary to provide talented people with the leisure vital to the development of art, science, and other forms of high culture.

Perhaps most importantly, this agricultural revolution helped change the German and the other northern Europeans' attitude toward nature. Whereas human beings had once considered themselves a part of nature, they were now able to think of themselves as nature's master. Modern western civilization would not have been possible without this radical change in attitude.

B. OTTO II: ADVANCES AND SETBACKS

The only son of the Emperor Otto I and Empress Adelaid to survive to maturity was also named Otto. To secure his succession, Otto I associated this son with him as king by arranging his election at Aachen in August of 961. Otto I also co-opted him as emperor in 967. Pope John XIII provided the necessary anointing and blessing in exchange for a promise of protection against rival Roman families. In attendance at the elevation of Otto II were Romans, Franks, Bavarians, Saxons, Alsatians, Swabians, and Lotharingians. Thus when Otto I died in 973, his son's position was unassailable.

During the first seven years of his reign (973-980), Otto II successfully put down various disturbances threatening the Empire. The first of these came from the West. Lothar, king of the West Franks (in what is now northern France), desired to acquire Lotharingia, going so far as to invade it with an army whose "erect spears seemed more like a grove of trees than weapons," as the contemporary historian Richar of Rheims reported. Lothar and his army went so far as to ransack Charles the Great's palace at Aachen. In 980, Otto had his revenge. He led an army to the gates of Paris and persuaded Lothar to abandon all claim to Lotharingia.

Otto was also faced with a plot hatched by Duke Henry II, "the Quarrelsome," of Bavaria. Duke Boleslav II of Bohemia and Duke Misko of Poland joined the conspiracy, but Otto's invasion of Bavaria put an end to their rebellious efforts. Otto bestowed Bavaria on the loyal duke of Swabia, a nephew also named Otto, but he also removed from Bavarian control several eastern marches including the Ostmark–later to become the duchy of Austria. Under the protection of these margraves still more new settlers moved east.

The empire's northern frontier was also threatened. The Danes, under their king, Harold Bluetooth, invaded imperial territory. Otto marched against the invaders so successfully that Harold offered not only treasure and a yearly tribute, but also his son as hostage. Otto built a fortress in the northernmost area of the Empire, and this bastion was the basis of extensive northward German settlement.

These successes were more than counterbalanced by a disastrous expedition to Italy. In this Otto II was following the example of his father, who had coveted the Byzantine and Arab possessions in the south of the peninsula and in Sicily. To legitimize this effort, Otto I had arranged the marriage of his son to a Byzantine princess, Theophano. Implicit in this marriage was a long-desired and long-denied recognition by the Eastern Roman emperors in Constantinople that the Western ruler was also a successor to the ancient Roman emperors. Theophano arrived in Rome in 972 and was wedded to Otto II.

The marriage benefitted both Otto and his bride. He was strengthened in his claim to Byzantine possessions in the toe and heel of Italy. In return Otto endowed Theophano with lands within his realm. The official document of endowment begins with an invocation of "the name of the holy and indivisible Trinity." God's will for humankind is then stated in elegant prose, reflecting God's "elegant creation":

> God, the creator and founder of all things that are, the creator of the greatest good, who brought forth primordial entities of nature in perfect elegance from the beginning of the nascent world, wished humans to attain to his own image and likeness. Since He did not wish the first man to remain alone, and in order that their posterity might be lasting, He created a conjugal helpmate from a rib taken from Adam's body and ordered that thereafter the two should exist as one flesh.

Otto then cited the wedding miracle at Cana to demonstrate Christ's blessing on all marriages.

The document reveals not only the theological education available in tenth-century culture, but also provides an insight into the flourishing economic and social life of the time. Otto enumerated the various lands he was ceding to Theophano "within the Italian borders and in the part of our realm beyond the Alps." These possessions were to come under Theophano's jurisdiction "together with castles, houses, farmers both male and female, lands, fields, vineyards, meadows, woods, mountains and plains, waters and streams, mills, fisheries, and all things belonging to those estates." It was a handsome wedding gift. Theophano responded to this generosity by producing three daughters and, in the summer of 980, a son who was to succeed to the throne as Otto III.

Otto II, having secured the Empire's frontier on the North, East, and West, then resolved to deal with the situation in southern Italy and Sicily that his father had not had time fully to address. By this time Arabs from North Africa had driven out the Byzantine Greeks from Sicily and had set their sights on Apulia and Calabria, the toe and heel of the Italian peninsula. Bishop Thietmar of Merseburg told of Otto's response to the expedition of Adu'l-Qasim, the Muslim emir of Sicily:

> Ascertaining that Calabria was suffering heavily from frequent incursions by the Byzantines and pillage by the Saracens, Caesar [Otto] called out the Bavarians and the battle-hardened Swabians to reinforce his army. But unexpectedly [the Saracens] proceeded in close ranks against our warriors and, on 13 July [982], defeated them. What a disaster!

Some 4,000 imperial troops died at Cortone. Otto escaped the massacre only by plunging his horse into the sea. He was rescued by a Jewish merchant whose ship was sailing nearby and who swiftly ordered the crew to rescue the emperor. The emir had been killed, but the emperor had been disastrously defeated.

Thietmar of Merseburg told the sad but edifying story of what happened afterward:

> At Pavia Otto fell seriously ill, probably of malaria. When he realized the end was near, he divided his money into four parts: one part for the church, a second for the poor, a third for his beloved sister Matilda, and a fourth for his sorrowing attendants and warriors. Then he confessed in Latin to the pope, to the pope's fellow bishops, and to the attending priests. He obtained the desired absolution from them and departed this life on 7 December 983.

Otto was buried in the atrium of Saint Peter's Basilica in Rome.

Otto's defeat by the Arabs dealt a shattering blow to German expansion in the East. Slavs all along the eastern frontier broke into open rebellion. Churches were destroyed and many Christians put to the sword. Hamburg, the principal ecclesiastical and trading center in the North, was plundered. The important civil and ecclesiastical centers of Brandenburg, Zeitz, and Havelberg were burnt to the ground. An army of Saxon lords assembled by the archbishop of Magdeburg was eventually able to check the Slav invasion, but this failed to restore German control over the Slavic territory or reestablish Christianity among the tribes that had reverted to paganism. The frontier established by Otto I would not be reestablished for several generations.

C. SOURCES OF STRENGTH

Even these devastating blows were not enough to cause the Empire built by Otto I to crumble. Enormous imperial wealth enabled it to survive these serious setbacks. The spoils of earlier wars, although considerable, were by no means the principal source of that wealth.

Imperial grants of land to bishops and their dioceses enabled those prelates to become counterweights to local rulers, as we have seen. Those grants provided the wealth with which bishops supported their ruler with warriors and replenished their supply trains laden with weapons, food, and horses, the last an especially expensive necessity. Moreover Otto I and his successors took monasteries under their protection and in return received substantial revenues from them. The dynasty benefitted as well from the lavish output of the silver mines it controlled.

The second most important source of Germany's wealth–after agriculture–was commerce. The Ottos encouraged this trade through grants of minting and market rights. In 975, Otto I granted his protection "to the merchants dwelling in Magdeburg and everywhere in our realm, and freedom to come and go unmolested." He also gave the archbishop of Hamburg the valuable right to hold a market in the town of Bremen: "We grant him jurisdiction, tolls, and a mint. We take under our special protection all the merchants who live in that place, and grant them the same rights as the merchants who live in other royal cities." In addition, both Otto I and Otto II forbade the destruction of bridges and any other obstructions to trade.

Both emperors established toll stations that enabled them to profit from that trade. Commerce was no longer merely domestic: international trade, especially with England, flourished. Under Ottonian rule the cities of Germany prospered, and the wealth of their rulers grew proportionally.

D. A FLOURISHING CULTURE

Intellectual life continued to thrive under Otto II's rule. He was himself much interested in philosophical and theological questions. In the year 980, while celebrating Christmas in Ravenna, Otto sponsored a disputation. Othrich, his chaplain and former teacher at the cathedral school at Magdeburg, was matched against a professor at the cathedral school at Rheims, Gerbert of Aurillac, the leading intellectual of the day and future Pope Sylvester II. The topic was the classification of the sciences, that is, the divisions of philosophy.

Still earlier Otto I's ambassador to the Byzantine court at Constantinople, Liudprand of Cremona, wrote of what he described as outrageous treatment at the hands of his hosts. Nevertheless, he brought back from the East political and cultural information that was eagerly received, especially in Lotharingia, which became a center for Arabic and scientific studies.

Theophano, Otto II's wife, contributed as well to the high cultural level at the imperial court. She had arrived in the West from Constantinople with a large entourage of scholars and an immense treasure. The artwork she brought to the West, particularly the ivory statues and devotional plaques, showed great artistic merit and served as models for German artists.

Chapter Four

A Vision of Christendom

A. THE EARLY YEARS OF OTTO III

The son of Otto II and Theophano was but three years old when his father died in 983. Henry the Quarrelsome of Bavaria sought to assume guardianship over the child, supported by most of the bishops and other great lords. But when, a year later, Henry demanded that those powerful men acknowledge him as king, the vast majority refused, and little Otto was elected. He was given into the guardianship of his mother, Theophano, a sophisticated and strong-willed lady. When she died in 991, the eleven-year-old Otto was entrusted to his equally intelligent and powerful grandmother, Adelheid, the widow of Otto I. In 994, an assembly of the leading men of Germany declared that Otto, now fourteen years old, had come of age and was fit to rule in his own name. On Christmas Day of 996, he was anointed king at Aachen by the archbishop of Cologne and the archbishop of Ravenna, representing Germany and Italy. In May of the following year, a new pope, Gregory V, a cousin of Otto elected through his influence, anointed Otto emperor.

Life at Otto's court was a curious mixture of Greek and Germanic customs and practices. Following the Greek practice learned from his mother, Otto dined alone from time to time, at a raised table instead of seating himself in the midst of his warriors, as was the Germanic custom. Despite Otto's assignment of Greek titles to many of his staff, the personnel of his administration functioned more like the traditional Germanic brotherhood band of warriors–even though many of his carefully chosen advisors and administrators were bishops and other clerics. Otto took very seriously his roles as Germanic warrior and Roman emperor. Like Charles the Great, he read and spoke Latin fluently. Otto outdid his revered predecessor in not merely reading but speaking and writing Greek. Otto made a pilgrimage to

Aachen to visit the tomb of Charles as a symbol of his personal commitment to the values of that bellicose Christian king and scholarly Germanic warrior. The sight that greeted Otto when the tomb was opened surely supported the young king's resolve: "He [Charles] was not found lying down, but sitting on a throne as if he still lived. He was crowned with a golden diadem and held a scepter in his hand. None of his members had been corrupted; [so Otto] rebuilt the tomb again and departed." The synthesis of Christian, classical, and Germanic values that Charles had achieved was Otto's goal, for himself and for his empire.

B. POPE SYLVESTER II

When Otto's cousin, Pope Gregory V, died in 998, Otto saw to it that Gerbert of Aurillac was elected pope. The son of a farmer, Gerbert had been recognized as a lad of exceptional talent by the monks of the nearby monastery of Aurillac, who took him in and gave him a splendid education. Gerbert's mastery of mathematics, and indeed of all the branches of learning–literary, philosophical, and scientific–led to his appointment as chancellor of the cathedral school in the northern French city of Rheims. It was in this capacity that he had come to the attention of Otto II, who invited him to participate in a discussion of the classification of the sciences. In 982, Otto II made Gerbert the abbot of Bobbio, a venerable but by this time disreputable Italian monastery, in hopes that he could reform the life there. Despite Gerbert's noble attempts, in the end he failed and returned to Rheims.

There, in 994, he was elected archbishop. However he withdrew from the post to calm a dispute arising from the claims of another cleric. Three years later Gerbert left Rheims for Rome and there became the fast friend of the emperor's son, who would become Otto III. That same year, 997, Otto the son addressed a letter to Gerbert that succinctly shows how much he revered him: "Otto, most faithful of pupils, offers his steadfast loyalty to Gerbert, a teacher beyond all others." Otto saw to it that his mentor was elected archbishop of Ravenna in 998. In the following year Otto arranged for his election as bishop of Rome. Gerbert's choice of Sylvester II as his papal name was no accident. The first Sylvester had been bishop of Rome at the time of the Christian refashioning of the Roman Empire by the fourth-century emperor Constantine. Otto and Gerbert saw themselves working together to establish a new Christian empire, becoming the new Constantine and the second Sylvester.

C. ADELBERT OF PRAGUE, BOLESLAV THE BOLD, AND STEPHEN OF HUNGARY

In Otto and Sylvester's time, the Christian church in Bohemia (now the Czech Republic) was still in its infancy. The second bishop of its capital, Prague, was a man of piety and erudition whose name was Voytech. Political rivalries forced the bishop into exile, and he entered the Roman monastery of Sant' Alessio as a simple monk–assuming the name Adelbert. While there he and Otto became fast friends, Adelbert often serving as Otto's spiritual counselor. Recalled to Prague in 992, Adelbert encountered the same opposition as before, and he resolved to embrace the life of a missionary. He aimed at introducing or renewing Christianity among the Bohemians, Hungarians, and Poles, but he met his death at the hands of pagan Prussians, a Slavic tribe, in 997.

In the winter of 999-1000, Otto III set out on a pilgrimage to Poland, to the tomb in which his friend Adelbert had been buried. Otto's entrance into the lands of Duke Boleslav the Bold of Poland could well have been taken as a massive threat to the duke's independence. But Otto brought with him a decree from Pope Sylvester that supported Otto's belief that his was an apostolic mission. The document established in Poland an archbishopric and three bishoprics, all of them independent of ecclesiastical or political control by the emperor. In addition to giving this document to Boleslav, Otto presented the duke with a replica of what was believed to be the Holy Lance, the spear that had pierced the side of Jesus. Otto then bestowed on Boleslav the title "Brother and Fellow Servant of the Empire, Ally and Friend of the Roman People." As a contemporary chronicler put it: "Otto turned Boleslav from a tributary into a lord." Otto's vision of Empire did not demand submission from the Polish ruler or people but their fraternal cooperation in a federation of Christian states. To that vision Boleslav subscribed, and he accompanied Otto to Aachen and presented the emperor with three hundred stout-hearted Polish warriors to strengthen his army.

The conversion of Hungary marked another step in the realization of Otto's vision of a Christendom united in a federation of Christian states and peoples. This time it was Pope Sylvester who took the initiative in realizing this part of his and Otto's vision. We hear little of the Hungarians after their great defeat in 955 at the hands of Otto I. Although a flood of missionary efforts followed that defeat, Geza the king, and many of his countrymen, remained pagan. However, Geza's son Wajk subsequently married a Christian noblewoman, Gisela, and was baptized, taking the name Stephen. As a wise diplomatic gesture, Stephen commended his kingdom to Saint Peter. In 1001, Sylvester, who saw himself Peter's successor, took Stephen, his people, "and the Hungarian nation under the protection of the Holy Roman Church." On behalf of Saint Peter, Sylvester replied to Stephen's donation:

"We return and convey [this land] to your prudence, to your heirs and legitimate successors, to have, to hold, to rule, to govern, and to possess." Sylvester also bestowed on Stephen the crown and title of king that he had requested. Beyond that, the pope declared that Hungary should have its own church structure with an archbishop and "other bishoprics." Otto agreed and supported the creation of another kingdom independent of his rule, and another church province independent of the German Church. Both the Hungarian kingdom and Church remained the eastern bulwark of Latin Christendom for centuries to come.

D. CHURCH REFORM AND ROMAN RESTORATION

Otto coupled his Christianizing efforts in Eastern Europe with the resolution to complete his forbears' intention to free Church institutions, both bishoprics and monasteries, from attempts at control by the lay nobility. To this end, and to strengthen imperial government, he completed the process of granting immunities from lay control begun by his grandfather and continued by his father. Sometimes he granted governmental powers over whole counties to bishops and abbots.

In Italy the lay nobility had, in Otto's time, achieved a great deal of influence over, and often complete control of, church institutions. In Rome, for example, a group led by Cresentius arrested Pope John XIV whom, in 984, they starved–or poisoned–in prison. His successor, John XV, was a tool of these nobles, much to the dissatisfaction of the priests and people of Rome. In 997, Otto reacted by deposing John XV and selecting his own cousin, Bruno of Carinthia, as pope, who was duly elected by the clergy and people of Rome. Bruno took the name Gregory V and, as we remember, anointed Otto as emperor. Gregory's goal was to follow in the footsteps of his famous predecessor and Church reformer, Gregory I, the Great (590-604). Bruno was deposed by the hostile Roman nobility but, in 997, Otto came back to Italy and reestablished him in the chair of Peter. Otto defended churches all over Italy from the power of lay lords by appointing *ministeriales* (lay administrators) to protect the lands and interests of monasteries and bishoprics.

Evidences of the close cooperation of Otto and Pope Sylvester II we have already noted. Their joint effort led Bishop Leo of Vercelli, once a chaplain at the imperial court, to applaud the success of their effort and proclaim them the luminaries of the age, exclaiming: "Our times are reformed by the pope under the aegis of Caesar." The reformation of the Church, the people of God, was intended to be accomplished by the renovation of both ecclesiastical and temporal institutions. In Otto and Sylvester's time, no sharp distinction was made between what we call Church and State since the emperor received his power from God through his election by the people and his consecration by the bishop of Rome. Otto and Sylvester jointly presided over Church councils throughout the Empire and jointly issued church documents.

Otto referred to himself as *imperator romanus*, Roman emperor. He sincerely believed that the Roman Empire had been bestowed on him by God for the purpose of protecting, nourishing, and expanding the Church, the people of God. He envisioned the institutions which served that end, the imperial government and the Church hierarchy, coexisting until the end of time. He himself was the servant of both, and as such he also functioned as "the servant of Jesus Christ, our Savior and Liberator."

E. INTELLECTUAL LIFE UNDER OTTO III

Reform of Church institutions and renewal of imperial power both required a revival of classical and Christian learning, which were considered two sides of the same coin. Otto, we remember, had command of both Greek and Latin, and had amassed a substantial library. He also surrounded himself with intellectuals such as Gerbert and Leo, the bishop of Vercelli, a distinguished rhetorician and enthusiast for all facets of Roman antiquity. Almost all of the bishops in the Empire had been classically trained, either in the imperial court or in the flourishing monastic and episcopal schools of the time.

As a result of his classical education, Otto himself possessed considerable critical acumen. For example, Otto declared a forgery the *Donation of Constantine*, a document declaring that the Emperor Constantine I had transferred political control over the Empire in the West to the pope.

Theophano, Otto III's mother, had brought with her from Byzantium a large following, among which there were artists working in all sorts of media: ivory, enamel, jewelry, gold, and illuminated manuscripts. These proved to be a rich source of inspiration to German and Italian artists of the late tenth and eleventh centuries.

In January 1001, there arrived in Rome the bishop of Hildesheim, Bernward. He had come to Rome to plead his case in a boundary dispute between himself and his archbishop, Willigis of Mainz. Pope Sylvester ruled in Bernward's favor, but the bishop returned to Germany with far more than a legal decision. Bernward had taken advantage of his time in Rome to survey its ancient monuments. That survey was to have a profound effect on his own plans for the beautification of Hildesheim. The grandest result of Bernward's artistic imagination was to be the Saint Michael's Church. The bronze doors there are splendid examples of his observation and adoption of classical forms and motives.

F. THE END OF THE REIGN

During Bernward's stay in Rome, the Roman nobility launched a campaign of resistance to Otto's rule. Otto reacted with a plea for peace made to his assembled "children":

> You have closed me out of your hearts. But in truth you cannot exclude me from them, for I shall not permit that you, whom I love with a fatherly love, should be exiled from my heart. I know the ringleaders of this uprising; everyone sees and knows them. However, I find it monstrous that my most faithful followers, in whose innocence I trust, are mixed up with these evil doers.

At this, most of the Roman nobility declared their fidelity, and "moved to tears by these words of the emperor, they promised satisfaction."

Fearing that the leaders of the Roman opposition might seize the moment to reassert their power, Otto left Rome. The beginning of 1002 saw him just north of Rome, where a number of powerful German lords awaited him with their troops. There Otto was stricken with a mortal illness, perhaps smallpox, and he died at the age of twenty-two on the twenty-fourth of January. His loyal followers carried his body back to Germany, where they buried him in the center of the choir of Saint Mary's Church at Aachen, also the final resting place of his idol, Charles the Great. A grand vision was apparently cut short, but it would be revived and continued by Otto's successor.

Chapter Five

Reform and Imperial Theocracy

A. THE KING AND EMPEROR

The dominant motifs of the eleventh and twelfth centuries in Germany were reform and theocracy–rule through God's chosen agents. These concepts had formed important roles in the life of Germany since the time of Henry I. Reform and theocracy, however, were only implicit in the working of the political and religious spheres of tenth-century life. In the reign of Henry II (1002-1020), they became explicit sources of German life and thought.

Henry II was well suited to assume a leadership role in this process. He was born in 972, the son of the duke of Bavaria, Henry the Quarrelsome, who, we remember, had caused so much trouble in the early years of Otto III's reign. The child was, on his mother's side, the grandson of King Conrad of Burgundy and, on his father's side, the great-grandson of Emperor Henry I. Thus he was the second cousin of Otto III. Consequently, when grown he was an obvious candidate to succeed the childless Otto. However, when still a boy Henry was destined for the priesthood and an ecclesiastical career. In cathedral schools he received a thorough education in the liberal arts, the literary, philosophical, and scientific tradition of antiquity. But, at the death of his father in 995, he was elected duke of Bavaria. In that role he was much involved in the conversion of Hungary and its creation as a Christian kingdom. When the emperor Otto died in 1002, the great lords of Germany decided "that Henry should become king with Christ's help and by hereditary right."

B. EPISCOPAL AND MONASTIC REFORM

The idea of returning to the purity of belief and practice of the early Church was not new in the eleventh century. Indeed, down through the ages since apostolic times, the prevailing position was that the Church, being composed of fallible humans, was always in need of reform. Roughly a century before Henry's accession to the throne, a number of reform ideas achieved considerable success. In 906, for example, Regino of Prüm completed a work called *Two Books on Ecclesiastical Discipline*. Book 1 is directed to the clergy, Book 2 to the laity. Both books contain an anthology of instructions in morality and in practical approaches to a good Christian life. The books were an immediate success in Germany, and a century later spread throughout the whole Latin Church.

During Henry's own time, between 1008 and 1012, another bishop, Burchard of Worms, composed a book, the *Decretum*, which instructed bishops on all facets of their spiritual obligations and authority. This book too was circulated in the entire Christian West and promoted the cause of episcopal reform.

Surely the best known movement for monastic reform had taken place at the Abbey of Cluny in the area of French-speaking Burgundy which neighbored Lotharingia. When William the Pious, duke of Aquitaine, founded Cluny in the year 910, he specifically forbade any temporal lord, including his own son, to exercise control over it or to appoint its abbot. This permitted a return to the practice of early monasticism, in which the monks themselves selected the head of their monastic family and thus could ensure the continuation of their efforts to live a life of prayer and study. The land that William donated he owned outright, and therefore it carried no obligations to any other lord. Thus freed of any yokes, Cluny's reform was so successful that eventually some two thousand monasteries, from England to Poland, joined in a federation under the abbot of Cluny. Only a few of these monasteries were in Germany, but the reforming spirit of Cluny caught hold there too.

Monastic reform in Germany took a different direction from that in France. In France, the first step in reform was to free monasteries from the control of local lords who often appointed unworthy men as abbots. In Germany, monastic reform–and reform in the whole German Church–was effected through the cooperative, supervisory, and supporting agency of the emperor.

Sometimes the initiative in reform was taken by the monks themselves. This was most obvious in the case of the Lotharingian monastery of Gorze, an abbey founded in the year 993. Gorze fostered a reform, a revival of the practices counseled by Saint Benedict in his sixth-century *Rule for Monks*, and that revival was extremely popular. Young men flocked to Gorze; numbers of young women also entered monasteries inspired by Gorze's reform.

Some 150 monasteries spread all over Germany were eager to imitate Gorze's observances. Many monasteries formed or reformed in imitation of Gorze's practices entered into a federation for mutual support. Still other new or revitalized monasteries created similar groupings.

There were monasteries whose monks refused reform, since they lived rather comfortably from the revenues generated from donated lands. These were nevertheless reformed by imperial order. Henry called on monks from reformed monasteries to assume command of recalcitrant communities, and took away from those houses land he deemed superfluous to their monastic life. Abbots adopting a reformed way of life were supported by the emperor, while those that refused were replaced or coerced by Henry or his bishops. Henry considered his reform efforts were incumbent on him as a ruler responsible to God and to his people.

C. IMPERIAL THEOCRACY

Like his predecessors, Henry saw to it that virtuous and learned men were elected bishops. Indeed, those promoted to the highest ecclesiastical posts–archbishops, bishops, and important abbots–were dependent on royal favor. About one half of these higher clerics had been trained in the royal court as scribes, administrators, and emissaries. Once selected and elected, bishops were expected to support the king's military expeditions by supplying troops, and the king rewarded their support by granting still more lands to their bishoprics.

The most notable of Henry's actions in supporting and controlling the Church was his unilateral establishment, in the year 1007, of a new bishopric at Bamberg. A contemporary chronicler, Cosmas of Prague, reported that

> Henry endowed it to such an extent with resources and honors that, in all of Franconia, it was considered not the first established but the second [after Mainz]. He also built there a temple of astonishing size dedicated to the Virgin Mary and Saint George. He likewise augmented it with endowments for the church, with ornaments of gold and silver.

Some of the lands bestowed on the bishopric were in alpine regions. This allowed the king–through the bishop–greater control over the strategically important passes into Italy. Another of Henry's motives was to provide spiritual guidance to the still considerable Slavic population of this eastern region, "so that the paganism remaining among the Slavs would be destroyed." Still another motive was to replace the powerful and rebellious margrave, Henry of Schweinfurt, with a dependable supporter. To this end whole counties were transferred to the new bishopric. For Henry II, governmental and ecclesiastical concerns were two sides of the same coin. Through both he thought himself bound to provide justice to his people.

Henry's intention to create the new diocese at Bamberg was revealed to the bishops of Franconia at a synod which he convened in 1020 in Frankfurt, and over which he presided. There Bishop Henry of Würzburg's objections were mollified by a donation to him of some 150 manors possessed by the crown. Henry then sent off his decision to the pope, and Benedict VIII joined the emperor in the dedication of the new cathedral at Bamberg.

D. THE MAKING OF THE THEOCRAT

The rationale for Henry's power is mirrored in the ceremony that celebrated the conferring on him of both imperial dignity and power. As the king of England was anointed and crowned by the archbishop of Canterbury, the highest ranking prelate of his land, as the French king would be anointed and crowned by the archbishop of Rheims, so too the preeminent bishop of the empire, the bishop of Rome, had the privilege and duty of presiding over the ceremony. A detailed description of Henry's consecration rite has been preserved. It is a rite paralleling almost exactly the ceremony of episcopal ordination, symbolizing, it was thought, God's bestowal on the recipient the spiritual and temporal powers necessary for the fulfillment of his duties.

According to the document outlining the anointing and coronation rite, the emperor-elect and his wife were to be first "received by the prefect of the city and the count of the Lateran palace," representing the Roman people and the pope's temporal administration. A grand procession of clerics–"bishops, cardinals, deacons, and other orders of the church"–led the royal pair to the pope, and the emperor-elect promised the "vicar of St. Peter the Apostle to be the protector and defender of all the interests of this holy Roman church." (We note that the pope is addressed as vicar of Peter, not, as he would later be known, as the Vicar of Christ.) Henry then swore to defend the Church of Rome, meaning the local church, not the Catholic Church as a whole. After a procession to Saint Peter's Church, the emperor-elect was seated next to the pope, who examined him "with great love about his faith in the Holy Trinity." This, explained the document, was so "that the ordained would receive instruction on how to conduct himself when raised to his lofty position, and thus justifying the laying of hands on him." The laying on of hands was the means of ordaining both bishops and priests, hence the emperor became an ordinand. This is clear from the description of the dress with which the emperor-elect was clothed: "They dress him in the amice, alb, and cincture, and take him to the pope who makes him a member of the clerical order and grants him the tunic and dalmatic," the vestments of sub-deacons and deacons. The next step was still more important to contemporaries: "the anointing with consecrated oil." As David had been anointed by Samuel, as Jesus "was anointed by the Father with the oil of gladness," so too was Henry anointed as "the man appointed to rule the Church."

Henry then received the symbols of his temporal office: first a ring, "the symbol of the holy faith, the very foundation of kingship." The pope then girded him with a sword, saying: "Receive this sword, conferred on you with the blessing of God, and with it may you succeed in resisting and expelling all your enemies and those of the Church of God. May you guard the realm entrusted to you and protect the fortresses of God with the aid of the invincible victor, Our Lord Jesus Christ." Following this, the pope conferred "the scepter, the emblem of royal power, the wand of virtue by which you shall govern yourself and with royal courage defend from evil men the Holy Church and the Christian people entrusted to you by God." Following this path, the pope declared, the emperor "may from the temporal kingship reach the eternal Kingdom."

Imperial theocracy did not deny that the bishops of the Church, under the leadership of the pope, were superior to layfolk, including the emperor, in purely spiritual matters. On the other hand, the bishops were subject to the emperor in all questions touching on matters temporal. In the eleventh century, in Henry's time, there were very few matters which did not touch on both the temporal and on the spiritual. Cooperation, not conflict, was the ideal and was the norm in Henry's time. The Church was seen as the entire body of the faithful whose spiritual needs were served by bishops and priests through the administration of sacraments and the spiritual direction given through public sermons and individual counsel. The temporal needs of the people of God, preeminently protection and justice, were to be provided by the emperor and the other officials of the empire.

E. THE GOVERNANCE OF THE EMPIRE

Henry's imperial administration continued to rely on the royal "chapel" as the central institution of governance. Some of the "chaplains" functioned as notaries, others as royal scribes. They drew up the documents issued to convey the ruler's wishes, generally in response to requests. Scribes were also needed to record grants, sometimes made by Henry's predecessors, sometimes recording the reclamation of lands forfeited by rebellion or recovered through the death of the grantee. Lists were made of the military contingents to be supplied by the powerful men of the Empire, both lay and clerical.

The court officials charged with fiscal matters were the emperor's chamberlains. Chamberlains were in charge of the royal treasure, including coin and precious objects. They also collected the moneys owed the state. The emperor rewarded outstanding chamberlains with high honors, sometimes numbering them among his closest associates and ranking them below only church prelates and lay princes.

The court received a constant stream of visitors. High-ranking and notable visitors, counts and bishops, were treated as friends and as sources of valuable information about the provinces. Henry II often agreed to serve as godfather or confirmation sponsor to their children, thus cementing a cordial relationship with the parent of the son or daughter so honored.

The imperial court continued to be itinerant, showing by the emperor's presence his power and exercising that power by "holding court." The king received requests and complaints, administered justice, made peace between enemies, and gave and received gifts, sometimes lavish ones. Some of the emperor's duties required more than a well-functioning staff and an efficiently managed administration. Matters of the highest importance to the empire demanded an assembly of the powerful men of the land. The protection due to the people of the land sometimes required expeditions to which the great lords were to give their approval and support. Bishops especially were called on to provide troops, though they were not expected to lead them. Matters affecting the Church and thus the nation were discussed in assemblies presided over by the king. These Church councils included not only bishops, but also lay lords. Conversely, bishops as territorial lords joined the lay magnates in influencing the king's choice of replacements to vacant duchies and counties.

F. UNIVERSALITY AND REGIONALISM

As well governed as Henry's realm was, there were revolts to be put down and wars to wage. In the West, Henry was faced in 1006 with the revolt of Baldwin IV of Flanders. Henry launched a retaliatory expedition with the support of King Robert of France. The following year Baldwin came to Aachen and took an oath of loyalty to the emperor.

Also in the West, Henry resisted the attempts of his wife's brothers to take control of Lotharingia. In 1005, one of the brothers, Dietrich, used force to claim the bishopric of Metz. In 1008, a second brother, Adalbero, attempted to follow Dietrich's example by claiming the archbishopric of Trier. Open warfare resulted, but Henry offered the brothers a compromise that brought about a sharing of power and lasting peace.

The immensely rich kingdom of Burgundy covered the greater part of today's southeast France. It was brought within the imperial orbit in Henry's time. Thietmar of Merseburg wrote: "Henry's mother's brother, Rudolf, the [childless] king of Burgundy, had promised him his crown and scepter in the presence of his wife, his step-sons, and all his nobles. And now this promise was repeated with an oath. This happened at Mainz in the year 1013." Henry's efforts to secure the crown, however, met with resistance by the Burgundians. Henry's efforts to incorporate Burgundy fully into the Empire were ultimately rewarded, but not until after his death.

Much more serious problems faced Henry on the eastern frontier of his realm. Duke Boleslav I Chobry of Poland was called by contemporaries "the Great" or "the Mighty." He extended his sway westward into lands under imperial control. He allied himself with some discontented German nobles, including the king's brother Bruno, the bishop of Augsburg. In 1003, Boleslav seized Bohemia and had its duke beheaded. Henry conducted three expeditions against Boleslav, but he was unable to realize complete victory because he was repeatedly called to Italy to settle matters there.

Eventually, in 1004, Henry did recover Bohemia for the Empire with the help of contingents from Saxony and Bavaria and troops sent by the German bishops. Boleslav sued for peace the following year. The defiance of the Polish king required Henry's action again in 1015 and 1017, and peace was finally attained only in 1018. As part of the settlement, the Liutizi, a pagan Slavic tribe, were granted their independence as a reward for their support against the Polish king.

Henry was thus able to deal with threats on the eastern and western frontiers of the Empire. Nonetheless it was the southern part of his realm, Italy, that occupied most of his attention and energies. Already at the beginning of his reign there were perils perceived by the pro-imperial party in Italy. Letters and envoys urged Henry to intervene in the rebellious north Italian region of Lombardy. The rebels went so far as to elect Ardwin, the margrave of Ivrea, as king of Lombardy, crowning him in the basilica of Saint Michael in Ardwin's capital city. Henry amassed an army composed of Lotharingians, Franconians, and Swabians, crossed the Alps, marched through Lombardy, and defeated Ardwin, by now abandoned by most of his former supporters. At Pavia, Henry was in turn elected king of Lombardy, anointed and crowned on Sunday, the fourteenth of May in 1004. Overcoming the remaining resistance, Henry held a royal council to bring about a settlement of the issues of this land, and, satisfied with the results, he wended his way back across the Alps.

Though Henry was king in Lombardy, the real power in the land was in the hands of the magnates, both bishops and lay lords, of a land continually agitated by warfare. Strife was also rampant in Rome, in both the city and the surrounding territory. The great Italian families fought and, when successful, named their adherents as popes, exiling the popes from other factions. By 1013, Henry had had enough and marched into Italy. At Pavia a throng of reform-minded bishops and abbots met to support the king who had done so much to aid their cause. Henry repaid their support by responding forcefully to the clerical corruption endemic to much of Italy. At Rome in 1014, he was anointed emperor, in the impressive ceremony we have seen described. On his way back to Germany, Henry secured his hold on the city of Florence and on Tuscany, the land in which that city lay. After crossing the Alps Henry relied increasingly on bishops as his agents in ruling his Italian lands.

A new threat to the peace of Italy came in 1021, this time from an army expanding from the Byzantine Greek holdings in southern Italy. A new German expedition faced hard fighting. This fight was for the most part successful, but disease prevented the expulsion of the Greeks from the extreme southern provinces of mainland Italy. On Henry's way back to Germany, a council presided over by pope and emperor once more addressed the issue of reform of the Italian church.

Reformation of the church, stabilization of government, and fostering good rule through providing his people with protection and justice were Henry's highest aspirations. His was a dauntingly complex task, and to his credit he largely succeeded in accomplishing his goals. The Germany over which he ruled was not a society of lords and vassals, like that of contemporary France, but a society of freemen jealous of their freedom. Though Henry remained first and last a German, he saw himself destined to bring the benefits of imperial rule to all his lands, from the Baltic to the Mediterranean.

Henry died childless on the twelfth of July in the year 1024 at the castle of Grone near Göttingen. He was but fifty-two years old. His body was buried in the cathedral of Bamberg, in the diocese he had created. In 1146, Pope Eugenius III declared Henry a saint.

Chapter Six

The Construction of a State

A. CHOOSING THE KING

We are fortunate in having a detailed description of the deeds of the emperor Conrad II. The author of this narrative, Wipo, was a *capellanus*, a royal chaplain to Conrad, and his narrative extends from 1024 to 1093, through all the years of Conrad's reign. Wipo's narrative is filled with biblical references and quotations, and is liberally seasoned with a generous salting of quotations from classical authors. Clearly, Wipo's education reflected the union of classical and Christian culture which characterized an ongoing renaissance.

Wipo wrote of Conrad's election:

> When the Emperor [Henry II] died without children, every great and powerful man among the lay princes strove either to become the first man or by some pact or other to become second. This state of affairs demands that I mention the names of the greatest men, bishops as well as lay princes, by whose counsels the realm was wont to elect kings.

Wipo did so–at great length–and then continued his narrative of the election:

> A long disputation took place as to who ought to rule. Some few were chosen from the many, and from the few only two [both named Conrad] were singled out. The rest of the noble men present vacillated long between these two men. The younger of them promised in no uncertain terms that he would render [to the elder] all the faithfulness owed to a king. Then the archbishop of Mainz, whose opinion had to be heard before all the others, with a full heart and a happy voice acclaimed and elected the older Conrad.

The other great lords, lay and clerical, followed suit, and so the elder Conrad was chosen emperor on September 8, 1024. Thus a new dynasty, called the

Salian, assumed the reins of power in Germany and the empire. It is called the "Salian" dynasty because Conrad was a Salian Frank, one of the Franks who had settled near the salty (Latin: *sal*) North Sea.

The archbishop of Mainz, the primate of the German Church, also presided at the anointing of Conrad as king. In his sermon, the archbishop counseled Conrad "to be merciful to those who lose your favor, to be merciful to those who sustain injuries." God wills, proclaimed the archbishop, "most of all that you render just judgment and thus bring justice and peace to the fatherland." God, he said, wants Conrad to be "the defender of churches and clergy, the guardian of widows and orphans." Moreover, the archbishop declared, in a statement to have repercussions before long: "You have come to the highest dignity. You are the vicar of Christ."

How seriously Conrad took these admonitions was shown, Wipo reported, by his actions preceding his consecration:

> During the procession of the king, three persons came before the king, each with a complaint. When the king began to hear their cases, some of the princes took him aside, pointing out that he should not delay appearing at his consecration. He responded like a true Vicar of Christ in a most Christian way: "It seems to me to be more virtuous to do what I ought than to hear from another what should be done."

Conrad continued this approach to his position throughout his reign, "hearing the complaints of many paupers and ruling on their cases. He declined to defer justice, since that was the very heart of governance."

B. THE GOVERNANCE OF THE REALM

To cement his power in the various regions of Germany, Conrad journeyed far and wide throughout his kingdom, "ordering most excellently the affairs of the commonwealth." His solemn procession took him first to the northern part of Lotharingia, specifically to the palace and cathedral of Charles the Great at Aachen. There "he held an assembly of the people and a general council in which he distributed spiritual and temporal rights with efficacious results." Conrad next traveled to Saxony, then Swabia, also "passing through Bavaria and eastern Franconia." Wipo commented: "In this progress, he bound those districts very firmly in a bond of peace and in royal guardianship."

To ensure uninterrupted continuity of the bonds uniting his realm, Conrad declared his son Henry his successor in 1026, only two years after his own accession to the throne. Two years after that, in 1028, he had Henry anointed king at Aachen. Henry had been entrusted to Engelbert, the bishop of Freising, when still a young boy. As the lad grew, Conrad gave him more and more responsibility–eventually turning over to him the administration of Burgundy and appointing him duke of Bavaria.

Conrad's wife, Gisela, was an essential helpmate in his administration. She was, Wipo tells us, "held in high esteem because of her prudence and counsel." The daughter of Herman, duke of Swabia, Gisela brought to her marriage "rich estates," and these and other great responsibilities "she was qualified to administer well." She was also Conrad's "necessary companion."

The royal pair was, of course, surrounded by a host of officials high and low: from chamberlains, in charge of the treasury and numerous other fiscal matters, to stewards and cupbearers, responsible for feeding the royal court. Conrad's biographer Wipo, as chaplain, was also a member of the court. Observing at close range the working of the court, he was particularly impressed with the quality of Conrad's central administration. He attributed it to the wise counsel of Bishop Bruno of Augsburg, Bishop Werinhar of Salzburg, and a lay court official and confident also named Werinhar.

The quality of Conrad's governance was greatly enhanced by his skillful handling of the great and powerful lords of the various territories comprising Germany. We have already seen how Conrad's predecessors countered the power of counts by assigning large parts of their authority to neighboring bishops. At times, however, one or another of the especially powerful bishops chose to obstruct the king's plans.

An example of this occurred even as Conrad was being elected king. The chief opponent of that election, Archbishop Pilgrim of Cologne, joined the dukes of upper and lower Lotharingia in opposition. Conrad resisted all three firmly and finally won over Pilgrim by asking him to anoint and crown his consort Gisela as queen, in a ceremony to be held in the archbishop's own cathedral.

The opposition of Adelbero of Eppenstein, duke of Carinthia, was longer lived. In 1027, Conrad presided over an assembly at which Adalbero put forth the claim that all the towns, villages, and farmers belonging to the Church of Aquileia owed him "the bread and wine, the meat and grain, and other services needed to feed and support his soldiers." To this the chief ecclesiastic of Aquileia, Patriarch Poppo, replied that "it was not true that they owed anything to dukes or margraves or counts, to judges or police officers." The court ruled in favor of Poppo, and Adalbero was admonished not to press this suit again on pain of an indemnity of "one hundred pounds of the purest gold." Adelbero did not forget his humiliation, as he saw it, at the hands of the emperor. He continued his opposition to Conrad until at last, in 1035, at an assembly in Bamberg, Adelbero was charged with treason, deposed, and deprived of his lands.

The repeated revolts of Duke Ernst of Swabia reveal even more clearly the profound change that Conrad introduced into his governance of the Empire. Conrad's biographer, Wipo, reported that when Emperor Conrad returned to Swabia, he took counsel about those who had betrayed the fatherland. Duke Ernst did not appear before the assembly as a suppliant, but relied on support of the great number of his very important men. Ernst first reminded them of their fidelity to him, and then exhorted them not to desert him, lest they forfeit their honor.

To this two of the counts accompanying the duke replied:

> "We do not deny that we promised fealty to you. But we are free men, and we hold that our king and emperor is the supreme defender of our liberty on earth. We are willing to obey whatever honorable and just command you make. But if you demand something contrary to this, we shall firmly revert to that condition [of independence] that we enjoyed before we began to follow you."

At that Duke Ernst "realized he was abandoned by his own men and surrendered to the emperor." The counts who had pledged their loyalty to the duke recognized the higher loyalty that they owed to their emperor. In return for their support, Conrad strengthened the relationship by transferring authority over many crown lands to the counts.

So it came about that bishops held counts in check, counts assisted the ruler against the dukes, and bishops, largely chosen by the king, rarely resisted him. And when members of any of these groups did choose to disobey the king, Conrad was sufficiently powerful to overcome their resistance with a force largely composed of episcopal troops.

Conrad's rule was immeasurably strengthened by a new group of administrators called in Latin *ministeriales*. Initially these were men obligated to remain in service to their lord, but otherwise free. In time, the ministerials' sons won total freedom through their fathers' and their own faithful and efficient service. Loyal grandsons received royal land grants from their king and themselves became lords. This is surely a remarkable example of upward mobility: from *Dienstmann* (serving man), to *Dienstherr* (serving lord), to simply *Herr* (lord). Conrad organized these men into an administrative staff, and made one such ministerial, Werner, his treasury secretary. Through men like Werner the lands of royal abbeys–those immediately dependent on the king–received the same efficient management as the lands belonging directly to the king. Ministerials also served a military function, as captains of the royal castles. They often lived in them–whereas the king typically resided in a much more comfortable but less formidable manor house.

Under Conrad disputes were settled and reconciliations fostered at assemblies of the people. The law thus enshrined in the memories of the people was organized into a coherent legal code by the ministerials. In important cases, for example, Conrad ordered an inquest, an investigation into the land ownership and rights pertaining to the case. Conrad would call on his officials to offer sworn evidence as to what lands belonged to whom.

Conrad's innovations extended to economic matters as well. With Conrad we see the growth of crown property and the beginnings of separation of public property from personal ownership by the king. Conrad also generously supported merchants, granting, for example, both Jews and Gentiles of the city of Magdeburg "the freedom to come and go everywhere in our realm, both in Christian and barbarous lands." Farmers as well as merchants were protected. Conrad issued decrees warning landlords not to ask their farm workers for excessive labor services and cash payments.

It was, of course, incumbent on Conrad to be a capable manager of his political subordinates, lords great and small, lay and clerical. And in this he was highly successful. To achieve this success he had to be a proficient military commander, a just man knowledgeable in the law, and an astute economic manager of both his and the realm's agricultural and industrial production and trade.

C. THE TRIUMPHANT WARRIOR AND DIPLOMAT

Without a doubt the most important addition to the Empire during Conrad's reign was the kingdom of Burgundy. Even though Burgundy had been willed to Henry II in 1013, Henry had been distracted from the task of fully incorporating Burgundy into the Empire by the many military fronts, from Bohemia to Italy, which engaged his attention. When Henry died in 1029, Conrad assumed the claim to the Burgundian kingdom. Wipo the chaplain told the story:

> In the year of the Lord 1032, Rudolf, king of Burgundy, died in peace. Count Odo Francigen, son of his sister, invaded the Burgundian realm and took some very well constructed castles and well-defended cities. In the year of the Lord 1033, Emperor Conrad, with his son King Henry, collected an army and entered Burgundy. At Zürich he was elected ruler of Burgundy by the greater and lesser lords of the kingdom, and, on the same day, was crowned as king.

Conrad led his army against Odo, who pledged to relinquish Burgundy but failed to give over all the territory he had promised. Conrad then besieged Odo's principal stronghold and took it by force, thus removing all opposition to his rule. Wipo continued:

> After all the princes of the [Burgundian] realm had been called together, Conrad presided over a general assembly, and for the first time made Burgundy taste the traditional Burgundian law, long disused and almost wiped from the books. Then, at the request of the leading men of the realm, along with all the people, the emperor handed the Burgundian kingdom over to his son, as co-ruler.

Burgundy would remain part of the Empire for centuries afterward.

Conrad was bedeviled by the same problems on the Empire's eastern frontier his predecessor had faced. Two events mitigated those problems. First, Boleslav Chrobny, the Polish king whose territorial ambitions had plagued Henry II, died in 1025. Secondly, Conrad had secured the loyalty of the Lausatians and Obodrites, pagan Slavic tribesmen living to the east of the Saxons and to the west of the Poles. In 1025, however, Boleslav's son Misko drove out his elder brother Otto and assumed the sole kingship of Poland. Five years later Misko led a Polish incursion into imperial lands, destroying 100 villages and taking captive 9,000 women and men in the process. Misko's forces were beaten off by Count Dietrich of Wettin, whose fortress served as a launching pad for Conrad's retaliatory expedition. Conrad had allied himself with Misko's banished brother Otto and with Yaroslav, the prince of Kiev. Conrad freed the lands of the Lausations, and Misko was dethroned in favor of Otto, whom Conrad recognized as the lawful duke of Poland.

The peace that resulted from Conrad's efforts on the Empire's eastern frontier gave impetus to new or much increased migration. The sparsely settled lands east of the Elbe River, then later east of the Oder River, were rapidly filled with pioneering families who sought new land to farm. These families needed the protection of local lords, often the younger sons of noble families attracted by the opportunities opening up in the East, who took an active role in the "Push to the East" (German: *Drang nach Osten*).

Conrad spent only some three out of the fifteen years of his reign in Italy. Still, the peninsula continued to be a thorn in the side of the Empire. Conrad's response would significantly change imperial governance in the Italian peninsula.

The strife endemic in Italy was partially due to past imperial policy. German rulers had relied on Italian bishops to keep the peace and, to that end, had donated to them control of lands, mints, markets, and tolls. The increasingly prosperous merchants of Italian towns considered their trade constrained by these episcopal powers. They likewise chafed under episcopal administration of law in their cities. Church law, they thought, did not take into account the special needs of their commercial world.

The power which the Italian bishops had amassed led some of them to defy Conrad's authority. A case in point is that of Aribert, archbishop of Milan. Aribert had pledged his support to Conrad in the very year, 1024, of Conrad's ascendance to the throne. Only two years later, in 1026, when Conrad led his first expedition to Italy, Aribert had changed his mind and declared in a session of the imperial court that he would not recognize the emperor's right to issue decisions affecting his territory. Aribert's subsequent imprisonment was cleverly foiled when an amply-robed monk came to visit him and during the night exchanged clothing with the archbishop, who calmly walked out of the prison. In 1037, Aribert was declared guilty of high treason and deposed–an effective warning to powerful bishops and lay lords alike.

Another source of unrest in Italy was the deteriorating relationship between high lords, lay and clerical, and between knights and lesser nobles. The knights saw themselves reduced to the status of employees who could be dismissed at a lord's pleasure. Conrad's biographer Wipo reported that "all the knights of Italy had entered into a pact, directed against their lords, not to allow anything done to them against their will go unrevenged. They said if their emperor did not wish to join them, they would enact laws for themselves." But Conrad did indeed come to the knights' aid and was reported to have said: "If Italy hungers now for law, God granting I shall sate it well with laws." At Milan, on the twenty-eighth day of May 1037, Conrad issued a decree aimed at reconciling "the minds of lords and knights so that they can be mutually harmonious." To accomplish this, Conrad decreed that no knight should be deprived of landgrants made by "bishops, abbots, abbesses, margraves, counts, or any who hold a grant from our royal property or from that of the Church without a fault being proved." Conrad also granted to all, whether high or lowborn, that when they died, their land grants would be inherited by their sons, grandsons, or brothers. Given this independence and the economic success that followed, more and more of the lesser nobility built or purchased houses in the towns of northern Italy, eventually becoming integrated socially with the urban manufacturing and trading class.

Conrad significantly promoted the success of north Italian mercantile activities. He issued a decree substituting the Justinian Code, a sixth-century compilation of Roman law, for the Lombard law which had until then prevailed in that land. The Lombard law code had been followed by the Germanic tribe that, in the sixth century, had settled in the Po river valley, which included most of northern Italy. Like other early Germanic codes it was primarily devoted to providing alternatives to private vengeance by the kinfolk of an injured, sometimes mortally injured, member of the tribe. Roman law operated on a completely different level: it presupposed city-states having an economic relationship within and between them. This law, bequeathed from antiquity, so greatly aided the economic growth of northern Italy that, in the centuries to follow, it would help the region become the most prosperous area in Europe.

D. CONRAD AND THE CHURCH

In 1032, when Conrad brought Burgundy into the imperial fold, the reform movement there was flourishing. The movement had by this time aimed not only at monastic and episcopal reinvigoration, but had set its sights on the spiritual renewal of all of society. The "Truce of God" was one of the means established to realize this goal. Councils of reform-minded bishops and abbots, supported by like-minded lay lords, forbade armed conflict on Sundays throughout the year and on major feast days like Christmas and Easter. A general and obligatory truce had already been adopted in Lotharingia, but its observance was sufficiently strengthened by the successful Burgundian practice that it became nearly universal in Germany.

Conrad supported monastic reform by granting monasteries imperial protection, so that, "perpetually remote from disturbance of all," the monks could "devoutly serve God." The abbots of these reform monasteries were granted the right to appoint lay administrators, who, were "restricted from having any power beyond what the abbot and his successors should grant them with the consent of the brothers."

Conrad also streamlined and thus strengthened the temporal support of the reform by combining the administrative resources of several monasteries. This reduced the cost and simplified the task of supporting the spiritual activities of the monks. This revival of monasticism found its crowning expression in Conrad's appointment of the head of a reformed German monastery to the abbacy of Monte Cassino, the Italian monastery founded by Benedict of Nursia in the sixth century and the mother house of western monasticism.

Conrad's support also extended to bishops and the other clergy serving the spiritual needs of lay folk. His concern was by no means limited to institutional reform; he also promoted personal reform. Wipo told a story illustrative of this point. He described a solemn procession of the king through his whole realm:

> When the royal entourage had been assembled, King Conrad first went to the place where the regal throne of state was set up by the kings of old, notably by Charles [the Great]. Sitting there Conrad set the affairs of the commonwealth in good order. He held an assembly of the people and a general [Church] council there. His fame gained strength because of his virtue. He prudently instructed every bishop and all other clerics to conduct well the affairs of their office. If he approved of their conduct he praised them warmly and courteously in public. If he found them remiss in their duties he admonished them in private, sometimes accompanied by a fitting punishment.

E. DEATH AND LEGACY

Inevitably Conrad's prudent reign came to an end. Wipo the chaplain wrote that

> in the year of the Lord's incarnation 1039, Emperor Conrad was confident that now the actual state of the kingdom, still more the hope for the Empire, had

been well placed in his son, King Henry. And when he saw that everything throughout his kingdom was functioning according to his wishes, he celebrated the holy day of Pentecost at Utrecht, a city of Frisia.

That evening, at a state dinner, Conrad suffered a painful attack. "He concealed his discomfort," Wipo related, "lest it disturb the happiness of so great a day." However, "the following day the mortal illness grew violent," and Conrad sent the empress for bishops who brought the eucharistic bread and wine to his bedside. After communicating, "he bade farewell to the empress and to his son, King Henry. He then departed this life." Conrad was buried in the crypt of the cathedral he had begun to have built at Speyer.

Conrad's legacy was manifold. One event that occurred in the very first year of his reign revolutionized the relationship between the person of the emperor and the office that he held. Again it was Wipo who recorded the story:

> There was in the city of Pavia a palace once built with marvelous workmanship by King Theodoric [a sixth-century king of the Ostrogoths] and afterwards much adorned by Emperor Otto III. When the death of the emperor Henry, the predecessor of King Conrad, became known, the Pavians razed the whole palace to the last stone of the foundation. Because of this a great and lengthy disputation was held between the king and the Pavians.

The Pavians claimed that they had been loyal subjects of Henry II, but that, when he died, there was no longer a ruler to be offended by their actions. Conrad replied:

> I know that you have not destroyed your king's residence because you had no king at that time. But you cannot deny that you have torn down a royal residence. Even if the king died, the kingdom remained. It was a state building, not a private one. You, then, have done wrong to the property of another; therefore you have incurred the wrath of the king.

To differentiate between public land and the private property of those who hold the public trust is a giant step forward in the understanding of the law.

If most of Conrad's contemporaries did not understand the force of his sophisticated argument, they certainly respected the power he represented and controlled as king. In March of 1027, both Knut, the king of England and Denmark, and King Rudolf III of Burgundy traveled to Rome to attend Conrad's anointing as emperor.

Partially by good fortune, but mostly by astute planning and resolute action, Conrad succeeded in creating a structure of governance for his whole empire. That empire now included Germany and its frontier lands to the East, Burgundy, and northern and central Italy. His was a formidable achievement at a time when mobility was measured by the pace of a horse and feeding the royal entourage required moving from one royal manor to another.

Chapter Seven

Apogee of Empire

A. THE ACCESSION OF HENRY III

Henry III received from his grandfather, Henry II, the legacy of a far-ranging vision of Church and society, commonly called Imperial Theocracy. From his father, Conrad II, Henry inherited a sophisticated and effective state structure.

Conrad also bequeathed his son extensive experience in rulership. Conrad had had his eleven-year-old son anointed and crowned king in Charles the Great's cathedral at Aachen on Easter day in 1028, having already (in 1027) named Henry duke of Bavaria. In 1038, the great magnates of Burgundy recognized Conrad as king and Henry as joint ruler. In 1038, the duchy of Swabia was added to Henry's honors.

Henry's suitability for kingship had been proven in battle in 1031, when he rode with his father in a successful campaign against the Poles. Conrad had also sent Henry to battle restive Slavs and rebellious Bohemians. In both missions he was successful. Henry had rapidly and well mastered the military virtues into which his father had had him initiated.

Henry was extraordinarily gifted in other ways. He had been well-educated under the tutelage of his cousin Bruno, bishop of Augsburg, and the caring direction of Bishop Egibert of Freising. Henry was also recognized by one and all for his sincere religious piety.

On Conrad's death in 1039, Henry's succession was clear, having been publicly designated king by his father as early as 1026. After having buried his father in the cathedral crypt at Speyer, Henry began an extensive royal progress at Aachen and from there traveled through Lotharingia, Saxony, Bavaria, and Swabia, showing himself to his people and settling local disputes.

B. THE GOVERNANCE OF THE REALM

At the time of Henry's succession, the population of Germany had increased to five or six million people–people for whom he was obliged to provide protection and justice. The personnel on whom Henry relied for governance changed little on his accession. Margraves, counts, and ministerials all played supporting roles, although the last were becoming increasingly important. Bishops were central figures in Henry's royal governance, although their responsibilities to their dioceses meant that they could not perform the day-to-day activities of royal administration. Abbots of reformed monasteries also served their rulers through their advice and counsel.

A major means of discovering and correcting problems were the great assemblies that Henry called three or four times a year. At these assemblies–which also served as Church councils–most of the political problems of the kingdom were brought into the open, discussed, and settled. Appointments to major lay and ecclesiastical offices were discussed and announced. Rebels were proscribed and their submission accepted. Delegations from far-off regions of the empire were received, as were ambassadors from foreign lands.

The king, with the support of the assembly, passed judgement on even the most powerful men of the land. For example, Henry intervened forcibly on behalf of Bishop Gebhard of Regensburg when, in 1053, he was attacked by Duke Conrad of Bavaria. On the other hand, Henry refused to support bishops Gerhard and Lietbert in their attempt to wrest control of the city of Cambrai from its count. Henry favored no single group over another.

Henry's search for justice extended beyond his immediate reach. He sent out chaplains from his court to act with his authority in bringing justice to people far removed from that court. They also traveled on diplomatic missions and often acted as intermediaries in quarrels between even the most powerful lords. These royal officials also presided in local assemblies of the people. These and other duties meant that the number of court chaplains increased markedly. Some of them were recruited from as far away as Italy. Henry appointed only those with a superior education and with impeccable morals. Those who were preeminent in their service were sometimes promoted to the office of bishop.

Henry's band of roving peacemakers and lawgivers was supported by a central administration housed at Goslar. This administrative center in the Harz Mountains of Saxony was heavily fortified by Henry. As in all the king's manors and castles, the overseer was one of the ministerials, men without noble ancestry who through their and the forefathers' service had been made members of the lesser nobility. One of Henry's ministerials, Benno, became the mayor of the imperial palace at Goslar and chief administrator of the crown lands. In 1054, as a reward for his outstanding service, Henry selected him to be bishop of Osnabrück.

All these institutions, Henry maintained, were means by which his people could come to live in justice and prosperity. He himself wrote: "It seems fitting that imperial skill should serve the people's welfare, and diligently provide those things useful and beneficial to coming generations."

C. DEALING WITH DUKES AND KINGS

In his campaign to provide peace and justice, Henry built on traditional structures while bringing them firmly under his control. For example, we have seen that Henry had been given rule in 1038 over the Kingdom of Burgundy by his father. His royal status was enhanced by his second marriage in 1038, to the high-born Agnes of Poitou, daughter of William IV, duke of Guienne. Although Henry made but three appearances in Burgundy, spending fewer than two years out of the sixteen years of his reign there, his conciliatory attitude toward the powerful men of the kingdom contributed effectively to the consolidation of his rule over this relatively new territorial acquisition. Henry created a separate chancery to provide administrative services to Burgundy, and, contrary to his father's action in Lombardy, revived traditional Burgundian law. His declaration that Burgundy was "its own country with its own law" won him the loyalty of virtually all the inhabitants of that land.

A much less welcoming response awaited Henry in the duchy of Lotharingia. The last ten years of Henry's reign witnessed a feud between the king and Duke Godfrey the Bearded. Godfrey's father had been duke of upper and lower Lotharingia, and, at the father's death in 1049, Godfrey claimed the succession. Henry recognized Godfrey's rule in Upper Lotharingia but wisely gave Lower Lotharingia over to Godfrey's brother Gozolo II. When Godfrey refused to accept this decision, he was deprived of his remaining duchy. In the struggle that followed, Henry was supported by the bishops of Liège, Metz, and Utrecht. Henry led an expedition into Upper Lotharingia, and this, strengthened by Pope Leo IX's excommunication of Godfrey, forced the latter's cause to fall into disarray.

Still another bishop, Adelbert of Hamburg, aided Henry by negotiating a treaty with King Swein of Norway and Denmark. Swein, an ardent Christian whose devotion to the faith matched Henry's, sent his fleet to the coast of Frisia in support of the emperor's pacification of his western provinces. Personal piety and the support of sympathetic leaders, both churchmen and lay lords, were factors in Henry's success in Lotharingia and elsewhere. Political acumen and the judicious use of force were equally crucial components of that success.

D. DEFENDING FRONTIERS

Germany's eastern frontier demanded much of Henry's attention. In 1040, Duke Bratislav of Bohemia invaded Poland. Henry rushed to the defense of his neighbor, but his first expedition suffered heavy losses. Even so, Lambert of Hersfeld reported that, in 1041, "King Henry entered Bohemia a second time and compelled its duke, Bratislav, to surrender. He made his territory tributary to Henry." Peace was secured, and Bohemia was once more attached to the Empire. In fact, when "the king celebrated Christmas at Goslar, the duke of Bohemia came to see him. Bratislav was kindly received by the king, honorably entertained for some time, and at length sent away in peace." As a result of Henry's victory over Bratislav, the Poles were able, with German help, to reinstate their exiled duke, Casimir.

To the south of Poland and Bohemia and to the east of the German duchy of Bavaria, lay Hungary. Lambert of Hersfeld recounted the story:

> Peter of Hungary was expelled by his own people and fled to Henry for whose aid he pleaded. Ouban, who had usurped the crown of Hungary, invaded Bavaria and Carinthia and took much booty. But the Bavarians united all their forces, pursued them, retook the booty, killed a great many of them, and put the rest to flight.

The next year, 1044, "King Henry led a campaign against Hungary and deposed the pretender, Ouban. After Henry had invaded Hungary, he received oaths of fidelity from the inhabitants of that land." The result was that the kingdom's easternmost frontier county (later Austria) was shielded from attack and was thus opened to secure and extensive settlement.

E. THE BENEVOLENT THEOCRAT

Like his namesake Henry II, the third Henry possessed deep religious convictions and a strong sense of his divine mission. His goal was to serve his people as a just king, and he strongly believed that that goal necessitated the king's oversight of the Church. Most of his contemporaries agreed. Abbot Ekbert of Tegernsee, for example, proclaimed that Henry was "the head of the Church."

As head of the Church, Henry pursued an unrelenting campaign to ensure peace within his realm. In October 1043, Henry, dressed in penitential garb, made an unprecedented appearance before an assembly of Swabians at Constance. From a pulpit Henry promised forgiveness for all offenses committed against him—including those of his nemesis Godfrey of Lotharingia. This was his royal restatement of the increasingly popular "Truce of God" being proclaimed by Church councils throughout Henry's lands. For example, a council presided over by the archbishops of Besançon and Vienne demanded that "all begin the truce from sunset every Wednesday to sunrise on Monday, from each Christmas to Epiphany [January 6] and during Lent and Easter." The council further declared:

> If anyone violates the truce and refuses to make satisfaction after he has been admonished three times, his bishop shall excommunicate him and shall notify, by letter, the neighboring bishops of this action. No bishop shall receive the excommunicated person. If any bishop violates this decree he shall be in danger of losing his rank.

This decree had teeth in it. Violators of the peace were to be denied the sacraments until they made peace with their neighbors. Clergymen, even high ranking clergymen, who refused to enforce this peace initiative would incur far more severe penalties, even deposition.

Henry showed great skill in supervising the affairs of the Church in his realm. He appointed the bishops, many of whom he chose from pious and learned members of his royal chapel. Though the German church observed the highest moral standards in contemporary Europe, Henry did not hesitate to reform with vigor the bishops and abbots who failed to maintain those standards.

Henry insisted, as had his predecessors, that prospective bishops receive the symbol of their pastoral office, the crozier or shepherd's staff, from his hand. Henry went still farther, insisting on bestowing on the newly ordained bishop a ring, the symbol of his marriage to his church. What is more, Henry declared that the customary payment to the king by the new bishop following his appointment was simony, traffic in spiritual offices. By this Henry willingly accepted a significant reduction in imperial revenue for the sake of reform.

F. THE REFORM CAPTURES ROME

For more than a century before Henry's time, popes had been appointees of aristocratic Roman families–at least when no German king or emperor controlled the "eternal city." The result was that the majority of the men who sat on the chair of Peter devoted much of their time to activities aimed at maintaining themselves in office and lived more like princes than pastors.

Henry's success in restoring Burgundy's government and in continuing the reform of its Church led the king to look to Italy to effect similar restoration and reform. When, in 1040, a group of Italian princes urged him to cross the Alps and bring peace to their country, Henry responded with characteristic vigor. His descent into Italy had a much more significant and lasting effect on that country, on the Empire, and, indeed, on all of western Christendom than the mere settling of the squabbles of petty princes.

In September of 1044, an uprising in Rome succeeded in driving the notoriously simoniacal Pope Benedict IX into exile. Benedict's spiritual inadequacies were probably less important to his ouster than the political quarrels between his own and other powerful Roman families. Benedict was replaced by the bishop of Sabina who was supported by a rival family and took the name Sylvester III. Sylvester found the strife in Rome so dangerous that he declared himself ready to abdicate if he were reimbursed for the money he had dispersed to buy the papal throne. The money was collected and the contributors chose a replacement who took the name Gregory VI. Even Church reformers accepted Gregory as pope–until word of the money transfers leaked out.

In 1046, Henry III crossed the Alps and presided over a Council at Pavia that was attended by northern Italian, German, and Burgundian bishops. The Council issued a wide-reaching prohibition of simony. The Pavia Council was followed by a crucially important council at Sutri, a town just north of Rome. This meeting, called to deal with the scandal of three popes, or rather three men all claiming to be pope, was described by an anonymous Roman chronicler:

> When the emperor came to the city called Sutri, he decreed that a great council should be held in the holy church at Sutri. After he had tried the case justly and according to church law, he made the right of the matter plain. He condemned John, bishop of Sabina, to whom they had given the name Sylvester. He also condemned John who as pope had been called Gregory–as well as Pope Benedict.

To succeed these three, Henry wished to appoint as pope his old friend and advisor Adelbert of Hamburg, who, however, refused the nomination, undoubtedly so that he could continue his missionary work in the northern regions of the Empire.

Undaunted, Henry "called together the multitude of the Roman people, the bishops and abbots, and all the clergy of Rome into the basilica of Saint Peter." Following Adelbert of Hamburg's advice, he appointed Suitger, the bishop of Bamberg, as pope. Suitger received the acclamation of the Romans and chose to be called Clement, the second of that name. The next day, on Christmas of 1046, Clement anointed and crowned Henry emperor.

Henry's action at Sutri and Rome was widely acclaimed by those who longed for Church reform. Henry had always maintained a close relationship with the leaders of the reform movement. For example, he had his son baptized by Hugh, the abbot of Cluny. Hugh's successor at Cluny, Abbot Odilo, proclaimed his support of Henry's action at Sutri. An equally important reformer, Peter Damian, founder of a preeminent reformed congregation of hermits, also lent his support.

Zeal for reform had captured Rome. But a seeming setback occurred only nine months and sixteen days into Clement's reign, for he then "left the terrestrial for the celestial kingdom." The Roman Church had previously granted the emperor "the right to create popes," and so the Roman people "sent messengers to Henry with a letter beseeching him to appoint for them a man of godly life as shepherd of the holy Roman Church." Henry responded by appointing Bishop Poppo of Brixen on Christmas day of 1047. Poppo, who took the name Damasus II, succumbed to a fever only twenty-three days after his installation, on August 9, 1048.

Henry's choice now fell on his cousin Bruno, bishop of Toul, a highly gifted and well educated proponent of reform. In February of 1049 Bruno entered the city of Rome dressed not as a potentate, but as a pilgrim. Bruno had informed the emperor that he would accept the Roman pontificate only with the support of the Romans. Henry's choice was confirmed by the clergy and people of Rome, and Bruno was seated on the chair of Peter as Pope Leo IX. Shortly thereafter, the Council of Rheims, under Leo's influence, regulated that all bishops should be chosen by the clergy and people of their diocese, as had been the case in the early Church. Leo himself wasted no time touring Italy, France, and Germany, presiding over reforming Church councils wherever he went.

At Mainz, Leo and Henry jointly presided over a council attended by some forty bishops, the chancellors of Germany and Italy, many lay lords and–all the way from Constantinople–the ambassador of the Eastern Emperor Constantine IX. The Council condemned simony and the widespread practice of clerical marriage. Henry later joined Leo's successor, Victor II (1055-1057), in presiding over a Council at Florence. There some 120 predominantly Italian bishops assembled and issued reform decrees mirroring those promulgated by the German bishops at Mainz. The reform had captured Rome; Rome now took a leadership role in reforming the whole western Church.

In 1056, Henry III, the man who had spearheaded all these reform activities, died. Peter Damian, perhaps the most vehement champion of reform, wrote of him: "It was he, after God, who snatched us from the serpent's insatiable maw, he who cut off the heads of the many-headed hydra of simoniacal heresy with the sword of divine courage." Another reformer, Adam of Bremen, declared, with more than a little hyperbole, that Henry had been the nineteenth emperor since Caesar Augustus. Great praise indeed, though very bad arithmetic. It is surely fair to say that Henry III successfully combined the vision and acumen of his predecessors, Henry II and Conrad II. He left to his successors the most powerful and best governed land in Europe, a government based on a comprehensive view of the future.

Chapter Eight

The Investiture Conflict

A. REFORM: THE SECOND PHASE

The reform movement had captured the see of Rome through the benevolent and vigorous actions of Henry III. Imperial theocracy, however, could only promote church reform if a theocrat like Henry saw to it that virtue and learning remained the leadership qualifications of the clergy. The danger, as many reformers believed, was that an emperor not as pious as Henry and his predecessors would undo the great strides the reform had made by appointing unworthy popes and other bishops.

In 1059, Archbishop Gerard of Florence was elected pope by the reform party. To avoid control by a powerful party of Roman nobles–who had already chosen their own subservient pope–the reformers met in Siena. With the help of massive military support from Duke Godfrey of Burgundy, the reformers were able to expel the nobles' chosen pope from Rome and restrain the ambitions of the anti-reform party.

In the same year, 1059, the new pope, who had chosen the name Nicholas II, called together the clergy of the city of Rome and its immediate environs. At this local church council, sometimes called a synod, the assembled clergy undertook to free their church from the control of lay nobles by reviving the ancient practice of episcopal election. They decreed that "on the death of a pope, the cardinal bishops should confer together concerning the election of a successor; then they shall summon the other cardinal clergy and the people to give their assent to the election." The cardinal bishops were the bishops of the suburban dioceses around Rome. Other cardinals were priests, the pastors of the most important parishes in Rome, and the deacons who served the pope as his chief aides. It is significant that the people of Rome were to approve the choice of the cardinals. This too was a part of the reform agenda, because the people of the early Church had elected their bishops. A reform-minded pope chosen by this method, it was thought, would appoint reform-minded cardinals and other clergy. At the death of the pope, the cardinals and people of Rome would elect another reformer as pope. This system worked well for more than a century.

Through a deliberately vague formula, the rights of the king in the choice of the pope were barely acknowledged by the Papal Election Decree. Even these rights were to be exercised only with the pope's consent.

The Papal Election Decree of 1059 was, in effect, the declaration of independence of the reform papacy. Two circumstances aided the reformers in maintaining this independence. First, Henry IV, as a boy of six, had only recently succeeded his father. He was clearly unable to lead a military expedition to Italy to respond to this challenge to imperial domination of the Church. Secondly, some Norman adventurers had by this time conquered most of southern Italy. Their leader, Robert Guiscard, sought the pope's recognition of his legitimacy as ruler and sanction for his conquest of Sicily. In return Robert promised "to be faithful to the holy Roman church and to you Nicholas, my lord pope." This alliance provided Nicholas and his successors with a powerful ally and a secure place of refuge in case of imperial invasion.

Still another momentous event occurred in that same year, 1059. Nicholas II, identifying himself simply as "bishop and servant of the servants of God," issued a decree with a potentially revolutionary effect. This letter was aimed not merely at the Roman church, but at the whole of the western Church. He directed his missive "to all Catholic bishops and to all the clergy and people," offering them "affectionate greetings and apostolic blessing." Nicholas decreed that "no cleric or priest was to receive a church from a lay man in any way, whether as a free gift or at a price." Furthermore, Nicholas declared: "No one shall be ordained or promoted to any ecclesiastical office obtained by simoniacal heresy."

Simony, the buying and selling of church offices, was clearly a violation of a moral or ethical pillar of the reform movement. To call it heresy, an erroneous theological position, shows more passion than theological precision. But the die was cast.

B. HENRY IV

The future king and emperor Henry IV had been born at Goslar in the year 1050. His father requested one of the most influential leaders of the reform movement, Abbot Hugh of Cluny, to preside at the baby's baptism, and Hugh did indeed perform the ceremony. When the boy was but six years old, his father died, leaving his mother, Agnes of Poitiers, as regent.

Agnes had neither taste nor talent for imperial politics, relying on the questionable advice of high nobles and clerics who sought their own interests rather than those of their young ruler. To win the support of the most powerful princes, Agnes allowed the tight control that Henry III had exercised over the duchies to dissipate. Rudolf of Rheinfelden, a Burgundian nobleman, was promoted to rule that land and also granted the duchy of neighboring Swabia. Agnes appointed a high Saxon nobleman, Otto of Northeim, to the duchy of Bavaria and the Swabian Duke Berthold of Zähringen to the duchy of Carinthia. She attempted to grant the duchy of Saxony to Ordulf of Billung, but the move backfired when Archbishop Adelbert of Hamburg-Bremen took issue with Agnes' choice.

Agnes herself chose to enter a monastery and thus in effect resigned the regency. This allowed Archbishop Anno of Cologne to assume that post, which he later shared with Archbishop Adelbert. Henry was taken to Cologne along with the symbols of imperial office. Neither Anno nor Adelbert stemmed the flow of power away from their royal protégé. Anno devoted himself to amassing power within the German church. Adelbert had loftier goals: missionary efforts in lands as far away as Finland, Greenland, and Iceland.

At the age of fifteen, in 1065, Henry came of age and assumed control of what royal power was left. In an effort to rebuild his position, he actually diminished it by granting the duchy of Lower Lotharingia to Godfrey, duke of Upper Lotharingia and of Tuscany. Left with only one duchy, Henry concentrated on building his power on the north German territory of Saxony.

Henry built castles all over Saxony to keep the Saxon nobility in check. He put ministerials from far-off Swabia in charge of these castles. The Saxon nobility were infuriated by Henry's power grab and by the fact that he imported foreigners of a lower class to curb their ambitions. Saxon farmers were equally furious, for it was they who were taxed ruinously to build the fortresses from which they were, they believed, governed unjustly. Oppression led to organized opposition, opposition to rebellion and warfare. Saxon knights on horseback were joined by farmers wielding weapons that, while home-made, were nevertheless effective. In 1070, the farmers were crushed by Henry's cavalry, but rebellion broke out again in 1073. The threats to the nobles' liberty led to their support of farmers resentful of the new dues and services Henry demanded. However, at the battle of Unstrut, in June 1075, Henry won a decisive victory. The mounted nobility were able to flee the scene, but the free Saxon foot soldiers were slaughtered by the thousands.

Henry's power was now threatened by a new foe: the reformed papacy. To support his limited power base and strapped financial condition, Henry had taken to selling bishoprics and abbeys to friends and other wealthy supporters, thereby defying this formidable adversary. From many of these bishops and abbots Henry would find support in the coming conflict.

C. THE BATTLE IS JOINED

In 1073, the Roman cardinals elected as pope the monk Hildebrand, whose chief aim as Pope Gregory VII was to complete the reform movement by freeing clergy everywhere from appointment and control by lay rulers. To accomplish this, Gregory sent out papal ambassadors called legates, who encouraged local and regional councils to attack practices considered abuses by the reformers and to elect and install only virtuous and learned clerics as bishops. Gregory also held a series of reform councils in Rome at which he repeatedly condemned simony, the buying and selling of church offices. The Roman synod of November 19, 1078 went still farther:

> We [the council fathers] decree that no clergyman may receive investiture of a bishopric, abbey, or church from the hands of an emperor, king, or any other lay person, male or female. If he should dare to do so, let him be informed that such investiture is annulled by apostolic authority and that he himself is under sentence of excommunication.

Investiture was the ceremony by which a clergyman was given the symbols of his office, for a bishop his crozier or shepherd's staff and the ring that signified his marriage to his church. The person who held the power of investiture clearly controlled the election of the bishop or other clergyman, thus ignoring the practice of the early Church–the Church that the reformers were striving to restore. Henry not only sold high church offices, but invested his choices with the appropriate symbols.

In the year 1080, Pope Gregory sent out a warning directed not only at Henry, but at all lay persons who practiced investiture:

> If any emperor, king, duke, margrave, count, or other lay dignitary or person should presume to confer investiture on bishops or other ecclesiastical officials, let him know that he is bound by the sentence of excommunication. Rather let the people, setting aside all worldly ambition, elect their shepherd according to God's will.

Excommunication brought serious consequences for notorious sinners. They were held to be outside (*ex*) the community (*communio*) of believers. Furthermore, since lay lords, including emperors, assumed their offices in a religious ceremony, excommunication could lead to deposition by a lord's superior or, in the case of the emperor, rebellion and deposition by his subjects. The whole foundation and structure of imperial theocracy was threatened.

Gregory, knowing that Henry was practicing both simony and lay investiture, had sent him a letter in December 1075. This letter reproached the emperor for associating with bishops whom Gregory had excommunicated for blatantly buying their offices from Henry:

> Bishop Gregory, servant of the servants of God, to King Henry, greeting and apostolic blessings–that is, if he has been obedient to the apostolic chair as is fitting for a Christian king. Considering and carefully weighing the strict judgement to which I shall be accountable for the ministry entrusted to me by Saint Peter, I have only hesitatingly sent you the apostolic blessing. For you are said to be in close contact with those excommunicated by the sentence of a synod. If this is true then you yourself know that you will not receive divine favor unless you cease to associate yourself with those excommunicated persons.

Gregory then offered Henry a path to reconciliation with the Christian community:

> I advise Your Highness to seek the advice of some properly elected bishop who will surely absolve you. God's long-suffering patience invites you to amend your ways. However, I warn you, out of paternal love, to recognize the authority of Christ and reflect on how dangerous it is to prefer your own honor to his. I counsel you strongly to cease impeding the freedom of the Church to which Christ has joined to himself in celestial union.

Henry had no intention of complying with this advice. The very structure of his government depended on his association with his chief administrators, the very same bishops who had purchased their office–a purchase that had aroused the ire of the reformers.

Henry's response to Gregory's admonition was a masterpiece of indignation, articulating a theory of Church governance by imperial theocracy that had become traditional under his predecessors:

> Henry, king not through usurpation but by God's holy ordination, to Hildebrand, not now pope but false monk. You have deserved such a salutation from us because of the disturbances you have created. You have left no order in the Church untouched, no class that you have not caused to share in confusion rather than benediction. You have dared to threaten to take our royal power away from us. As if we had received the kingship from you! As if the kingdom and all the empire were in your hands and not in the hands of God!

It was God, Henry believed and asserted, who had chosen him king and made him his anointed. Henry disdained to employ the papal name Gregory, for his adversary was but a monk–and a monk false to his peaceful vocation who has falsely claimed Saint Peter's chair. In the emperor's view, Hildebrand, in rejecting his monastic vow to retreat from the world, had usurped a worldly authority and attacked God's anointed one:

> All this even though our Lord Jesus Christ did call us to the kingship but not you to the priesthood. By trickery you have gained wealth, through money influence, by the sword [Peter's] chair of peace. You have attacked me, one who, though unworthy, has been anointed to kingship. The true pope, Saint Peter, exclaims: "Fear God; honor the king." Since you do not fear God, you dishonor me, his appointed one. I, Henry, king by the grace of God, together with all our bishops, say to you: Descend, descend, to be damned through all the ages.

Henry spoke of all his bishops, and there were a number of bishops who did support him, some of them because they had purchased their bishoprics, some to gain or keep power, some out of a genuine concern that Gregory had gone too far in attacking imperial theocracy. Some even accused Gregory of "cohabitation with a strange woman." The woman was Mathilda, countess of Tuscany, whose support for the reform and for Gregory made her the object of false accusations. In 1081, Mathilde was placed under an imperial ban, divesting her of all dignities and forbidding all communication with her. Henry seized a good number of her domains and held them for more than a decade.

At a synod in Rome, Gregory retaliated by declaring that Henry "had withdrawn from the Church in an attempt to split the Church wide open" and had thus excommunicated himself. Gregory declared that Henry "had deserted God by associating with excommunicate men." The excommunicates were the bishops who had simoniacally purchased their posts and who were the king's staunchest supporters. Gregory went further:

> On behalf of God Almighty, Father, Son, and Holy Spirit, I forbid King Henry, who has rebelled with unheard of insolence against the Church, to govern any part of the kingdom of the Germans or of Italy. I absolve all Christians from any oath of loyalty to him that they have taken or shall take in the future.

This statement was a radical denial that the ruler of the Empire was beyond criticism, to say nothing of resistance or rebellion.

Henry replied in kind. In 1076, he called for an assembly of German bishops at Mainz to excommunicate Gregory. This tactic led to the defection of many clergy and layfolk. It also rekindled the smoldering Saxon resentment at what they perceived as their lord's oppressive rule. Opposition to Henry snowballed, and was expressed formally at the Diet (parliament) of Tribur in October of 1076. There the assembly declared that Henry must extricate himself from the sentence of excommunication within four months or face the loss of his crown. Assuming that Henry would refuse this action, the assembly invited Pope Gregory to their next year's meeting to advise them on their choice of a new ruler.

In 1077, Henry evaded his rebellious subjects by crossing the Apennine mountains to a castle at Canossa. It was there that the pope was wintering on his way to Germany. A contemporary named Bruno told the story:

> Henry came to the pope. He was barefoot and dressed in woolen garments. He declared that he loved the heavenly kingdom more than the earthly, and he promised that he would undertake any satisfaction for sin which the pope wished to lay upon him. The pope rejoiced at such humility. He counseled Henry to avoid living with or even speaking to excommunicated persons. Henry promised to do this, and the pope absolved him from the sentence of excommunication.

Henry seemed to have lost this round in his fight with Gregory, but he, in fact, came away from Canossa as the victor, freed from the most powerful constraint the pope possessed. Gregory had been suspicious of Henry's motives, but, as a priest, he was bound to give absolution to a man professing penitence.

On his return to Germany, Henry returned to his practice of simony and lay investiture. When Gregory sent word of a second excommunication, Henry led an army to Rome and installed his own appointee as an anti-pope, who in turn consecrated Henry as emperor. Gregory found refuge in Salerno as guest of his Norman ally, Robert Guiscard. He died in exile on May 25, 1085, his last words a sad rephrasing of Psalm 44: "I have loved justice and hated iniquity–and so I shall die in exile."

Henry's victory was hollow. His excommunication was renewed by Pope Paschal II, and Conrad, Henry's eldest son and choice as his successor, went over to the reform side. When Conrad died, Henry's second son, also named Henry, summoned a general assembly at Mainz and there declared his father's abdication. King Henry continued his struggle to regain power but died at the age of fifty on August 7, 1106.

D. THE ROOTS OF THE STRUGGLE

To his dying day Henry continued to claim that his office derived its authority from God. This none of his contemporaries, including Gregory, would have denied. But Henry claimed much more: that he could not be judged for his actions by anyone except God. For Henry the crown was to serve society in all ways physical, including the organization of the Church. The clergy were subject to the ruler in all matters save the one function proper to them: prayer for the world. Imperial theocracy was the intellectual foundation of this view.

There was, of course, a practical reason why Henry resisted the reformer's attempt to eliminate lay investiture. What meant freedom for the Church to Gregory and his reforming predecessors and successors meant to Henry the destruction of the empire. The imperial constitution was at stake because the king governed largely through his bishops and abbots. If Henry gave up his power to appoint his higher clergy, he could not be sure of the loyalty of his chief administrators.

For Gregory, however, the freedom of the Church from simony and lay investiture transcended all material considerations. Appointment of church leaders by lay lords, including the emperor, meant that the leadership qualifications of the early Church, the possession of both virtue and learning, would always be in danger of being ignored. The only way, Gregory thought, to ensure the continuing reform of the Church was to return to the primitive Christian practice of free elections of its clerical servants.

Chapter Nine

The Great Settlement

A. HENRY V ASCENDS THE THRONE

In 1106, Henry V was able to depose his father and assume the throne through a powerful combination of disparate forces. Henry V's rebellion against his father had won him the allegiance of his father's political opponents in Saxony and Thuringia. Henry received the support of Pope Paschal II by swearing to end the practice of imperial investiture of bishops. Paschal freed him from his oath of loyalty to his excommunicated father, and that gained Henry the support of those clerics and laity loyal to the reform movement.

Accession to the throne was one thing; maintenance of that position was quite another. Henry set out to bolster his weak power base by returning to his father's practice of selecting and investing men loyal to him as bishops. Pope Paschal tried to forestall tension over investiture by confirming many of Henry IV's appointments, but Henry V's continuing installation of his choice of bishops was too much for both Paschal and the reformers. Twelve years of fruitless negotiations followed which led Henry to declare that "this quarrel will not be settled here in Germany, but in Rome with swords." He resolved to lead an expedition to Italy to force concessions from the pope.

The expedition was delayed by warfare with Germany's eastern neighbors and by unrest within Germany, but, in the autumn of 1110, Henry invaded northern Italy with an army perhaps 30,000 strong. The pope's traditional allies, the Normans and Countess Mathilda of Tuscany, offered Pope Paschal little more than token support. Paschal was thus left defenseless when Henry and his army reached Rome in February 1111. On the fourth day of that month an agreement was reached–or extorted as some contemporaries asserted.

In the document which resulted, Pope Paschal first offered an explanation of the problem:

> In parts of your kingdom, bishops and abbots are so occupied with secular concerns that they are compelled to frequent the court and provide military service. Ministers of the altar are thus made ministers of the royal court, since from kings they receive cities, duchies, margravates, manors, and other things necessary for the service of the king.

From this reality, continued Paschal, "has arisen the practice–intolerable for the Church–that elected bishops cannot receive consecration unless first invested by the hand of the king."

Paschal's solution was straightforward. He commanded all bishops to surrender "those rights, privileges, and properties that manifestly belonged to the kingdom in the time of Charles the Great, Louis the Pious, and any of your predecessors." Furthermore, Paschal forbade any bishop or abbot to acquire any rights, privileges, and properties involving or implying secular responsibilities. On the other hand, Paschal decreed that "the churches should remain free of royal control, along with the offerings and the possessions handed down to them that clearly did not belong to the kingdom." In return, Henry was to renounce the right of investiture.

What seemed so simple a solution to Paschal proved to be impossible. How was one to determine which lands and possessions had been "manifestly" bestowed on individual churches for their services to the ruler and his government? Which lands and possessions were "clearly" the results of pious donation? Three hundred or more years of these rewards and gifts, many of them unrecorded, had resulted in an insolvable confusion of rights and privileges. Indeed, on February 12, when Paschal began the imperial coronation rite and had his decree read, a near riot resulted. Bishops and princes alike loudly rejected Paschal's decision. Henry's reaction to it was a forceful demand for the imperial crown and the right of investiture. Paschal refused the latter, so Henry arrested both the pope and the cardinals and led them out of Rome as prisoners.

A few weeks later, on April 13, 1111, the imprisoned Paschal issued another document that completely reversed his earlier stand. In it, he addressed Henry as "glorious king of the Germans and, through the grace of almighty God, august emperor of the Romans." The second title clearly expressed Paschal's abject submission to Henry's demand for papal consecration as Roman Emperor. Paschal continued:

> You shall freely confer investiture with the ring and shepherd's crook on bishops and abbots of your kingdom who have been chosen without violence or simony. After the investiture they shall receive canonical consecration from the bishop under whose authority they stand. If anyone, moreover, shall be

elected by the clergy and people without your consent, he shall not be consecrated by anyone unless first invested by you.

The document constituted a complete capitulation on Paschal's part. Henry would now have papal sanction for his selection of any persons he preferred as the chief pastors of clerics, monks, and layfolk.

The reaction by the church reformers was immediate. In 1112, at the pope's cathedral, Saint John Lateran, a synod attended mainly by Italian clerics renewed the ban on lay investiture, having declared Paschal's decrees null and void because they were extorted by force. In Burgundy, a synod, called by Archbishop Guy of Vienne and attended by two German cardinals, excommunicated the emperor.

In Germany, still in the year 1112, the most powerful lords of Saxony formed a coalition opposing Henry, decrying not only his treatment of the pope, but also his increasing employment of ministerials and other lesser nobles in the administration of their duchy. Archbishop Adelbert of Mainz, the primate of Germany, also joined this group. Together they protested Henry's church policy, the threatening practice of erecting castles along the Rhine, and installation in them of members of the ministerial class. Henry had Adelbert arrested and imprisoned for three years, freeing him only after a rebellion by the citizens of Mainz.

Still another city, Cologne, joined its archbishop, Fredrick, in opposition to Henry. The *Annals of Cologne* record the battle between the townsfolk and the imperial forces that took place in the year 1114:

> The people of Cologne called together under their standard great numbers of their most valiant young men, who awaited the emperor's attack with stout hearts. When a great cloud of arrows came showering down from the side of the people of Cologne, the knights of their imperial enemy fell dead or wounded. It was Count Theodoric, a brave knight, to whom the victory was largely due, since he pressed forward with his followers like a lion.

Townsfolk, nobility, and clergy all found common cause in opposing Henry. Even the bishops that he had invested with the symbols of their office broke away from him, having been absolved by the pope and papal legates from the excommunication incurred by their submission to Henry's policies and actions.

Paschal died in 1118, and the final resolution of the conflict had to await the pontificate of his second successor, Callixtus II. That settlement was the product of a lengthy dialogue which had gone on since the days of Henry IV and Gregory VII.

B. PURSUING A COMPROMISE

Both Gregory and Henry had adopted extreme positions in their conflict over investiture. As the successor to Saint Peter, Gregory had claimed the right to depose emperors. Henry, of course, had rejected this, claiming that God's choice of him as the supreme ruler of all Christendom entitled him to create and depose all bishops, including the bishop of Rome. The prolonged struggle between these two positions led to an exchange that brought precision and eventual conclusion to the conflict. The polemics, however, proceeded only slowly toward consensus.

About the year 1102, Hugh, a monk of the abbey of Fleury, wrote a *Treatise on Royal Power*. Hugh was convinced that "a king, inspired by the Holy Spirit, could appoint a pious cleric to the honored position of prelate." However, Hugh asserted, the "care of souls" ought to be conferred through ordination of the king's nominee by the archbishop of the appropriate ecclesiastical province. "If indeed," Hugh explained, "a bishop is elected by the clergy and people reasonably and according to church custom, the king ought not to use force against the electors but rather give his consent to the electee's ordination." Hugh seems to have contradicted himself. Perhaps he meant that after a free election by clergy and people–the practice in the early Church–the ruler had the right to approve or disapprove the choice to safeguard his control of his principal political subordinates.

In 1107, a conference was held at the French city of Châlons. Representatives of Henry V and the pope, Paschal II, participated. An excellent account of the exchange of views was recorded by Suger, abbot of the French royal monastery of Saint-Denis, near Paris.

Suger first recorded the emperor's position as expressed by his envoys. In every choice of a bishop, the envoys declared, "the election must be brought to the emperor's attention before it is publicly announced." The emperor could then indicate his choice among the candidates. Afterward,

> the election must be proclaimed at a general meeting as having been carried out by the clergy with the ratification of the people. The person, thus freely chosen without simony, must present himself to the emperor to be invested with the symbols of his temporal office, the ring and the staff, to pledge his fidelity and pay homage.

It is clear that the "free" election advocated here is free only for the emperor. The pledge that the election should be free of simony meant that the candidate need not, indeed could not, purchase the emperor's approbation.

Although this pro-imperial proposal contained important concessions, they were not sufficient to satisfy the pope's representatives. On their behalf the bishop of Piacenza replied:

> The Church, redeemed and made free by the precious blood of Jesus Christ, may in no way be made a slave again. Now if the Church cannot choose a prelate without the permission of the emperor, she is subject to him. To invest with the ring and staff, since these pertain to the altar, is to usurp the powers of God himself.

The imperial delegation's focus was on "free election." The papal representatives agreed. "Free election" was clearly the goal of both. What makes an election free was the sticking point.

Around 1080, Manegold of Lautenbach wrote *A Book for Gebhard* that maintained an extreme view of papal power:

> The Roman church is distinguished with such great authority and power that it excels all the principalities and powers of this world in its singular and incomparable dignity. According to the harmonious witness of the ancient and holy fathers, no one is permitted to judge its judgements or reverse its sentences, and no one may rightfully claim the power to disobey its decrees. Accordingly, anyone who has not remained in communion with the Roman Church is a stranger to, and an enemy of God.

Despite this radical exaltation of the power of the papacy, Manegold did not assert that the popes have the authority to choose or to depose a king. The power to elect a ruler God has given to the people. This, Manegold affirmed, is ascertained by use of the God-given faculty of the human intellect, which should "inquire into the causes of things with rational judgement."

By rational reflection, then, it was clear to Manegold that

> the people raise someone over them to rule and govern them. By virtue of this just authority, he is to apportion to each what is his own, to protect the good, to repress the wicked, and to deal out justice to all. If, however, he breaks the compact by which he was elected and ruins and confounds what he was established to order correctly, reason justly considers that he has absolved the people from their duty of obedience to him. This is because he himself first broke the bond of mutual fidelity by which he was bound to them and they to him.

The one who governs "must, then, exhibit still greater virtue than others and should be careful to exercise the power committed to him without partiality."

Reason, thought Manegold, reveals the right of the people to resist a tyrant, "for the people did not exalt him in order to grant him the unlimited power of tyrannizing over them, but rather to defend them against the tyranny and wickedness of others." Power then, is to be bestowed by a contract that the ruler breaks at his peril:

> When he who is chosen to repress evil-doers and to defend the just begins himself to cherish evil, to oppress good people, to exercise over his subjects

the cruel tyranny that he ought to ward off from them, is it not clear that he deservedly falls from the dignity conceded to him and that the people are free of his lordship and from subjection to him? Is it not evident that he first broke the compact by virtue of which he was appointed? No one can justly or reasonably accuse the people of a deliberate breach of faith when it is evident that he first broke faith with them.

Manegold offered his contemporaries a political theory based on rational analysis rather than theological disputation. He offered the idea of a social contract and the principles enshrined in the modern world in the American Declaration of Independence.

Ivo of Chartres took another tack. Ivo was a brilliant canon lawyer and professor whose contributions to the question of investiture led to his appointment as cardinal. In his letter of 1097 to Archbishop Hugh of Lyons, then papal legate to France, Ivo defended Daimbert, archbishop of Sens, who had accepted investiture by the king of France. Ivo wrote that he could not see how the faith or the Church were injured by the king's conferral on a bishop of the symbols of his office, since such investiture "does not have the force of a sacrament in the making of a bishop."

Ivo held that it was ordination, not investiture that constituted the essential activity in the making of a bishop. Ivo wrote:

> Why should it matter whether installation is accomplished by the king's hand or by his gesture, by his word or by the touch of his staff? Why should it matter when the king does not intend to bestow anything spiritual but only to add his assent to the petition of the people or to confer on the person elected the estates and other worldly goods which churches receive through the gift of the king?

Ivo thus made clear that bishops in effect wore two hats. They were both spiritual shepherds and temporal lords. Their pastoral office was conferred through ordination, their lordship through the king's investiture.

C. THE RESOLUTION

Despite the efforts of theologians, canon lawyers, and political theorists to settle the deep differences between Henry V and his contemporary popes, the struggle went on for decades. After Pope Paschal's death in 1118, his successor, Gelasius II, fostered the reformers' opposition to lay investiture. Henry countered by setting up an anti-pope. At this, as much as half of Germany rose in rebellion. On the other hand, the Roman nobility and the political power-holders of northern Italy opposed Gelasius, who fled to the safety of the reform abbey of Cluny, where he died in 1119.

The cardinals accompanying Gelasius selected a new pope, who won the support of the cardinals remaining in Rome. Their choice fell not on a Roman or an Italian, but on Archbishop Guy of Vienne, who took the name Callixtus II. Callixtus had proved himself a zealous reformer, and his family was also related to the German royal house. Efforts at compromise between Henry and the reformers failed at first, but in 1121 a group of German princes produced a "law-finding" that recommended a nation-wide meeting. Under intense pressure, Henry agreed to call the parliamentary Diet. Callixtus II sent an embassy with far-ranging powers, led by Lambert, the cardinal-bishop of Ostia.

On September 23, 1112, an agreement, later called the Concordat of Worms, was made public. It consisted of two parts: the grant of the pope and that of the emperor. The imperial document began:

> In the name of the holy and undivided Trinity I, Henry, by the grace of God august emperor of the Romans, for the love of God, of the holy Roman Church, and of the lord pope Callixtus, and for the health of my soul, do surrender to God, to the holy apostles of God, Peter and Paul, and to the Holy Roman Church all investiture through the ring and crozier. I do agree that in all churches throughout my kingdom and empire there shall be canonical elections and free consecration of bishops and abbots.

Henry's privilege was issued "by the consent and counsel of the German princes, archbishops, bishops, abbots, dukes, margraves, and counts."

The papal document had two parts, one for Germany, the other for Burgundy and Italy. The first reads:

> I, Bishop Callixtus, servant of the servants of God, concede to you, beloved son Henry–by the grace of God august emperor of the Romans–that the election of bishops and abbots in the German kingdom shall take place in your presence–without simony or any sort of violence. If any discord should arise you may–with the advice and judgement of the appropriate archbishop and the other bishops of that province–give your assent to the person who seems to have the better case.

Then followed a decision on the all-important question of investiture: "The candidate elected may receive the symbol of his temporal office from you through the conferring of the scepter, and he shall discharge his lawful duties to you." The symbols of the new bishop's spiritual office were then to be bestowed by fellow churchmen through a ring, proclaiming his marriage to his diocesan church, and a crozier or shepherd's crook, signifying his role as pastor.

Although the election of a bishop in Germany was to be free, as all agreed, the fact that it must take place in the presence of the emperor meant that he had an opportunity to influence the outcome. The emperor's conferral of the scepter before the church ceremony bestowing the pastoral staff and ring clearly implied the possibility of an imperial veto. These procedures and their consequences applied only to German areas of the empire.

In Burgundy and Italy another procedure was to prevail. Callixtus wrote:

> The man elected in other parts of the empire shall, within six months, receive the symbol of his temporal office through the conferring of the scepter. In return, he shall then discharge his lawful duties–excepting all things known as the Church's sphere of competence. If you complain to me about any such matter and ask for my help, I shall aid you to the extent that my office allows.

No veto power was allowed the emperor in the western and southern parts of his realm. His only recourse was an appeal to the pope, who alone could judge the emperor's cause. The Concordat of Worms allowed the virtual independence of the Italian and Burgundian bishops, though it kept a tighter imperial rein on the bishops of Germany. Still, the imperial theocracy of Otto I and his successors had everywhere disappeared. The reform movement had won freedom for the Church for at least a century–but not without continuing struggle.

Chapter Ten

Kings, Cistercians, and Crusades

A. LOTHAR THE SAXON

Henry V died at the age of 31, probably of cancer. Since Henry was childless, the choice of a successor was not obvious and considerable controversy erupted. The duty of assembling an imperial parliament or diet charged with the election of a king fell to the archbishop of Mainz, the arch-chancellor for Germany. In 1125, Archbishop Adelbert called together the great lords, ecclesiastical and temporal, to meet at Mainz, on Saint Bartholomew's Day, to take the necessary action to elect a successor. "I ask you," he wrote, "to bear in mind the oppression of the Church in these last days and pray that this election may result in the freeing of the Church from this yoke of servitude." Adelbert's reference to the "yoke of servitude," imposed as he thought by Henry V, was a factor in the election of Henry's principal opponent, Lothar, count of Supplinberg, duke of Saxony.

Lothar had been the leader of several rebellions against Henry, and he was known to be a supporter of Church reform. He was also fifty years old and, like his predecessor, childless. Surely some of Lothar's supporters welcomed the prospect of another open election on his death.

Lothar met with considerable opposition centering around Henry's nephew, Frederick of Hohenstaufen, the duke of Swabia. For nine of his twelve year reign, Lothar faced the opposition of the Hohenstaufen clan, who went so far as to elect Frederick's younger brother, Conrad, as anti-king. By 1135, however, both Frederick and Conrad had submitted to Lothar. Their cause had been rejected by Pope Honorius II, on behalf of the reformers, and by Henry the Proud, duke of Bavaria and head of the powerful Welf family.

Lothar's authority, however, was largely limited to Saxony and Thuringia, the heart of his family lands. Like the other lords, temporal and spiritual, of that northern area, he was a leader in a revived "push to the East" (*Drang nach Osten*). The first wave of settlers included Cistercian monks who, in search of simplicity of life, established their houses in forests, swamps, and other marginal lands. The Cistercians drained swamps with windmills, harnessed streams with dams, and cleared forests. Farmers from as far away as Holland followed, settling the lowlands along the Baltic Sea and the rich, largely untilled farm lands on the frontier. Young men of knightly class–often second or third sons whose elder brothers inherited their father's castles and lands–migrated east to be granted lordships by the high nobility–counts and margraves–who had established regional authorities. Missionaries moved eastward as well, serving sparsely settled Slavic territories. These lands also saw an influx of Germanic peoples that led to frequent intermarriages. The establishment in the East of church structures–archbishoprics, bishoprics, and parishes–was a reflection of the eastward movement of clergymen to serve the spiritual needs of these folk.

Equally attractive opportunities for a growing German population offered themselves in pockets of thinly settled areas in the western lands of Germany. For example, the Black Forest area of western Swabia was a largely unsettled area until the twelfth century. The lords of this area, Conrad of Zähringen and his successors, brought about a radical change in their political fortunes by offering unsettled land near and in the mountains that paralleled the Rhine plain to those who paid a relatively low rent. Conrad went one step further by offering land, protection, and self-government to merchants and manufacturers who migrated to the new towns he sponsored. Conrad profited from the taxes the towns paid him, and they profited from the freedom and security he provided. Two of these towns are still named Freiburg (free city).

When Lothar died in December of 1137, he left behind a prosperous and peaceful Germany. It was, however, a Germany not of tribal duchies, but of territorial lordships. There were dukes, to be sure, but they were not subject to royal and imperial power to the extent that they had been under Otto I. There were many lordships that almost equaled and sometimes surpassed ducal power. The most successful of the territorial lords, the Zähringers, for example, adopted the title duke. Under Lothar too, there was a flowering of cooperation between emperor and pope, a flourishing of the reform ideal–now taking a new form.

B. CISTERCIANS AND THE THIRD STAGE OF THE REFORM

In Germany the first stage in the medieval reformation was directed from above, by the king-emperors who were thought to be appointed by God. They were to encourage and direct spiritual leaders in correcting abuse and restoring the pristine purity of the early Church. In the second stage, the reformers recognized that the imperial theocracy of the first stage would bring about their goal only if the theocrat, the emperor, were devoted to the goal of reform and consequently appointed virtuous and learned bishops and popes to serve the Christian community. Their experience of the reigns of Henry IV and Henry V led reformers to change the direction of their cause toward what they saw as essential: freedom of the Church to be accomplished through free election of bishops. That goal had been largely realized by the Concordat of Worms, and this success led to a third reform stage which built on the second. This third stage was less oriented toward institutional reform and much more concerned with personal reform and the pursuit of individual and collective happiness. This goal gave rise in turn to new institutions intended to help Christians attain their individual goals in a society configured to help accomplish them.

It was this longing for a more complete and fulfilling form of Christian life that led, in the late eleventh and early twelfth centuries, to a wide variety of individual and institutional responses that together constituted the third wave of reform. By far the most popular new monastic institution of the time was the Order of Cîteaux, founded in 1098.

Cistercian monks and nuns aimed at the sustained pursuit of an intensely Christian life of love. They spent between three and four hours a day in communal prayer, singing hymns, chanting psalms, and listening to readings from the Bible and the early Christian writers. Time was also given for private prayer and meditation on Scripture. Architectural simplicity and restraint in speaking gave the monks freedom from visual and aural distractions. Manual labor was a central part of the Cistercian day, for they refused to "live off the sweat of other men's brows."

The popularity of the Cistercian way of life led to the founding of myriad Cistercian monasteries from Norway to the Holy Land. Medieval Germany was home to hundreds of houses of Cistercian monks and nuns. Although each monastery was self-governing, it received support from an annual visit by the abbot of its mother house, the monastery by which it had been founded. An annual meeting of all Cistercian abbots, the Chapter General, also supported each house in maintaining a vigorously committed life of personal and institutional reform.

Despite the relative isolation of their monasteries, Cistercians extended their loving concern through prayer for all of society and through a flurry of letters and spiritual writings. The spiritual leadership that Cistercians exercised led many church communities to elect Cistercians as their bishop, thus bringing deeply spiritual values to an increasingly wide section of society. A Cistercian monk was elected bishop of Rome in 1145 and served in that leadership position as Pope Eugenius III.

By far the most influential Cistercian monk in the early twelfth century was Bernard, the abbot of Clairvaux, a Cistercian monastery in the county of Champagne. Though Bernard was not a subject of the emperor, he had an enormous influence within the Empire. In his letter of 1132 to Conrad, duke of Zähringen, Bernard urged that ruler to refrain from war with his southern neighbor Amadeus I, count of Geneva:

> If you set out to invade his territory, destroy churches, burn down homesteads, and shed human blood, there can be no doubt that you will seriously anger the God who is "father to the orphan and gives comfort to the widow." If he is angry it would not be to your advantage to fight, no matter how great your military strength. Not that I believe your enemy to be stronger than you, but I know that the omnipotent God is more powerful than either one of you and that he "resists the proud and gives grace to the humble."

Bernard sounded a more positive note in the first words of his supportive letter to the Emperor Lothar:

> Blessed be God who chose you and raised you up to be a sign of salvation for us. This was for the promise and glory of his name, for the restoration of the glory of the Empire, for the support of the Church, and for the work of salvation. It is God's doing that the crown of your glory is daily augmented and elevated, wonderfully growing and progressing in beauty and splendor before God and humankind.

Even though Bernard claimed he was "but an insignificant person," he was quite willing to offer both support and advice to powerful rulers like Lothar and Conrad in their quest to provide justice to their people.

C. THE SCHISM OF 1130

Two men were elected pope in 1130, and each refused to yield to the other. Of course there had been more than one pope before this, but, generally speaking, one had been appointed by the emperor, the other elected by reformers. The 1130 schism was something new: both claimants had been chosen by cardinals and both were reform-minded. The newly elected Innocent II and Anacletus II both announced their election to Lothar, the German king. Under the influence of Bernard of Clairvaux, Lothar decided for Innocent and agreed to accompany both Innocent and Bernard to Rome.

Lothar's army numbered only some 1,500 knights, a force inadequate to root out Anacletus's Roman forces ensconced in the area around Saint Peter's. So it was at the cathedral of Rome, Saint John Lateran, on June 4, 1133, that Innocent anointed and crowned King Lothar and his wife Richenza as Roman emperor and empress. Soon after Lothar left Rome to return to Germany, the Norman ruler of Sicily, Roger II, drove Innocent out of Rome in favor of Anacletus, who had previously crowned Roger king of Sicily.

Bernard called for Lothar's help once more. Another Italian expedition became possible when the Hohenstaufen opposition to Lothar was relieved by that family's submission. As a sign of reconciliation, Frederick of Hohenstaufen retained his duchy of Swabia, and his son, the future king Conrad III, was made imperial standard bearer. Augmented by the Hohenstaufen force, a powerful expedition succeeded in taking the strongest cities of southern Italy, stemming the ambitions of Roger of Sicily to expand his domain northward. Those ambitions and the endemic conflicts in southern Italy revived immediately when Lothar set out once again for Germany. On his way back home in December 1137, the emperor died while crossing the Alps, and the papal schism came to an end when Anacletus II died in January of 1138.

D. THE REIGN OF CONRAD III

The election that followed Lothar's death was irregular in that the archbishopric of Mainz, responsible for calling an election, was vacant. Alberic, the archbishop of Trier and a friend of Bernard of Clairvaux, took the initiative, and Conrad of Hohenstaufen was elected king on March 7, 1138. A papal legate presided at Conrad's anointing a few days later. Conrad's sympathy for the cause of Church reform was strengthened by his chief advisor Wibald, abbot of Stablo and later of Corvey.

At first Conrad's election was generally recognized, but resistance to his rule by the powerful Welf family quickly developed. Welfs controlled the two most powerful duchies in the empire, Bavaria and Saxony, and they resented Conrad's insistence that a single family should not hold more than one duchy. When the imperial German territories were joined to the possessions of Conrad's Hohenstaufen family, they formed a barrier to Welf unity that cut across Germany from southwest to northeast, from Swabia to Thuringia. Not until 1151, one year before Conrad's death, did the intermittent struggle between the two families end through a peace treaty between the king and Duke Welf, the sixth of his name. Five years earlier, in 1146, the two had temporarily ceased hostilities to join forces against what was seen as a grave threat to the Empire and to all of Christendem.

E. CALLING A NEW CRUSADE

On Christmas Eve of the year 1144, the citizens of the several states established in the Eastern Mediterranean in the wake of the First Crusade received a telling set-back to their self-confidence. The county of Edessa–located in what is today south-central Turkey–had fallen to the forces of 'Imād-al-Din

Zengi, the ruler of Mosul and Aleppo–now in Syria. A retaliatory expedition was to wait for the response to a crusading call from the newly elected pope, Eugenius III, a call issued on December 1, 1145. This Cistercian pope entrusted to his former abbot, Bernard of Clairvaux, the task of preaching a crusade to rescue the Holy Land from the dangers threatening it.

In the course of launching the crusade Bernard enrolled the hosts of a willing–indeed, eager–King Louis VII of France. At Speyer, in December of 1146, Bernard enlisted the army of the hesitant king and emperor-elect Conrad III. Conrad was understandably reluctant. Tensions between his family, the Hohenstaufen, and the supporters of his old enemy, Duke Welf VI, had once more approached a state of civil war. Bernard's influence, apparently aided by that of his Cistercian confrère, Abbot Adam of Ebrach, won Welf's support to the same cause as Conrad and enabled both sides to join the crusading pilgrimage.

Strange as it may seem to us, Bernard preached the crusade in the cause of peace, the peace and tranquility of a Europe Bernard saw as bursting with the militant energies of all-too-often indiscriminating and badly motivated warriors. He wrote to Archbishop Arnold of Cologne, Bishop Manfred of Brixen, and "all the archbishops, bishops, clergy, and people of Franconia and Bavaria":

> Your land is well known to be rich in stout men and filled with robust youth. For this you are praised throughout the world, and the fame of your virtue fills that world. Gird yourself manfully, then, and take up arms with joy and zeal for your Christian name. Stop your former violent actions–better described as malicious than military–by which you try to cast one another down and destroy one another. Why this miserable, savage desire? The bodies of your neighbors are impaled on the sword, and souls may perhaps perish. Stop what I see as madness not virtue, not daring but daftness.

The crusade, Bernard thought, offered an outlet for this military energy and manly prowess, for "the Church in the East now cries out in misery, so that whoever does not have complete compassion for her cannot be judged a true child of the Church." The solution to the Church's dilemma and the misdirected military energies of his German audience was clear to Bernard. He proclaimed: "O mighty soldier. O man fit for war, you now have a place where you can fight without danger to your soul, where to win is glory and to die is gain." That glory and gain were not to be won by killing Muslims simply because they were Muslim. Bernard recognized, however, no option other than to engage in combat with these Muslims, since he saw their invasion destroying both peace and justice.

F. THE JOURNEY TO THE EAST

Conrad's preparation for the crusading expedition necessarily included provision for ruling Germany in his absence. He decided to entrust the kingdom to his ten-year-old son Henry and had him anointed. Knowing that Henry's age made him unequal to the task, Conrad appointed the archbishop of Mainz as the boy's guardian and regent. Conrad also enlisted the support of Pope Eugenius, who assured him that "I do not wish Henry's honor to suffer any damage or diminution during his father's absence, and so he shall be under the protection of Saint Peter." Conrad also strengthened his son's hand by proclaiming an imperial peace that threatened dire consequences to those who broke it.

Early in 1146, Conrad wrote John Comnenus, the Eastern Emperor at Constantinople, advising him that he had proclaimed that peace and that it had been accepted by Welf VI, thus bringing the forces of all Germany behind the crusading effort. Conrad also informed the Eastern Emperor that France, Spain, England, and Denmark had promised to carry out "our imperial mandate." John Comnenus received this news gratefully, as his empire was menaced by Muslim rulers in the East and by Normans in Sicily. In the middle of May 1147, the German army–composed mostly of Franconians, Bavarians, and Swabians–marched from Nuremberg to Vienna. From there their route passed through Hungary, crossed the Balkans, and peacefully entered the eastern Roman Empire–often referred to as Byzantium. By September 10, the German army had camped outside Constantinople; then, without waiting for the French army to catch up, they plunged into Asia Minor. There the Germans met one defeat after another. At Dorylaeum, for example, the Turks ambushed the German column. Wave after wave of German cavalry hurled themselves against the Turks, who, by retreating, led the Germans away from the main force that the Turks then attacked, inflicting terrible losses. When the German army finally reached Nicaea at the beginning of November, it broke up. Most of the army went home, but Conrad joined the French forces and exhausted himself in one unsuccessful foray after another. In 1149, worn out by fighting and having suffered serious illness, Conrad returned to Germany. There he found that Welf VI had arrived before him, and, breaking the peace that he had sworn to uphold, had taken up arms against him.

The crusade had been a total failure. As Pope Eugenius put it, "it was the most severe damage to the Christian name that the Church of God has suffered in our time." Eugenius however, conceived a plan to enlist Conrad's support against the Romans who had meanwhile risen in rebellion against papal rule. Conrad was to come to Rome, receive anointing and coronation as emperor, and then lead his army against King Roger of Sicily, who continued to threaten the Italian lands to the south of Rome. The death of Conrad III on September 15, 1151 brought all those plans to naught.

G. THE OTHER CRUSADES

Conrad's reign had, however, seen some notable successes. While he and his army had been taking the long, slow land route to the East, crusaders from Flanders, Frisia, and Cologne–joined by French-speaking warriors from Normandy–had set out by sea. Their first stop was in eastern England, where they were joined by Englishmen and Scots. Together these sea-faring folk sailed along the coasts of Spain and Portugal. They found King Alfonso I of Portugal preparing to besiege the Moors controlling Lisbon. The members of the naval expedition decided that Alfonso's campaign was also a crusade and joined the fray. The walls of Lisbon were finally breached on October 24, 1147, and the Moors gave up the fight. Most members of the crusading expedition agreed to sail on to the East, having achieved at least one success.

Germans embarked on another crusade at this time, one that took place far to the north and east of Portugal. The Wends, a Slavic people who lived to the east of the Elbe river, were pagans whose conversion was the goal of both Pope Eugenius and Bernard of Clairvaux. In Bernard's letter to crusaders about to attack the Wends, he wrote: "I forbid you to enter into a treaty with them–in any way or for any reason whatsoever, not for money, not for tribute, until, through God's assistance, either their religious observances or their nation be destroyed."

This statement seems to contradict Bernard's other words on the subject of forced conversion: "Heretics are to be caught rather than driven away. They are to be caught not by force of arms but through arguments through which their errors may be refuted." The apparent inconsistency was resolved in Bernard's mind by distinguishing between the peaceful dissent of heretics and the danger from those whom he feared would launch an armed attack on the line of march to Jerusalem. The conversion of the Wends was Bernard's chief concern: only if the Wends were to attack those who had taken the crusading cross as "the sign of salvation" should they, in turn, be attacked. Pagans "who are not spurred on by such a love of God as the Church experiences," must be evangelized, not eliminated.

As it turned out, the Wendish crusade led to very little armed conflict. In 1147, a small army of crusaders moved east against a Slavic chieftain who quickly retreated to his fortress and agreed to accept baptism. Another crusading contingent advanced across the Elbe to the fortress of Stettin. When Prince Ratibor of Stettin agreed to accept Christianity, the crusaders went home.

Earlier, in 1145, when Bernard had been preaching the Second Crusade in the Rhineland, he had heard disturbing reports. It seems that a monk named Rudolf was going about the area around Cologne, preaching the crusade. But Rudolf asserted that the extirpation of the infidel in the Holy Land might suitably be preceded by the slaughter of infidels closer to hand. As a result, Jews in some of the towns along the lower Rhine suffered severe persecutions–until Bernard came to their rescue.

Bernard took quite literally Saint Paul's assertion in his letter to the Romans (11:25-26), that all Israel will one day be saved. This is why Bernard could thunder that "Jews must not be persecuted, slain, or cast out." Persecution, he concluded, is "the foulest heresy, a sacrilegious prostitution, impregnated with the spirit of lies. It is conceived in sorrow and gives birth to injustice." Bernard even forbade attempts to convert Jews to Christianity, for Jews, he thought, attain salvation by living up to the covenant that God made with them in and through the Old Testament Law. That Bernard's admonition did indeed bear fruit is shown in a letter of a contemporary rabbi in which he extolled Bernard's efforts on behalf of the rabbi's Jewish coreligionists.

Chapter Eleven

Three Gifted Germans

A. ANSELM OF HAVELBERG AND THE IDEA OF PROGRESS

The reform of monasticism initiated by Bernard of Clairvaux and his Cistercian contemporaries was matched by the reform of the canonical life by his friend Norbert of Xanten (1080–1139). A canon was a priest attached to a church whose pastoral needs were served by several clergymen. As an indication of a priest's commitment to this particular church, he inscribed his name on the clergy list (or canon) of that church and was therefore himself called a canon. As a part of the reform movements of the eleventh and twelfth centuries, many groups or "chapters" of canons advocated what they called the "apostolic life." This was a conscious attempt to live the life of early Christians, as recorded in the biblical book *The Acts of the Apostles*. The canons prayed together, shared a common purse, and supported each other's pastoral and educational ministry. The canons sought to institutionalize their "apostolic life" by adopting a rule (*regula* in Latin), and thus were called "regular" canons. Most chapters of canons adopted the *Rule* of Saint Augustine, a rule based on that fifth-century bishop's spiritual instructions to a community of women.

Norbert was born around 1080. His father was the count of Gennep in the duchy of Cleves; his mother was a cousin of Emperor Henry IV. He first became a canon at the lower Rhenish city of Xanten, and, after a profound religious experience, sought to convince his fellow canons to embrace a life more harmonious with the Gospel. In this he failed, and so he left Xanten for the life of an itinerant preacher. He gradually gathered a group of like-minded men and in their name accepted a gift of property in the beautiful but desolate valley of Prémontré some twelve miles from the northern French city of Laon. The life of these reformed regular canons attracted so many men that new Praemonstratensian (from Prémontré) foundations were made, hundreds of them in Germany and Central Europe.

The reform movements of the twelfth century, notably the Cistercian and Praemonstratensian reforms, went far beyond the institutional framework of traditional monasticism or canonical life. Traditionalists found these changes and, above all, the more rigorous life-style of these reformers, to be unnecessary, impudent, and downright insulting. One such traditionalist, Rupert, a Benedictine monk of Deutz, a monastery across the Rhine from Cologne, asked of the innovators:

> Why should there be so many novelties in God's Church? Why all these new orders? What is the point in having so many sorts of monks and canons? Who would not be scandalized by so much diversity? Is not a religion contemptible that is continually agitated by so many new laws, new customs, new rules, and what-not? How can a wise man consider anything so changeable and variable worth imitating?

Anselm of Havelberg was admirably suited to answer these charges. A Praemonstratensian, he was a disciple of Norbert of Xanten, and, like his mentor, became a bishop in the eastern frontier area of Germany (1129) and an advisor to emperors. Anselm also had to defend himself against the charge of novelty when he undertook missions to Constantinople, in 1135-1136, on behalf of the emperor Lothar and again in 1153 for the Cistercian pope Eugenius III. At the capital of the Eastern Roman Empire, Anselm engaged in friendly dialogue with theologians of the Greek Church who found the western positions on the Holy Spirit, the use of unleavened bread in the Lord's Supper, and the primacy of the bishop of Rome to be unacceptable innovations.

In response to the charges of traditionalists abroad and at home, Anselm undertook to show, in a book called *Dialogues*, that the history of the relationship between God and humankind is an evolutionary process. This process calls for continual change in the institutional expression of truth (new religious orders, for example) and in how people understand and express their Christian beliefs. In this way the Church is continually being renewed and remains perennially youthful. The faith remains essentially the same, but each age must understand and express it in ways intelligible to that age.

From this position, Anselm elaborated a theory of history in which the unifying thread was a continual, progressive movement of reform in the Church. Most ancient cultures had seen history as a process of decline, often expressed as golden, silver, bronze, and iron ages. Most ancient thinkers concerned themselves with the logic of things as they are at a given moment, not as they become over the course of time. By and large, Anselm and the other thinkers of the twelfth century accepted and adopted the ancient analytical approach, but they also adopted and articulated a concern with development in time that enabled them, as they thought, to use the past to see the present and the future more clearly. As Bernard of Chartres, a contemporary of Anselm's, said, "We are like pygmies who stand on the shoulders of giants [the ancient writers], and we are thus able to see much farther than they." Owing in large part to the thought and writings of Anselm of Havelberg, medieval thinkers continued to acknowledge their debt to antiquity, but viewed their own, their "modern" world as still better. This is surely at least the germ of the idea of progress.

B. HILDEGARD OF BINGEN: THE SIBYL OF THE RHINE

Hildegard was born in 1109, the last of the ten children of Mechthild and Hildebert of Bermershausen, lesser nobility of the Rhenish area near Metz. When still a small girl, she was sent by her parents to live with a hermitess, Jutta of Spanheim, herself the offspring of a noble family and only six years Hildegard's senior.

Hildegard served as handmaid and companion to the recluse, and also as her pupil. She learned how to read the Latin Bible, concentrating on the Psalms that were central to the monastic prayer cycle the two followed. Other women were attracted to the life led by Jutta and her pupil, and the hermitage became a monastery of nuns professing the *Rule* of Saint Benedict. Although Jutta was the abbess, the life of her monastery was overseen by the nearby abbot of the ancient monastery of Disibodenberg. In 1136, Jutta died, and, at the age of thirty-eight, Hildegard was elected abbess of the growing community. Eventually the supervision by the abbot of Disibodenberg became burdensome, so Hildegard and her nuns moved to the Rupertsberg, a site high above the village of Bingen-on-the-Rhine.

From an early age. Hildegard experienced visions. She wrote of this in her work *Scivias (Know the Ways of God)*:

> From the time I was a little girl of about five, I was conscious of a mysterious hidden power and experienced wonderful internal visions. During the time before the grace of God wished them to be known, I hid them under strict silence. The visions that I saw were not in sleep or dreams, not in my imagination or through bodily eyes or ears, but in watching, aware with the pure eyes of the mind and the inner ear of the heart. I received these visions while wide awake, as God wished. How this happened is difficult for mortal man to understand.

In another place in her *Scivias*, Hildegard tried to convey to her readers her "mode of seeing":

> In my vision, my soul, as God commands, rises up high into the vault of heaven and into the changing sky and spreads itself out among different peo-

ples, although they are far away in distant lands and places. I do not hear them with my outward ears, nor do I perceive them by the thoughts of my own heart or by any confirmation of my five senses, but in my soul alone.

In this exalted state, Hildegard wrote, she saw "the reflection of the Living Light." "Sometimes," she wrote, "I see within this reflected light another light, which I call 'the Living Light,' and I cannot describe when and how I see it, so I feel like a simple girl instead of an old woman."

Hildegard was sure her visions resulted in an intuitive understanding of Scripture:

> In the year 1142, it happened that a great light of brilliant fire came from the open heavens and overwhelmed all of my mind, my heart, and my breast. It was not so much like a flickering fire, but rather like the glowing heat of the sun. Suddenly I had the power of explaining Scripture.

Despite a physical weakness brought on by her visionary experiences, Hildegard lived an extraordinarily active life. She wrote several other works of theological significance, such as *Various Expositions on the Gospels,* an *Explanation of the Theology of Saint Athanasius,* and a *Commentary on the Rule of Saint Benedict*. She also wrote an ethical treatise entitled *The Book of Life's Merits*. Her scientific contributions extend from cosmology, *On the Activity of God,* to *A Study of Nature,* with chapters on plants, trees, precious stones, animals, and reptiles. Her medical treatise, entitled *Causes and Cures,* provides information on various illnesses and their treatment. She also composed poetry and music for use in divine worship, and her songs were later compiled under the title *A Symphony of the Harmony of Celestial Revelation*.

Some three hundred of Hildegard's letters survive. In them she sought to support and strengthen–and sometimes to correct–her reader. Four popes and numerous monarchs, including Henry II of England and his queen, Eleanor of Aquitaine, received letters from her. She wrote to the Emperor Frederick I Barbarossa, rebuking him fiercely for bringing about a papal schism. She wrote to Thomas Becket, the soon-to-be-martyred archbishop of Canterbury, and to Bernard of Clairvaux, the highly influential Cistercian abbot, as well as to a number of lay folk.

Not all of Hildegard's contributions to the world were made from within her cloister. She conducted some four long preaching tours, the first of them when she was sixty years old. She spoke frequently to monastic communities and sometimes to clergy and layfolk crowding their town squares. She spoke humbly but forthrightly, urging her audience to embrace personal reform. In this she saw herself as "a small sound of the trumpet for the Living Light."

In 1146, Hildegard wrote to Bernard, asking him to confirm her life and ministry. She asked that he "pour consolation upon me from your heart."

Bernard replied: "I am filled with joy at the grace of God that is in you. Since you have the inner knowledge and the anointing that teaches all things, what can I teach or counsel you?" For Bernard it was none other than the Holy Spirit who had anointed her and infused into her a profound knowledge of reality. Shortly after this 1147 exchange of letters, Pope Eugenius III, Bernard's monastic son, appointed a commission charged with examining Hildegard's teachings. The pope himself read everything she had written in her *Scivias* to that point. He not only approved of all that she had written, but also encouraged her to continue writing down "everything that she had learned from the Holy Spirit."

Hildegard outlived both Bernard and Eugenius, both of whom died in 1153. On the seventeenth of September 1157, Hildegard herself died peacefully in the midst of her monastic daughters.

C. OTTO OF FREISING OFFERS A MIRROR FOR PRINCES

Otto was born sometime between 1111 and 1115, the fifth surviving son of Leopold III of Babenberg, the margrave of Austria, and his wife Agnes. Otto was thus a scion of the high nobility of Bavaria. His family connections were impressive: he was the grandson of the emperor Henry IV, the brother-in-law of Henry V, the half-brother of Conrad III, and the uncle of Frederick I, often referred to as Barbarossa, the Red Beard. Otto's father, Leopold, was widely known for the piety that led to his canonization as a saint, and his son Otto was equally religious, a proper virtue for a young man destined for a post in the Church.

Otto was one of the most learned men of his day. In 1127, when still a teenager, he set out for Paris to study at the cathedral school there. As a result, Otto was able to engage in confident and competent–indeed often sophisticated–expositions of philosophical questions and conclusions in his biography of the Emperor Frederick I. Otto's mastery of the classical literature of Latin antiquity was extensive, so extensive that he often quoted Roman authors without identifying them–generously assuming that his audience knew the classics as well as he.

In 1133, Otto and a group of companions left Paris to return home. After they stopped for the night at the Cistercian abbey of Morimond, Otto resolved to stay at this "school of love." Only four years later he was elected abbot.

However, in the same year, 1137, he was elected bishop of Freising, so key a post in the Church in Bavaria that he thought it mandatory to accept. As a bishop, Otto continued to live the life of a monk, symbolized by his continued wearing of his Cistercian habit. Nor did he give up his intellectual interests and pursuits: one of his first acts as bishop was to introduce into his cathedral school the study of Aristotle, who was being rediscovered in the Latin world.

Perhaps Otto's most important literary work was *The Deeds of Frederick Barbarossa*. This work provides an account of only the beginning of Frederick's reign, since Otto died in 1158 and Frederick continued to rule until 1190. But the work is much more than history. Otto's underlying intention in the *Deeds* was to enlighten the reader–and especially Frederick himself–on the duties and necessary virtues of a ruler. Otto judged that Frederick had made a good start at this, though Frederick's activities after Otto's death surely would not have pleased his uncle.

Otto saw that the first and most pressing need of any society is peace. He informed his readers that Frederick's perceived ability to provide peace between the warring factions that had so disturbed his predecessor's reign, had been the reason for his election as king:

> The princes considered not merely the achievements and valor of the youth, but also that, as a member of both warring families [the Welfs and the Hohenstaufen], he might–like a cornerstone–link these two separate walls. They therefore decided to select him as the head of the realm.

Frederick, Otto wrote, was quite anxious to settle all disputes troubling his realm without recourse to bloodshed, but, when necessary, he was willing "to deflect harm from his subjects with the sword." One of Fredrick's first acts as king, Otto reported, was to proclaim a universal peace, a peace he rigorously enforced.

To provide his people peace, Otto wrote, the ruler must efficiently exercise authority, the power his subjects bestow on him. The reward for the ruler who maintains peace is a prominent place in the hearts of his people.

The security engendered by peace enables the ruler's land to enjoy the fruits of the justice he must also provide. Otto and his contemporaries defined justice as did the Roman orator Cicero: providing to each and every person what he or she deserves. Otto pointed to Frederick's response to the bravery of a sergeant in his army during a siege:

> I must not fail to mention the valor, the downright audacity of a soldier. Wearied by the long siege [of Milan], he wished to set the others an example by scaling the citadel. Wielding only his sword, and shield, and carrying a hatchet, he ascended the height. The continual clatter of spears and rocks that showered down from the citadel did not deter him. He reached the top and there, fighting manfully, laid low a knight in full armor. The king later called the soldier into his presence and decreed that for so noble a deed he should be honored with the order of knighthood.

If deeds well done are in justice to be rewarded, deeds ill done are to be punished by the just king. Otto told the story of the fate of Archbishop Arnold of Mainz and a count by the name of Herman who had "terrorized a section of Franconia by pillage and fire." They were brought to trial and "both were found guilty, together with their accomplices." Frederick spared the archbishop "because of his old age. The other was made subject to the penalty he deserved." Frederick assigned as a penalty

> an old custom that has gained the status of law among the Franconians and Swabians. Whenever a noble has been found guilty of offences like this, before he is punished by death, he is obliged to carry a dog from one county to the next as evidence of his shameful conduct. The Emperor, observing this custom, compelled the count, a great prince of the realm, together with his accomplices, also counts, to carry dogs for a mile.

This punishment provided an effective example: "When this stern justice was promulgated, everyone decided to keep the peace rather than promote the confusion of warfare."

Peace and justice could not prevail, in Otto's eyes, unless the ruler preserved harmony between the temporal and the ecclesiastical authorities. The concept of "church versus state" has led many, if not most, nineteenth- and twentieth-century historians to see the relationship as a controversy between religious and secular views of the world. Otto would not have understood this. For him the concept "church" embraces all members and institutions of society. The Church, the People of God, is served by two institutions, one of them spiritual, one of them temporal. Both are religious institutions; neither is "secular." Otto's view is succinctly summarized by his description of Frederick's consecration and coronation:

> On the same day and in the same church the bishop-elect of Münster was consecrated by the same bishops who consecrated the king. This was a sign that, in the one Church, one single day saw the elevation of two sorts of persons who are the only ones who are sacramentally anointed according to the mandates of the New and the Old Testaments.

Otto viewed the coronation as an occasion offering incentive to the German bishops to follow the admonition of his fellow Cistercian, Pope Eugenius III, urging them "to endeavor by your exhortations to influence my very dear son Frederick to preserve the liberty of the Church."

To fulfill their calling, Otto insisted rulers must themselves be virtuous. The prerequisite virtues are vigor, prudence, and piety. The pursuit of peace and justice, Otto affirmed, requires the virtue of vigor. Otto underscored Frederick's own vigor in battle: "No one fought more energetically than this prince. No one, not even a novice knight, was quicker to take up arms. No veteran soldier was more ready to undergo dangers." Otto warned, however, that the ruler's vigor must not be unbridled. Vigorous action in an unjust cause is no virtue at all. Vigor must be employed prudently, and must be based on good judgement.

Prudence is the product, Otto thought, of good counsel. Since the structure of the twelfth-century state and society was based on tradition rather than written law, the prudent response to the problems of governance is most often found in the minds and memories of wise advisors. One example, of many, concerns the disputed election of the archbishop of Cologne in 1156. Otto noted with approval that the dispute was settled with the "advice and judgment of the bishops and princes."

But, Otto declared, no ruler, no one at all, will be able to heed the call to prudence unless possessed by the virtue of piety that enables one to realize one's dependence on God. The ruler's piety pleases "the Ruler and Creator of all, without whom nothing is well begun, nothing is successfully completed."

For Otto, the virtues of vigor, prudence, and piety are received by the ruler as gifts from God "for the greater good of the whole world." According to Otto, the ruler's happiness is achieved precisely by doing all within his or her power to further the happiness, ultimately the salvation, of his or her subjects by providing them peace, justice, and harmony between the spiritual and temporal powers.

The twelfth century saw Cistercians, like Otto, Bernard, and Pope Eugenius III, giving expression to the values of the third wave of medieval reformation. Otto provided a significant contribution to political thought that belongs to a whole genre of manuals for the education and edification of rulers, often referred to as mirrors for princes.

Chapter Twelve

The Red-Bearded Ruler

A. THE LONG REIGN BEGINS

The future king and emperor, Frederick I, was linked by kinship to the rival houses of Welf and Hohenstaufen, the two most powerful families in Germany. Frederick's father, Frederick of Hohenstaufen, was King Conrad's elder brother. His mother, Judith, was the sister of Henry the Proud, leader of the Welf clan often at odds with the Hohenstaufen. Before his death on February 15, 1152, King Conrad could have put forward his own son as his successor for the throne, but he had recognized that the Empire would not be well served by a boy king only six years of age. Not only that but, as Otto of Freising reported, German kings were "chosen not by lineal descent but through election by leading men of the realm." Those leading men, the princes of the realm, agreed with King Conrad's assessment: "Considering not merely the achievements and the valor of the youth Frederick, but also his being a member of both the chief contesting families, they decided to select him as head of the realm." Frederick was only twenty-seven when elected. Nevertheless, his chivalric reputation and his demonstrated empathy for the lower nobility, as well as his excellent prospects for uniting the higher nobility, made him the virtually unanimous choice when the vote was taken on March 4, 1152.

Frederick readily–indeed eagerly–accepted the challenges of high office. His imperial agenda became obvious almost immediately. He was determined to bring peace and order to his people by asserting his imperial authority. He also set his sights on re-imposing imperial authority over the Church. Moreover, he aimed at restoring imperial claims over Italy and especially over Rome.

On April 15, 1152, Frederick was anointed and crowned king by Archbishop Arnold of Cologne. Almost immediately, Frederick dispatched a company of highly placed clerics to Rome to announce his election, promise his obedience to the pope, and declare his readiness to protect the Holy See. The letter that the distinguished ambassadors conveyed to the pope read:

> To his most beloved father in Christ, Eugenius, pope of the holy Roman Church, Frederick, by the grace of God king of the Romans and Augustus, sends filial love and reverence. Following the custom of the Roman emperor, I have sent ambassadors to you to notify you of my election and of the condition of the Church and the realm.

Frederick then described the process of king-making in his realm: election by the principal nobles and churchmen at Frankfurt and the enthusiastic response of the people. "Five days later," he wrote, "I was anointed at Aachen by your beloved sons, the archbishop of Cologne and other venerable bishops, and elevated to the throne with their solemn blessing." Frederick then declared his intention "to love and honor the pope, defend the holy Roman Church and all churchmen, maintain peace and order, and protect widows, orphans, and all the people committed to my care."

Within two days Pope Eugenius' response was northward bound. The letter began with the traditional papal salutation:

> Eugenius, bishop, servant of the servants of God, to his beloved son in Christ, Frederick, illustrious king of the Romans, greetings and apostolic blessing. I heartily approve of your election, and I shall labor for your advancement and exaltation, as is the duty of my office. Likewise, I admonish you to defend the Church of God, to keep peace and order, to protect the widows and the fatherless and all your people. Then will all your subjects rejoice, and you will win glory among all your people and eternal life with the King of kings.

There was no mention of papal confirmation of the election in either Frederick's letter or Eugenius' response. The separate spheres of spiritual and temporal authority were asserted, though their mutual support was affirmed.

B. BUILDING A POWER BASE

The accomplishment of the goals held mutually by pope and king was not a foregone conclusion. Although Frederick, as king, possessed great theoretical authority, he could exercise little of the power needed to achieve his aims. He was the duke of Swabia, to be sure, but the Swabian duke held much less power within his duchy than did the dukes of Saxony or Bavaria. Just west of Frederick's family and ducal lands were the extensive holdings of the rival Zähringen family, the head of which was now addressed as "duke."

Frederick worked successfully to consolidate his family and ducal possessions. He transferred his lands in the Harz Mountains of northern Germany to the duke of Saxony, Henry the Lion, and in return received the dowry of Henry's first wife, Clementia of Zähringen. These lands, located in southern Swabia, were an excellent bridge to the newly acquired Burgundian lands of Frederick's wife Beatrix.

By marrying the sixteen-year-old Beatrix in 1156, Frederick had extended his influence into Burgundy. As the heiress to extensive possessions in Upper Burgundy, she brought to the alliance lands which gave Frederick real imperial power in that area. Beatrix presented Frederick with ten children, eight of whom were boys, thus assuring continuation of his dynasty. After their marriage in 1157, the king received the homage of the Burgundian magnates at the Diet of Besançon.

Frederick laid still another foundation for his imperial power by living up to his coronation oath to bring peace and order to his realm. In 1152, he promulgated a general land peace (*Landfrieden*) for Germany that all but outlawed private warfare. Breaches of the peace were met with strict penalties. Murder and grand theft were punished with death, lesser offences, such as assault or petty larceny, by fines or flogging. Disputes over land were settled by humane though strict legal procedures. In 1158, at the Diet of Roncaglia, Frederick extended this peace to his entire empire. All men between the ages of eighteen and seventy were bound by oath to maintain the peace, and their oath was to be renewed every five years. These provisions were understandably popular, especially among the vast majority of people incapable of providing protection and justice for themselves.

C. CAPTURING THE CHURCH

It had been over a hundred years since the approval, by both ecclesiastical and imperial parties, of the Concordat of Worms that governed the election of German bishops. During that time, the privileges of the king or emperor had been largely ignored by the temporal rulers themselves. The provision of the Concordat that, in case of a disputed election, the ruler could intervene and choose "the person who seems to have the better case," was ignored. The imperial veto implicit in the ruler's mandated conferral of a scepter had fallen into abeyance.

Frederick recognized this disadvantage and he insisted on his rights under the Concordat. Moreover, he exerted his influence on episcopal elections by determining the nomination procedures. He also insisted on being present at key episcopal elections, a practice long discontinued. Frederick took a tough stand too on disputed or double elections, sometimes choosing a third candidate, thus violating a clearly expressed provision of the Concordat. During a vacancy following the death of a bishop he appropriated the governing duties and confiscated the movable property of the deceased prelate. Perhaps most significant was Frederick's insistence that bishops and abbots of major monasteries swear fealty to him and provide troops to imperial armies. The large armies employed by Frederick during his several Italian expeditions would be provided largely by compulsory levies on his high churchmen.

D. TAMING THE MOST POWERFUL

By far the most serious threat to the success of Frederick's plans was the power possessed by the dukes of Bavaria and Saxony. To make his own position tenable, Frederick had to win over the Saxon duke, his cousin Henry the Lion. This Frederick accomplished by supporting Henry in a territorial dispute with Albert the Bear, margrave of the Nordmark, a territory on the Saxon frontier with the Slavs. Frederick then won over Albert by adding the nearby county of Plötzkau to his domain.

Frederick also ruled in favor of Henry the Lion's claim to the duchy of Bavaria against the claim of the current duke, Henry Jasomirgott. Then to placate Jasomirgott, Frederick detached the Bavarian frontier counties and awarded them to the displaced duke, who now became ruler of the newly created duchy of Austria. Frederick's astute balancing act left Henry the Lion with power greater than his own, but it kept Henry occupied governing his extensive possessions.

E. THE FIRST ITALIAN EXPEDITION AND THE DIET OF BESANÇON

Six times Frederick led an army southward into his Italian possessions. Sixteen of the thirty-eight years of his reign were spent there. The areas of special interest for Frederick was the city of Rome as well as Lombardy, the northern area of Italy centering on the Po valley, and its largest and most prosperous city, Milan. In the Treaty of Constance that he made with the pope on March 23, 1153, three more reasons for Frederick's campaign were evident. Both pope and emperor were troubled about the rebellious citizens of Rome, the ambitions of the Norman king of Sicily, and the equally expansionist policies of the Byzantine Emperor. The king had one of his ministerals swear on his behalf to assure the pope that

> he will not make peace or a truce with the Romans or with Roger of Sicily without the consent of the pope. The king will employ all the power of his realm to reduce the Roman people to the control of the pope and the Roman Church. He will never grant any land in Italy to the king of the Greeks.

In the same treaty, Pope Eugenius III promised that

> he would ever honor the king as the most dearly beloved son of Saint Peter and that he would bestow on him the imperial crown whenever he should come to Rome for it. The pope will not grant any land in Italy to the king of the Greeks, and will drive him out if he invades that land.

This agreement to provide mutual cooperation set the stage for Frederick's expedition through the Tyrolean Alps and down onto the plain of the Po River. Frederick's army numbered only 1,800 knights. With such a limited force, he was unable to confront directly the rebellious and defiant Milanese. He did, however, range up and down northern Italy, attacking and destroying several small towns, including Tortona, a key ally of Milan.

The situation in Rome, however, had changed dramatically. A rebellion led by Arnold of Brescia established a communal government in Rome. By the time Frederick and his army succeeded in reaching the eternal city, Eugenius had died, as had his successor. The reigning pope, Hadrian IV (1154-1159), laid an interdict on Rome, suspending all but the most necessary services of the Church during Holy Week, the week before Easter. The merchants of Rome, hard hit by the loss of the usual income stemming from pilgrimages to Rome at Easter time, dissolved their commune and pledged obedience to the pope. Frederick cooperated by capturing Arnold and turning him over to papal officials.

Frederick's reward was his imperial coronation. On Saturday, June 18, 1155, the pope awaited Frederick on the steps of Saint Peter's basilica. Frederick approached the church at the head of his army, entered, and, accompanied by the pope, venerated the tomb thought to be that of the apostles Peter and Paul. The pope then anointed Frederick with oil, placed a crown on his head, and pronounced him Roman Emperor.

Rather than meet an invasion from the South by the Norman king of Sicily, William I, Frederick then decided to lead his small, malaria-infested army back home. Left defenseless, Pope Hadrian concluded a treaty of mutual support with William at Benevento. Both pope and emperor thus repudiated the cooperation pledged through the Treaty of Constance of March 25, 1153.

The resulting hard feelings were raised to a still higher degree in October 1157 at the Diet of Besançon. Frederick had called the parliamentary meeting in order to strengthen his hold on Burgundy, the huge territory that his wife Beatrix had brought to their marriage. Pope Hadrian's motivation in sending papal ambassadors to Besançon was quite different. The legates, Cardinal Rolando Bandinelli and Cardinal Bernardo of San Clemente, presented a letter of complaint from Hadrian to the emperor.

The letter rebuked the emperor for having failed to punish the brigands who had assaulted and captured Archbishop Eskil of Lund on his way back from Rome to Denmark. Hadrian's letter reads in part: "I do not regret that I have fulfilled in every way possible your ardent desire [to be crowned emperor]. But even if your Excellency had received still greater *beneficia* from me, I would have rejoiced and not without reason." The imperial chancellor and archbishop of Cologne, Reginald of Dassel, read out his translation of this document, deliberately rendering *beneficia* as "benefices." Reginald's reading implied that the pope claimed to have bestowed the Empire on Frederick, thus asserting the pope's overlordship. "When this interpretation was read out," reported Frederick's biographer Rahewin, "the princes present were moved to great indignation." Cardinal Rolando barely escaped the meeting with his life.

Frederick immediately took advantage of the furor by writing to the bishops of Germany:

> I have no wish nor power to overstep the limits that the good customs of our predecessors and fathers have established. I have no wish and no power to overstep the limits that they set on the Church. I gladly show due reverence to our father the pope, but I regard the free crown of our Empire as a benefice from God alone.

With this letter Frederick successfully aroused ire against the pope of those prelates who had not been present at Besançon.

Pope Hadrian hastened to reply to Reginald's translation of *beneficium* and Frederick's indignant assertion of imperial rights:

> On account of a certain word, *beneficium*, your mind is said to have been moved to anger. Although this word is used by some in a different sense, it should have been accepted in the sense that I attributed to it and which was its original meaning. This word is derived from *bonus* and *factum*, and a *beneficium* is thus a "good deed."

Despite Hadrian's explanation, Eskil of Lund was not freed, and Frederick did not punish Eskil's captors for breaking the law.

F. THE SECOND ITALIAN EXPEDITION AND THE DIET OF RONCAGLIA

Frederick did not make the same mistake in 1158 that he had five years earlier. This time he arrived in Italy with an overwhelming force of 10,000 knights. Frederick's goal was to assert imperial rights of governance over northern Italy. Lombardy had become an area of independent communes in which each city regulated its own governmental affairs. Most of these communes acknowledged Frederick's claim to authority over them, but Milan resisted. The city had become wealthy and powerful. Its expansionist policy had led to its military, economic, and political domination of its smaller neighbors. Frederick besieged the city, forcing it to capitulate on September 7, 1158.

Frederick insisted that all of Milan's citizens swear loyalty to their emperor–for whom they were ordered to build a palace. The city was also to provide the emperor with 900 marks of silver annually. Three hundred hostages–nobles, knights, and commoners–were also demanded of Milan. Frederick did allow the Milanese the right to elect their own governing consuls, but these had to be confirmed by the emperor before entering office. Milan's defeat marked the summit of Fredrick's power in Italy.

In November of 1158, buoyed by his success, Frederick convened and presided over the Diet of Roncaglia. Before this great assembly of bishops, nobles, and citizens of northern Italy, Frederick asserted his intention of recovering control of the region. His biographer, Rahewin, summarized the results of the Diet:

> Guided by divine counsel, Frederick appointed over each district a judge, chosen not from the city concerned but from his court or from another city. Moreover, he received the agreement and consent of everyone that he would appoint the chief authority in each city, and the consuls, and the other magistrates, with the assent of the people. Those appointees must be loyal, upright, and competent to maintain the emperor's honor and worthily to do justice to the city's citizens and the surrounding district. Then a general peace was sworn to so that no city might attack another or any man attack another, except at the command of the emperor.

This assertion of supreme power Frederick supported by a reference to Roman law as codified in the sixth century by the emperor Justinian. Rahewin described the proceedings that applied that ancient law to the current situation:

> First the emperor inquired into the issue of royal jurisdiction and imperial power. "These," he said, "had been lost to the Empire by the insolence of usurpers or the neglect of kings." When they could find no excuse for this state of affairs, the bishops, nobles, and citizens with one voice resigned the imperial power into the emperor's hands—the Milanese being the first to make the surrender. When asked what was the law in this matter, all declared that imperial power was superior to that of duchies, margravates, counties, and consulships. Imperial power included control of coinage, tolls, appointments to office, the imposition of customs and harbor fees, charges for open passage, mills, fish ponds, bridges, river passage tolls, and annual taxation levied not only on the land but also on their own persons.

Frederick had established a claim to power beyond that enjoyed by any of his predecessors since the days of Charles the Great.

Churchmen since Gelasius I (pope 492-496) had spoken of the "two institutions by which the world is ruled, the sacred authority of the pontiff and the power of the ruler." Under the influence of Roman law, Frederick claimed rather that the laws of the emperor were to be revered "as if they were divine oracles."

It was not long before several cities, led by Milan, chafing at this new definition of imperial power and the tight control Frederick imposed, joined in a revolt. Ignoring the moral support lent to the Lombard cities by Pope Hadrian, Frederick led his forces, now augmented by fresh troops from Germany, in besieging the Lombard city of Cremona. Despite hard-nosed resistance, Cremona fell in January of 1160. The city was razed to the ground. By 1162, the Lombard forces had been defeated. The walls of the Lombard cities were demolished, and Milan was also razed. Having accomplished his goals, Frederick returned to Germany in 1164.

G. THE THIRD AND FOURTH EXPEDITIONS

One of the bulwarks of anti-imperial resistance, Pope Hadrian IV, had died in late 1159. All but two of the cardinals who gathered to elect Hadrian's successor voted for Rolando Bandinelli, a canon lawyer who, as a cardinal, had faced the emperor at Besançon. Bandinelli took the name Alexander III. He was adamant in his resistance to the exalted claims of imperial power that Frederick had proclaimed at Roncaglia. The two cardinals who had opposed Alexander's election constituted themselves a pro-imperial party and elected their own pope, who took the name Victor IV. When Alexander excommunicated Victor, the emperor forced Alexander into exile. He fled to France where he won the support of King Louis VII, who, in turn, won support from King Henry II of England. When the pro-imperial Victor died in 1164, Reginald of Dassel, the archbishop of Cologne and imperial chancellor, procured the election of a papal successor who took the name Paschal III. Meanwhile, Alexander had established contact with the League of Verona that had been formed at the instigation of the powerful maritime city of Venice.

There were three results of the controversy. First, almost all of the German bishops, who had supported Victor but were now cowed by Frederick's dramatically enhanced claims to power, shifted their allegiance to Pope Alexander. Secondly, in 1165, Frederick caused the solemn exhumation of the body of Charles the Great from his tomb in the cathedral at Aachen. Reginald of Dassel then raised Charles, who had tightly controlled the Church, to the status of saint.

The third factor in the continuing struggle between the emperor and the north Italian cities–the latter supported by Pope Alexander–was Frederick's third expedition to Italy. Alexander's position was strong. He not only had the support of the Lombard cities, but now had the backing of all of Western Europe from Norway to Spain. In Italy, Alexander had won the strong support of William I, the Norman king of Sicily. Alexander even had contact with Constantinople, where his claims were viewed with favor by the Byzantine emperor. Given the widespread support for Alexander, Frederick did not bother to recognize the election of yet another pope, Calixtus III, at the death of Paschal III in 1168.

In view of the strong and growing coalition opposing him, in the fall of 1166, Frederick once again crossed the Alps with a large army that included mercenaries from Brabant (now in Belgium). In the spring of 1167, he won battles in central Italy at Ancona and near Tusculum. He occupied Rome by the end of July. Paschal III was then solemnly enthroned at Saint Peter's, and, on August 1, he bestowed the imperial crown on Frederick's wife, Beatrix of Burgundy. A few days later, however, malaria broke out in the imperial army. Over 2,000 knights were said to have perished. Frederick caught the disease himself but recovered. After a difficult withdrawal from Italy, Frederick remained north of the Alps for some seven years.

The north Italian cities, with Byzantine support, reconstituted themselves as the Lombard League. Milan was rebuilt, and, in May of 1168, the League established a stronghold near Tortona. The fortress city was named Alessandria in the pope's honor.

H. THE FIFTH AND SIXTH EXPEDITIONS

In 1174, Frederick resolved to return to Italy. He did so at the head of an army of 8,000 knights and a considerable contingent of mercenaries. The chief object of Frederick's attack on northern Italy was the fortress of Alessandria, but his winter-long siege (1174-1175) did not win success. When a Lombard relief army approached, the emperor saw himself outmatched and entered into negotiations that led to the Truce of Montebello. The treaty established an arbitration commission consisting of the representatives of the Lombard League and three delegates named by the emperor. In anticipation of a successful outcome, Frederick sent a considerable portion of his army back to Germany. This was a mistake. In the fall of 1175, the conflict broke out anew. On May 29, 1176, at Legnano, northwest of Milan, the foot soldiers of Milan won a devastating victory. In the confusion of the battle, the emperor himself lost his way and for several days was thought dead.

Frederick was more astute in negotiating peace than he had been in waging war. He succeeded in driving a wedge between the Lombards and Pope

Alexander that led to the Treaty of Anagni of November 1176. Frederick acknowledged Alexander as the rightful pope and committed himself to return all the rights and properties he had appropriated from the papacy. In return the pope released Frederick from excommunication, acknowledging him as emperor and his son Henry as king. At the formal cessation of hostilities, through the Treaty of Venice (July 1177), the emperor promised a six-year truce with the Lombards and a fifteen-year peace with Sicily. Lastly, Frederick's appointees to German bishoprics were approved by Pope Alexander. With great fanfare the resultant peace was proclaimed:

> The lord emperor and the lord pope will mutually aid each other in preserving the honor and rights of the Church and the Empire. The lord pope, as a benign father, will aid his devoted and much beloved son, the most Christian emperor. The lord emperor, on the other hand, a most devoted son and most Christian emperor, will aid his beloved and reverend father, the Vicar of Saint Peter.

Despite this abundance of superlatives, the fundamental issues separating League, emperor, and pope remained unresolved.

The chief point of contention separating the emperor and the Lombards was the continued existence and independence of Alessandria. The city had been built as a challenge to imperial rule, and it remained a symbol of the desire for north Italian autonomy. But both sides were exhausted by the continuing controversy, and the result was the Peace of Constance of June 23, 1183. The imperial decree by which the peace was proclaimed contains fundamental concessions:

> I, Frederick, Roman emperor, and my son Henry, king of the Romans, grant in perpetuity, to you, the cities of the League, the power to rule yourselves, in your strongholds and your suburbs. You may assert without opposition the customary rights that you claim, in military service, in fortification of your cities, in jurisdiction over both criminal and civil cases.

Even so, the emperor continued to exercise supervision through a consul appointed by him or through the bishops of the League's cities.

The Peace of Constance also contained many clauses that specified the duties of the Lombard cities to the emperor. When he entered Italy they were to provide forage for his horses, rebuild inadequate roads and bridges, and sell sufficient supplies to his army. In return for the cities' largely independent status, a sum of 15,000 marks was to be paid at once, followed by a yearly tax of 200 marks. Through these payments the Lombards recognized imperial sovereignty while retaining almost total self-government.

That settlement left open the question of the Tuscan lands left to the papacy by Countess Mathilda at her death in 1115. According to the Peace of Constance these lands situated around the city of Florence were to be occupied and administered for fifteen years by the Empire. Frederick proposed to Alexander's successor, an aged man who took the name Lucius III, that the Empire absorb Tuscany and compensate the papacy with a tenth of all imperial income from that land. Frederick also demanded that his son Henry, already king, now be anointed emperor. The papal curia rejected the first proposal because it feared the control that comes from financial dependence.

This stalemate led to Frederick's sixth Italian expedition. His meeting with the pope at Verona in September 1184 brought a new approach to his Italian policies. He arranged the engagement of his son Henry to Constance of Sicily, the daughter of the late king Roger II. Roger's successor and Constance's nephew, King William II, was eyeing expansion into Byzantine lands to the east and needed an ally to cover his rear. The marriage was celebrated in a seemingly unlikely spot, Milan. Frederick had concluded a compact with that city that included the marriage and Henry's coronation as king of Italy by the patriarch of Aquilia.

The death of Lucius in 1185 led to the election of the archbishop of Milan as Pope Urban III. Urban was known to oppose Frederick's ambitions in central Italy, so the emperor sent his son Henry south into Roman territory. Urban's response was a compact with Philip, the archbishop of Cologne, who led the German opposition to the emperor, an opposition that included several bishops and some lay princes. Frederick feared that Henry the Lion, the powerful duke of Saxony and Bavaria, would join the coalition, and so, in the summer of 1186, he hastened back to Germany.

J. THE DEFIANCE OF HENRY THE LION

Frederick, we remember, had ruled in 1154 that Duke Henry of Saxony was also the duke of Bavaria. As a result, Henry's power had become as great as, or greater than, Frederick's own. Henry's duchies were both on eastern frontiers, and he was busy keeping his subordinates from expanding their power at his expense.

Henry had only belatedly participated in Frederick's second expedition to Italy in 1158. He did not accompany Frederick at all on the third and fourth expeditions. When, in 1176, Frederick made a personal appeal for Henry's support against the Lombard League, Henry replied that he would go along only if Frederick ceded to him the stronghold of Goslar. This Frederick denied, and Henry renewed his refusal to join in the expedition.

The hard feelings between the cousins was brought to a head in 1179 over the accusation of Bishop Ulrich of Halberstadt that Henry had unjustly deprived him of his diocese. Archbishop Philip of Cologne joined the suit, claiming that his nephew's Saxon inheritance had been confiscated by Duke Henry. Frederick allowed a local court to adjudicate these claims. When

Henry refused the summons of the court, he was declared an outlaw. At this point Frederick initiated a royal trial of Henry, at which, in January 1180, the princes assembled and deprived Henry of both his duchies. They then assigned Frederick the task of disposing of them.

At an imperial court in April of 1180, Frederick divided Saxony into two parts. The western part, now called the duchy of Westphalia, was bestowed on the archbishop of Cologne. The eastern part of Saxony went to Bernard of Anhalt. The court granted Bavaria to Frederick's long-time and loyal supporter, Otto of Wittelsbach. To reduce the power of Bavaria, however, Frederick and the court separated from it its southwest territory of Styria, which was made a duchy in its own right. Although Henry the Lion was exiled for a time to the court of his father-in-law, King Henry II of England, he was allowed to keep his family possessions in Braunschweig and Lüneburg. Thus the area once held by Henry was divided into five duchies. Smaller duchies, Frederick knew, were easier to control.

K. THE THIRD CRUSADE

The story of Frederick's role in the third crusade is well told by the *Chronicle* of Otto, a monk of Saint Blaise. Otto's story begins in the Holy Land:

> In the year 1187, Saladin, king of the Saracens, thought the time favorable to conquer all of Syria and Palestine. With a very large army from all over the East, he made war on the Christians. Attacking them everywhere in Palestine with fire and sword, he took many fortresses and cities and killed or took prisoner all their Christian inhabitants. The king of Jerusalem and other nobles collected a large army and went out to meet Saladin. The true cross was carried at the head of the army. They were defeated, however, and many thousands of Christians were slain. The true cross, alas, was captured by the Saracens, Jerusalem was taken, and the holy places were profaned.

News of those events profoundly disturbed western Europeans, and King Philip II of France and King Richard I of England responded to the pope's urging by undertaking a crusade. Yet it was Emperor Frederick who first set out for the Holy Land.

At a Diet held in Mainz in March of 1188, "Frederick offered to go to the aid of Jerusalem, and he and his son, Frederick, duke of Swabia, took the cross." At a Diet at Regensburg, Frederick turned over the symbols of his imperial power to his son, King Henry. "And so," Otto of Saint Blaise continued, "with a very large army, well equipped and organized, he set out for the East to attack Saladin and all the enemies of the cross." The army passed through Hungary, Bulgaria, and the European part of the Byzantine Empire. They passed the winter near a very hostile Constantinople, but, claimed Otto, "the Crusaders overcame Greek treachery with strength and German bravery."

Frederick and his army then marched through Asia Minor, opposed, often nightly, by the Saracens but supported by Christian Armenians. However, "after part of the army had crossed a river, Frederick went into the water to refresh himself, for it was very hot. He was a good swimmer, but the cold water overcame him, and he sank. He died in the thirty-eighth year of his reign, the thirty-fifth of his rule as emperor. His bones were carried to Antioch and buried with royal ceremony." The month was June, the year 1190.

L. THE LEGACY

The reign of Frederick Barbarossa had been, in many respects, a watershed in the history of medieval Germany. It marked the culmination of the power of the emperor in Germany, Italy, and Eastern Europe, but it also revealed signs of a fracturing political structure. Economically, Germany was prosperous, but that prosperity was increasingly centered not on the land but in urban areas. Barbarossa's reign saw an intensification of social movements already underway when he came to power. The ministerial class continued its upward movement, castle building became ever more widespread, and the knightly class and its training more clearly defined. In an urban culture Jews became increasingly important members of medieval German society. Movements in intellectual life multiplied or intensified.

The primary political units of Germany prior to the reign of Frederick had been the duchies. When Germany went to war, each duke led his own contingent; now the army was an imperial force. The duchy of Swabia was in effect dissolved as a governmental unit after 1058. As we have seen, Bavaria and Saxony were divided into at least five major–and more minor–parts with the fall of Henry the Lion. Frederick deliberately singled out as princes a group of high nobility and clergy whom he endowed with expanded powers, raising them above most counts and lesser nobility. The number of counts was increased markedly, but this had the effect of reducing the power of each.

Germany flourished economically in the last half of the twelfth century. Trade expanded and new mints were established to facilitate that trade. Many new towns were founded, and many of these sponsored fairs that served both local and international commerce. The population of the German kingdom rose to some seven or eight million inhabitants.

A major social change that had been in the making for at least a century came to full fruition in the latter half of the twelfth century. Ministerials, who, we remember, had started out as only half free administrators of a lord's estates, were by now fully integrated into the knightly class of warriors. In 1151, the archbishop of Cologne granted his ministerials a charter of rights. The document reads in part:

> If anyone invades the territory of Cologne and the lands of the archbishopric, all the ministerials shall assist their lord in defending his lands. The ministerials are bound to go with their lord, the archbishop, on his expeditions across the Alps for the coronation of the emperor. After they reach the Alps, the archbishop shall give each knight one silver mark each month for his expenses.

Ministerials now belonged to the knightly class, and their positions were inherited by their eldest sons when they died. Even a second son had a right to enter the service of the lord if he "came with his war-horse, shield, and lance to the court of the archbishop and offered his oath of fidelity." Ministerials served the empire south of the Alps as major figures in imperial administration. Indeed, some ministerials attained positions comparable to those of the high nobility.

Jews too had become increasingly more important contributors to medieval German society. At the beginning of the century, some cities in Germany had seen their citizens, sometimes even their bishops, inflamed by the preaching of the First Crusade, inflict suffering, exile, or even death on their Jewish neighbors. A similar danger showed itself in connection with the Second Crusade. In 1146, in the course of his preaching of that Crusade in Germany, Bernard of Clairvaux heard disturbing reports that a renegade monk named Rudolf was fanning the flames of hatred by asserting that the extermination of the infidel in the Holy Land might suitably be preceded by the slaughter of infidels closer to hand. The result for the Jews of the area was severe persecution—until Bernard came to their rescue.

Bernard was a confident adherent of Saint Paul's conviction, stated in his letter to the Romans, that all Israel will be saved. This is the reason Bernard thundered that "Jews must not be persecuted, slain, or cast out." "Persecution," he continued, "is the foulest heresy, a sacrilegious prostitution, impregnated with the spirit of lies. It is conceived in sorrow and gives birth to injustice." Bernard even forbade attempts to convert Jews to Christianity, for Jews, he thought, attain salvation by living up to the Covenant that God made with them in and through the Old Testament Law.

In 1157, Frederick Barbarossa issued a charter to the Jews of the city of Worms. In it he commanded:

> No bishop or count shall exercise any authority over the Jews, only those whom they choose from their own number. No one shall take from them any property. No one shall interfere with their right to erect buildings against the walls of the city. They shall have the right to exchange money, to travel in peace and security throughout the whole kingdom for the purpose of buying

and selling. No one shall exact any toll from them or require them to pay any other public or private tax.

Frederick's charter did not concern itself simply with the economic well-being of Jews. He also wished to safeguard their religious conscience: "No one shall baptize Jewish children against their will. If anyone captures or seizes a Jew and baptizes him by force, he shall pay twelve pounds of gold to the royal treasury."

Frederick also decreed that the Jews of Worms should be essentially self-governing: "If Jews there have any suit or any matter to be settled among themselves, the case shall be tried by their peers and by no others." In disputes between Jews and Christians, "each party shall follow the process of his own law. The Jew has the same right as the Christian to prove his case." Under this condition of legal parity, Jews enjoyed virtual independence, a status affirmed by several bishops who urged Jews to seek legal as well as moral decisions from their rabbis.

Frederick, we are told, had an exceptional command of the German language. He read and understood Latin well, although his command of the spoken language was apparently not good. That did not prevent him from amassing a substantial library in his palace at Hagenau in Alsace. The collection included saints' lives, histories, law books, and philosophical and medical works, Gottfried of Viterbo informed his readers. Frederick commissioned his uncle, Otto of Freising, to write a lengthy account of his deeds, as we are already aware.

Frederick was by no means alone in fostering higher culture. In 1166, his cousin and longtime opponent, Henry the Lion, commissioned a bronze lion to be set up in Braunschweig, perhaps the first substantial piece of free-standing sculpture in the medieval West. One of Frederick's Italian subjects was Burgundio of Pisa (c. 1110-1193), who was well acquainted with the Greek language and culture. He served as an ambassador and judge for his town, but is best known for his excellent translations of Greek works of theology, philosophy, medicine, and law.

It was to the knowledge of ancient law that Frederick made his most notable contribution. In 1158, he brought four professors of Roman law from the nascent University of Bologna to the Diet of Roncaglia. These scholars were masters of the sixth-century compilation of Roman law issued by the Emperor Justinian. That law asserted that the emperor was the sole source of law, a position which Frederick enthusiastically embraced.

Frederick also supported higher education. In November of 1158, he issued a document called the *Privilegum scholasticum* that reads in part:

> I grant the favor of my dutiful love to all scholars who are traveling for the sake of their studies–and especially to teachers of divine and sacred laws–that

they may come to the places where classical literature is studied and may live safely in these cities. Henceforth, no one should be so bold as to do any injury to scholars. Moreover, if anyone presumes to bring suit against them on any matter, scholars shall be allowed to choose to cite them before their own dean or master or before the bishop of the city.

M. ASSESSMENTS

The contemporary views of Frederick's reign that have come down to us are uniformly positive. Witness this ecstatic comment by Otto of Freising: "To the present age, Frederick has brought so great a felicity of peace to the entire transalpine empire that he may rightfully be called not only Emperor and Augustus, but the Father of his Country." Rahewin, who continued Otto's biography, was equally enthusiastic about his subject: "So widely and so nobly has he waged wars throughout the whole world, so great are his deeds in peace and in war, that he who reads his history will think these achievements not of one king or emperor, but of many." This is clearly twelfth-century hyperbole, but next to Charles the Great, Frederick the Red Beard still ranks as the most popular ruler of the German middle ages.

Chapter Thirteen

The Flowering of Medieval German Literature

The wealth that Germany enjoyed in the twelfth and thirteenth centuries enabled German architects, sculptors, painters, and poets to flourish. Medieval German literature was the product of two fruitful cultures: aristocratic and agricultural. The worlds of the knight and the farmer were very different, but, as we have seen in the case of the ministerials, it was possible for someone with an agrarian background to become a knight.

A knight was a heavily armed and armored cavalry man. If a man fit that definition, he was a knight, no matter what his wealth or political position or power. A knight was a military man: the Latin word for knight was *miles*.

To become a knight a young man had to develop, then possess and exhibit certain virtues or powers. Foremost among these was, of course, military prowess. His role as a knight demanded great physical strength and skill in horsemanship and the use of arms. In addition, he was expected to exhibit courage and steadfastness, loyalty and integrity, moderation and constancy, humility and generosity–moral qualities of a high order.

A young man who aspired to be a knight sought out the patronage of the lord of a castle. The lord, often the aspirant's maternal uncle, sometimes his baptismal godfather, took the young man in and subjected him to a physically and ethically taxing training. This sort of education was an apprenticeship: the young man observed the battle tactics and techniques of his lord and then imitated them through long practice.

Military training was not the only education afforded him at the lord's castle. The lady of the castle was responsible for the aspirant's intellectual and social development. She arranged for the castle's chaplain to give knightly aspirants lessons in Latin. Some aspirants learned barely enough Latin to follow the Mass, though there were some, like the emperor Frederick

I, who mastered written Latin. There were even a few who became fluent in speaking it.

The lady of the castle also took charge of training the aspirant in the social graces necessary for knighthood. She insisted on proper reverence for the clergy, respect for other knights, and concern for the welfare of those who served the castle life as servants or farmers. She insisted on proper table manners and gentility toward all, especially women. To please his lady, a knight was often expected to have the ability to compose poetry, and sometimes to sing it.

The poetry the lady desired to hear–either from the young men at her court or from wandering minstrels–was not the tales of war and military adventure her husband preferred. The lady wanted lyrics, often love lyrics, and she got them. Women–already influential because they controlled the education of future military and political leaders–began to be praised and exalted as noble creatures whom men should long to serve. From the pen of one knight, Walther von der Vogelweide (c. 1170-1230), came this verse:

> When a lady chaste and fair,
> Noble and clad in rich attire,
> Walks through the throng with gracious air,
> As sun that bids the stars retire,
> Then where are all your boastings, month of May,
> What have you beautiful and gay
> Compared with that supreme delight?
> We leave your loveliest flowers
> And watch that lady bright.

Walther's lady is both physically and morally attractive. She leads him to a love that is both human and divine, a love that should draw him to God. Walther wrote in his poem *I Saw the World*: "Who fears not God, your gifts to take and then your Ten Commandments break, lacks that true love that should be his salvation." In the same poem, Walther also penned his loving embrace of all humankind: "Christian, Jews, and pagans all serve God, and he holds all of them in His care."

In the twelfth and thirteenth centuries, a major source of the material which formed the subject matter of German poetry was Celtic in origin. From Wales, French poets took over and reworked stories, many of them dealing with King Arthur or with a quest for the Holy Grail. Frederick I's Burgundian wife Beatrix played a major role in bringing this material to Germany, for much of Burgundy spoke a form of northern French. Frederick's longtime foe, Henry the Lion, had married Matilda, the daughter of King Henry II of England, who also ruled much of what is today France. Like Beatrix, Matilda brought with her the poetry of French troubadours.

Much of the Celtic material which inspired these French poets was only marginally Christian, and the twelfth-century poets did not always succeed in resolving all the tensions between pagan and Christian values in their literary sources and imagination. It was left to the German love poets, the *Minnesänger*, to complete the process.

An example of this literary transformation is the *Parzifal* of Wolfram of Eschenbach, a knight and poet who wrote over the years 1195 to 1225. Wolfram retold a story of the quest for the Holy Grail, a tale that the French poet Chrétien de Troyes had left unfinished. At one point in Wolfram's work, Parzifal is torn between his commitment to seek the Holy Grail and his deep love for his wife: "Once again Sir Parzifal his fair wife could not but recall her chasteness and her sweetness." The knight's faithfulness to his lovely wife was a reflection of his "great constancy, his manly heart, his body strong, till to no other could belong his love and his endeavor." In distress Parzifal chose to leave behind the love of his life. He donned his armor and "saddled, all alone, his horse. Shield and lance he took perforce. All present wept as he departed." Parzifal's quest was successful: through his labors he gained insight into the two-way bond between God and man–revealed in the person of Christ–and between service to his lady and the fulfillment of marriage.

Not all medieval German literature was based on Celtic and French sources. The epic poetry of Hartmann of Aue is a case in point. Born about 1170, Hartmann died sometime between 1212 and 1222. As a boy he received an excellent education. His command of Latin was excellent, as was his familiarity with the texts of the Bible. He also steeped himself in the works of the poets of Latin antiquity and of contemporary France. In the preface to his story, *Poor Henry*, Hartmann identified himself as a knight of no small learning:

> Once there was a knight who was so learned that he could read in books whatever he found therein. His name was Hartmann, and he was in the service of the House of Aue. He began to search in various books to see if he could find some story with which to wile away tedious hours more pleasantly. He sought topics that reflected the glory of God and with which he could please his fellow humans.

Hartmann then pleaded with readers for their prayers, "for the one who intercedes for another intercedes for oneself as well."

Hartmann's tale is of Sir Henry, whose "honor and conduct were without the slightest fault." Henry embodied all the qualities of a courtly knight, including wisdom. His lofty state turned, however, to misery when he fell victim to leprosy, sharing, as Hartmann said, the fate of Job. However, "the disease and tribulations that Job suffered led him to praise God. Alas, poor Henry did not at all react in this manner, and the heart that once soared up with joy now sank into gloom and depression."

Henry set off for the best medical schools of his time, at Salerno in Italy and Montpelier in France. At Salerno he learned that there was but one cure possible. The only solution was "to find a virgin of marriageable age who would be willing to suffer death for your sake."

Convinced that "it would be impossible to find anyone who would willingly die for him," Henry journeyed home. There "he began distributing his lands and possessions, enhancing the wealth of his poor friends and relations and giving alms also to the needy whom he did not know." He kept only one farm, to which he retreated to remain alone. That land was managed by a farmer who "spared no means to make Henry comfortable."

One day the farmer and his lovely and virtuous daughter asked Henry why he did not seek a cure, and Henry told them of the doctors' verdict. The girl resolved to sacrifice herself for her lord's sake, and no argument from her father or mother could dissuade her. No one, however, not even the surgeons at Salerno, agreed to cooperate with the girl's willingness to sacrifice herself.

Then, Hartman wrote, "the Searcher of Hearts saw clearly her devotion and distress. Christ, the holy one, made manifest how dear to him are devotion and compassion. He freed them both from all their miseries by cleansing Henry of his leprosy. After a long and happy life, they both gained possession of the eternal kingdom." Hartmann concluded his tale with these words: "May God help us to attain the reward that they received. Amen."

Hartmann's story offers valuable insight into the virtues and deeply held beliefs of the twelfth- and thirteenth-century knightly class. But within fifty years of Hartmann's death, another literary work reflected a different insight, a different view of the world–this time the world of medieval German farmers.

Throughout the late eleventh and twelfth centuries, the German frontiers steadily expanded to the East. Hitherto sparsely inhabited lands, such as mountainous districts in the interior of the country, were increasingly settled. In both cases those who owned or had rights over the land needed laborers to work it. This need led most lords, among them knights, to offer farmers increasingly favorable terms to work their land, most often through paying fixed rents in money. Prices of the goods required or desired by the knightly class rose steadily throughout the thirteenth century, but the lord's income remained fixed by contract. The potential consequences appear in a work, *Farmer Helmbrecht*, by a poet who called himself Wernher the Gardener. His work depicted, albeit with considerable exaggeration, the social conditions of the thirteenth century.

The protagonists in the poem are father and son, both named Helmbrecht. The father is a pious, hard-working, and prosperous farmer who wishes some day to hand his farm over to his son. The boy's mother and sister spoil him with gifts of splendid clothing decorated with bells, a sword and dagger, and a doublet made of chain mail. Thus decked out, he approaches his father, who reluctantly acquiesces to the young man's demand for a horse to carry him to court. The father counsels the boy, however, to follow the honest life of a farmer: "Take to the plow and till with me the field; then you'll live and die a respected man. See how I live: faithful to my calling, respectable and honest. Each year I pay my tithes, and my whole life long I have not known hate or envy or betrayed a trust." The father also admonishes his son to give up his planned trip to court, warning him that there "you'll suffer hunger, your bed will be hard, and you will have to do without love. You will surely be the butt of the jokes of the genuine court folk."

Despite the father's pleas, the youth rides off to join the company of a group of brigands who know little of the values, service, and honor of true knights. Joining them in cattle-rustling, the young man steals from farmers, then tortures them by gouging out their eyes, slashing their bodies open, tying them to anthills, and stringing them up in trees. The outlaws finally meet their fate at the hands of lawmen, despite the fact that they outnumber "the officers of right." Young Helmbrecht's companions are hanged, and he is both blinded and maimed. Worse yet, his parents refuse him refuge. Some farmers whose houses he has plundered, whose daughters he has raped, and whose babies he has smothered, hang the wretch from a tree–though only after allowing his confession.

Surely Wernher's tale is not a description of a degeneracy infecting the whole of the knightly order. It is, however, a poem that celebrates the virtuous life and growing wealth of the thirteenth-century farmer. It also describes an economic threat to the lowest levels of the nobility. Thus Wernher added this admonition: "If there are children, still at home with father and mother, who wish to seek knightly glory, let them be warned by Helmbrecht's fate."

Chapter Fourteen

The Turning Point

A. HENRY VI, AN AMBITIOUS EMPEROR

When word of the death of Frederick I reached the West in 1190, his son and imperial regent, Henry, was twenty-five years old. Henry had been born in 1165, the son of Frederick and Beatrix of Burgundy. He had been but three years old when elected king of the Romans–the title by then commonly conferred on the imperial heir apparent. The boy was then anointed and crowned at Aachen on August 15, 1169. In Milan, fourteen years later, Henry married Constance, the aunt and heiress presumptive of King William II of Sicily. One year later, Henry was crowned king of Italy. Since Pope Urban III refused to anoint him co-emperor, Frederick conferred on him the title "Caesar."

In 1189, the same year that Frederick had departed for the Holy Land, William II, Constance's nephew and king of Sicily, died. When the news reached Henry, he set out for Italy. There he learned of the Sicilian nobility's support for Tancred of Lerra, the illegitimate grandson of William's predecessor. Henry reached Rome in 1191, and there a new pope, Celestine III, anointed and crowned him Roman emperor. Henry then attacked Tancred's mainland stronghold at Naples. The siege dragged on, and with delay came disease and death. Henry had no other choice than to raise the siege and make his way back to Germany.

During the year 1192, a rapidly growing alliance of German princes, both lay and ecclesiastical, joined with Tancred of Sicily, Pope Celestine, and even Richard Lionheart of England in opposing Henry. The emperor's situation was dire, but he was saved by a happy accident. While returning from the Holy Land in December 1192, Richard Lionheart, though disguised, was captured by knights loyal to Duke Leopold V of Austria and held for ransom.

As a condition of his release, Richard was forced to pay Leopold and his emperor 50,000 silver marks. Henry also forced from Richard an oath of fidelity and an annual payment of 5,000 pounds of silver.

Another fortuitous event in Henry's reign was the death in 1195 of Tancred of Sicily. After being ferried across the Straits of Messina by the fleets of his allies, Pisa and Genoa, Henry captured the Sicilian capital, Palermo. There on Christmas Day in 1194, Henry was anointed and crowned king of Sicily.

Secure now in his position in Germany, Burgundy, and Sicily, Henry possessed the foundation for his great dream of a European and Mediterranean empire stretching from the North and Baltic seas to the Holy Land and even beyond.

As king of Sicily–which included one third of the boot of Italy–Henry adopted the ambitions of the Norman predecessors of his wife Constance. With part of Richard Lionheart's ransom, Henry purchased the loyalty of Cyprus and Armenia, lands far to the East. He fixed his eye on the kingdom of Aragon and threatened the African territories around Tunis and Tripoli. Henry's ambitions extended even to the acquisition of the Eastern or Byzantine Empire with its capital at Constantinople. In short, he sought the reunion of the two halves of the ancient Roman Empire. With this grand plan in mind, on March 31, 1195, Henry pledged himself to launch still another crusade.

In June of 1195, before embarking on his new crusading venture, Henry returned to Germany with the goal of uniting his kingship in Sicily with the imperial throne. This required making succession to the Empire hereditary, as it was in Sicily. To accomplish this, as the annals of the abbey of Marbeck recorded, "the emperor wished to confirm with the princes a new and unheard of decree in the Roman Empire, that kings should succeed him by hereditary right." At a Diet in Würzburg in April of 1196, Henry bullied the majority of the princes present into agreeing with his plan. In return, lay lords were to receive unrestricted rights of inheritance not only in the male line but also in the female line, or, failing these heirs, even nephews were to inherit. In any of these cases, the emperor gave up his long-asserted right to the territory in question. Furthermore, Henry promised that bishops' personal possessions were no longer to be forfeit to the emperor on their death. This practice had been long forbidden by agreement of both emperors and churchmen, but Henry's father, Frederick Barbarossa, had rigorously exercised it.

Opposition to Henry's plan soon gained strength under the leadership of Archbishop Adolf of Cologne. Henry ignored this and began negotiations with the pope for approval of his intentions. This was necessary because the pope, as the chief bishop of the Empire, had the responsibility to anoint and crown the emperor-elect. To secure the approval of the pope and cardinals, Henry proposed a scheme by which an enormous yearly payment was to be made by the German churches to the pope. Pope Celestine III refused to agree, sure that the plan would eventually result in imperial control of the Roman Church.

To add to the emperor's troubles, a revolt broke out in Sicily. Henry succeeded in cruelly suppressing it. But it was August of 1197 before he was able to rejoin his crusading force. He fell mortally ill, perhaps of typhus, and died in Sicily on September 26, 1197. He was buried in the cathedral of Palermo, leaving behind a two-year-old son, Frederick.

B. POPE INNOCENT III

Lotario dei Conti was born in 1160 or early 1161 in the castle of Gavignano, just below the hill-top town of Segni, some fifty miles southeast of Rome. Both his father, Trasmondo, and his mother, Clarice, came from upper class families. Lotario received an excellent education in Rome under the direction of Peter Ismaele, abbot of the monastery of Sant' Andrea. With Ismaele as tutor, Lotario gained a wide knowledge of biblical texts and allusions as well as a talent for liturgical chant. The pope appointed this learned lad a canon of Saint Peter's basilica in Rome while he was still in his teens.

The young canon left Rome for Paris where he stayed for some six years and earned a Master of Arts degree (roughly equivalent to a modern Ph.D.). His studies at Paris included classical Latin literature and the logic of Aristotle. He also had time for courses in theology but did not stay for a degree in that discipline. Instead, sometime in the mid 1180's, he migrated to Bologna, whose fame in canon (church) law matched that of Paris in theology.

In 1189 or 1190, Pope Clement III appointed the twenty-nine-year-old Lotario a cardinal deacon. His chief duties were hearing appeals to Rome from persons and institutions not satisfied with the judgment of a local ecclesiastical court. His name also appeared often as a witness to papal documents. Of this period in his life, Lotario wrote: "In my duties I am impeded by such a rush of cases and ensnared in such a tangle of business that I find neither leisure for reflection nor peace for writing."

Despite this claim, Lotario did take time to pen a number of treatises. In one of his works, *The Four Kinds of Marriage*, Lotario wrote that the first kind was that between a man and woman, the second that between Christ and his Church, the third between God and the individual soul, and, finally, the fourth between the Word of God and human nature in the incarnation of Christ. Meditation on any one of these, he wrote, can lead to illumination of all the others.

This work and several other spiritual treatises seem to contrast sharply with his active career as cardinal and pope, but are essential to an understanding of it. For Lotario, action in the world was necessary, but the purpose of that activity was the spiritual welfare of Christians, and its success could be measured only by reward in the next world.

Four months after the death of Henry VI in September 1197, the aged Pope Celestine followed his erstwhile enemy. The cardinals assembled to elect his successor and chose Lotario, at the time not even a priest. On Sunday, February 22, 1198, Lotario was seated on the episcopal chair at his cathedral, Saint John Lateran, and ordained bishop of Rome. He took the name Innocent III.

C. THE MUCH-DISPUTED SUCCESSION

Only a year after the death of Henry VI, on November 27, 1198, Queen Constance followed her husband to the grave. Earlier that year she had seen her three-year-old son Frederick crowned king of Sicily. On her deathbed Constance named Innocent III as the boy's guardian.

North of the Alps, Frederick's cause was supported to some degree by his previous election as king of Germany, an election Henry had forced on several of the leading noblemen of that land. More important were the efforts of Philip of Swabia, Henry's younger brother, to hold together the fragile support for his nephew. In March 1198, faced with the opposition of a growing group of high nobility collected by Archbishop Adolf of Cologne, Philip reversed his course and managed to have himself elected King of the Romans at a meeting at Mülhausen, a town on the upper Rhine. The opposition soon met at Cologne and elected Otto of Braunschweig, the son of the former Welf leader, Henry the Lion. Perhaps not unexpectedly, Otto also had the support of his uncle, King Richard Lionheart of England. Civil war ensued.

At first Pope Innocent refused to take sides in the dispute. He was distressed, however, by Philip's professed intent to take control of papal territory in central Italy and assert his rule over the kingdom of Sicily. At the same time, Innocent was heartened by Otto's pledge not to do the same. Philip rapidly gained power and, in the process, alienated Innocent still further by what the pope saw as his highhanded treatment of the German Church.

Both claimants to the throne submitted their case to the pope. Innocent responded that he "did not wish to claim the rights of the princes to elect a king who is subsequently to be promoted to the dignity of emperor." On the other hand, the pope argued, as the bishop charged with anointing and crowning the emperor, he had the right and the duty to examine the qualifications of the persons nominated.

In 1201, Innocent issued his decision. In a fine example of the scholastic method he had learned at Paris and Bologna, the pope weighed the evidence, balanced the authorities pro and con, and resolved the question by an appeal to logic. According to Innocent, authority is bestowed on a ruler so that he can provide justice to his people. Frederick was thus ruled out because, as a child, he was not able to provide that justice.

In Philip's favor was the fact that he had been the choice of the majority of the electors. Still more important, he was "so strong in wealth and supporters" that he was well able to fulfill the duties of a ruler. Even so, Innocent ruled Philip out because, though able, he had not proven himself willing to provide justice.

Against Otto was his relatively weaker strength and the smaller number of electors who had supported him. Innocent decided for Otto, however, because he had been "elected by as many or more of those electors who have the best right to elect the emperor and because he is much better suited to rule than Philip." In Innocent's eyes, then, the function of the imperial office–providing justice–determined the basis for his choice.

Philip refused to recognize Innocent's decision and seemed poised to triumph over Otto when, in 1208, he was murdered by some unknown assassin. For the sake of peace, the German princes then recognized Otto as king, and in 1209 the pope anointed and crowned him emperor. The new ruler, however, repudiated his coronation promises and attacked the kingdom of Sicily held by Frederick, the pope's ward and Henry VI's legitimate successor to that throne. Innocent III wrote to the bishops of Germany that "the sword I myself have forged has dealt me grievous wounds." Innocent declared Otto excommunicate and lent his support to Frederick's kingship in Germany. In 1211, the German princes elected Frederick, now seventeen years old, as emperor.

D. THE END OF THE OTTONIAN EMPIRE

To confirm his hold on the Empire, Frederick set out for Germany in 1212, but he refused to give up his rule in Sicily as he had promised both the pope and the German princes. Frederick's position in both Germany and Sicily placed both the northern Italian towns and the papal territories in central Italy in a vise.

Frederick's reign was devoted to tightening that hold. To accomplish that end he built up a highly centralized bureaucratic state in Sicily with himself as its absolute ruler. Frederick repeatedly attacked both the northern Italian towns and their papal ally. Repeatedly issued excommunications followed. In 1228, while under one of these sentences of excommunication, he set out on a crusade. Frederick concluded a treaty with the ruler of Jerusalem, Sultan al-Kamil, and placed on his own head the crown of the kingdom of Jerusalem, defunct since 1187. Perhaps even more sensational was his capture of several cardinals and other prelates sailing, in August 1241, to a Church council called by Pope Gregory IX.

The all-consuming focus of Frederick's interest and energies was his Sicilian kingdom. During his thirty-five-year reign he spent little more than nine years in Germany. His acquisition of the imperial crown was intended only to insure his safety from German attack. To the extent that he ruled Germany at all, he did so through the regency of his son Henry. In 1232, when Henry attempted to reestablish Hohenstaufen dominance north of the Alps, Frederick refused his support to his rebellious son and gave his wholehearted approval to the cause of the German princes. Henry was deposed as regent and imprisoned in 1235. After quelling Henry's rebellion, Frederick returned to Sicily and did not appear north of the Alps for the remainder of his life.

Frederick left a Germany no longer under the rule of the Emperor. In 1220, he issued a *Privilege in Favor of the Ecclesiastical Princes*. Frederick began his decree by enumerating the many favors bestowed on him by the bishops: "promoting me to the summit of the Empire, upholding me in that position after my promotion to it, and, later, electing my son Henry to be your king and lord." On the other hand he noted, "abuses burdensome to you have sprung up as a result of the long period of disorder in the Empire, in the form of new tolls, new coinage, wars between lay administrators of ecclesiastical lands who have usurped the power of the churches, and innumerable other evils."

Frederick then promised "that on the death of an ecclesiastical lord I shall never claim any part of his personal possessions." The Emperor also undertook "not to introduce new tolls or new coinage but rather to preserve and guard in their entirety the ancient tolls and coinage rights granted to their churches." Nor would Frederick "receive into my cities men fleeing the bishops' service," but would "shun any persons whom the ecclesiastical princes have excommunicated." The list continued and, in effect, made the bishops independent rulers in the territories they had governed, at least nominally, as agents of the Empire.

In 1231, Frederick granted further favors, this time to all princes, ecclesiastical and lay. Among the many provisions of this *Statute in Favor of Princes* he promised "that I will not construct any new fortress or city or any new markets that would interfere with the old ones." Most importantly, Frederick granted to the princes courts and jurisdiction over all counties and their subunits. In effect, all the lands of the lords of Germany were now administratively independent.

Frederick died in 1250. Owing to Pope Innocent IV's declaration that Frederick's son Conrad was as unfit as his father to rule justly, Conrad was not elected emperor. It was just as well that Conrad's chief interests lay in his Sicilian kingdom, but even there his hopes to carry on the absolute rule of his father were frustrated. At his early death in 1254, Manfred, Frederick's illegitimate son, tried to assume imperial status, but his true interests lay in dominating Italy by employing the resources of Sicily. The resulting warfare led a powerful French count, Charles of Anjou, to accept the invitation of another Frenchman, Pope Urban IV, to assume rule over Sicily. On February 26, 1266, Charles defeated Manfred, who died that same year. There was still one more Hohenstaufen to be reckoned with: Conradin, the youthful grandson of Frederick II. Conradin cobbled together an expeditionary force of all sorts of malcontents–Sicilian, Tuscan, and Spanish–and succeeded in capturing Rome. On August 23, 1268, he entered into battle with Charles and was decisively defeated. Overtaken in flight, Conradin was put on trial by Charles, who had him beheaded. With Conradin the Hohenstaufen dynasty died. There would not be a universally acknowledged Roman Emperor again until 1273.

During the time of Otto I and his successors, for some 250 years, Germany had been the most unified state in Europe. It would be now reduced to an agglomeration of petty states numbering eventually–according to some reckonings–1,200 sovereign states.

Chapter Fifteen

Political Reconstitution

A. THE FAILURE OF IMPERIAL RULE

During the thirteenth, fourteenth, and fifteenth centuries, England and France experienced growing centralization of power in the hands of the king. During the same centuries, Germany experienced an increasing disintegration of central authority.

After the death of Frederick II in 1250, Germany was left without a resident ruler for twenty-three years. During this period, called the Interregnum, there were indeed kings elected, sometimes more than one at a time, but the only capable candidates for the position were foreigners. Both Richard of Cornwall, the brother of King Henry III of England, and King Alfonso X of Castile were elected by a minority of the German princes, the most influential of them having been richly bribed. Alfonso did not so much as venture to set his foot in Germany. Richard did make three visits and was crowned king of the Romans by the archbishop of Cologne. He won some small support in the Rhineland, but in the end he returned to England to bolster his brother's power and to replenish his own purse.

Pope Gregory X (1271-1276) longed for a united Germany to serve as a counterweight to the threatening power of Charles of Anjou, ruler of Sicily. At Gregory's urging, the German princes decided to fill the ancient throne. Their choice fell on Rudolf of Habichtsburg, a name later shortened to Habsburg. The Habichtsburg (the Sparrowhawk's Castle) was situated on the Aar River, positioned advantageously to defend the city of Bern, and the Swiss territory beyond it, from any incursion by the count of Geneva. Rudolf's lands stretched from the Alpine passes northward to southern Alsace, but he was by no means one of the great princes of the empire. Indeed, that was the major reason why the princes chose him, thinking that they were safe from threats to their positions by a powerful ruler.

The great princes misjudged Rudolf's intentions and abilities. From the very beginning of his reign, his intent was to repossess the imperial crown lands that had been seized by the princes during the reign of Frederick II and the Interregnum. The Imperial Diet that Rudolf called to meet at Nuremburg in November of 1271 enacted decrees supporting his position but left it to him to enforce its decisions. The Diet also decreed that Ottokar, the king of Bohemia, had forfeited the land he held of the crown by his stubborn resistance to the king's authority. Ottokar was the most powerful prince of the Empire; to stand against him, Rudolf required aid from the very same princes who had seized the imperial lands he coveted. To win their assistance against Ottokar, Rudolf could not press too vigorously his claims to those lands. A substantial portion of the territories formerly belonging to the Empire were lost in this way.

Through diplomacy and warfare waged against Ottokar, Rudolf did succeed in 1282 in capturing the extensive and powerful eastern duchies of Upper and Lower Austria, Carinthia, Carniola, and Styria. These territories Rudolf attached to his family's possessions; but he did not transfer them to the imperial domain. This action provided a model for his successors. Thereafter, the principal motivation for seeking election as king of the Romans (and thus emperor-elect) would be the opportunity that post afforded to acquire additional family lands. Rudolf desired still more: to see his son Albrecht as his successor. At the Diet of Frankfurt, a few weeks before his death in 1291, he placed his proposal before the princes of the Empire. His plan was rejected because the princes feared allowing too much power in the hands of one family, and on Rudolf's death they elected Adolf of Nassau.

Adolf's election was won at the price of extensive and expensive concessions. To Siegfried, archbishop of Cologne, for example, he declared: "If the archbishop votes for me, I shall surrender many fortresses and strongholds so that he can better defend and preserve the rights of the kingdom and empire." Adolf also cancelled the debt that the archbishop owed the empire and instead promised the transferal of 25,000 silver marks to him. "If I should act contrary to my promises," he wrote, "I should be deposed and lose my kingdom." And this is precisely what the princes of the Empire did in 1298, after Albrecht, the Habsburg ruler of Austria, had risen up in rebellion.

The dead King Rudolf's son Albrecht was then elected emperor and pursued his father's goal of making the empire a hereditary monarchy. To accomplish this, he sought the support of the French monarch. The French goal was to annex German territories; Albrecht obligingly ceded to France lands west of the Meuse River, already occupied by French troops, as well as allowing French penetration of the duchy of Burgundy. In return, the king of France, Philip the Fair, sent troops to support Albrecht's subjection of the archbishoprics of Mainz, Cologne, and Trier, as well as the lands of the Count Palatine of the Rhine. Albrecht then reversed his policy, hoping that by allying himself with Pope Boniface VIII against Philip, he could win the pope's support of his goal of hereditary succession. The death of the eighty-year-old pope, after being manhandled by a French expedition to Italy, changed Albrecht's tactics once more. He decided to pursue Habsburg territorial expansion in the East, and he did indeed secure Bohemia and Moravia in 1306. Two years later, however, he was assassinated by three young nobles, one of whom was his disaffected nephew, Duke John of Swabia.

In the confused political maneuvering that followed the death of Albrecht, the Hapsburg candidate was rejected by the electors who saw him as too powerful. The king of France was determined to place his own candidate, a fellow Frenchman, on the throne. A compromise candidate was a minor count, Henry of Luxemburg, who was chosen by the relieved electors and crowned at Aachen in early 1308. Henry made no attempt to assert the rights of the crown, but instead pursued dynastic interests, establishing his family in Bohemia and Moravia in 1311.

Henry also turned to Italy, seeking to gain there the power base he had surrendered in Germany. The cities of northern Italy were still nominally part of the Empire, but were in actuality governed by the wealthy and powerful families of each city, who were continually faced with schemes, conspiracies, and insurrections. Henry arrived in Italy with a relatively small contingent of knights. His solemn proclamation of peace was almost completely ignored, and his small force was incapable of overcoming the determination of Florence and Bologna to impede his efforts to reach Rome. Although Genoa and Pisa supplied fleets to transport Henry's army, he found, on his arrival in Rome, that the troops of King Robert of Naples had taken over a large part of the city. Nevertheless, Henry was crowned by a papal legate at Saint John Lateran in Rome on June 23, 1312, the pope having transferred his residence to Avignon.

Rebellions in northern Italy forced Henry to leave Rome. His subsequent siege of Florence proved a failure, and his condemnation of his enemies at a Diet at Pisa was ignored. Henry then marched his now small force to southern Italy. At Benevento he fell victim to malaria and died on August 24, 1313.

Once more controversy erupted over succession to the kingship. The Habsburg candidate was Frederick of Austria, son of the late King Albrecht. The Luxemburg faction would have put forth John of Bohemia, but he was still a minor and therefore ineligible. The enemies of the house of Habsburg were the Wittelbachs, so the Luxemburgers threw their votes to that house and its candidate, Louis. An eight-year period of controversy over this election finally ended in 1322 at the battle of Mühldorf. The Habsburgers were defeated, and Frederick captured. Surprisingly, Louis freed Frederick and even made him his co-ruler with right of succession, Louis hoping thereby to secure the approbation of Pope John XXII.

In 1323, the Pope responded that he, not Louis, had the authority to decide who should be king of the Romans and emperor-elect. He gave Louis three months in which to lay down the power of governance, to appear before the papal court at Avignon, and to assume royal power only after and if he had secured papal confirmation. Louis protested with vehemence against the pope's assertion that the throne was still vacant. On March 23, 1324, the pope excommunicated Louis. Four years later, Louis led an army to Rome and there was crowned emperor, not by the pope but by Sciarra Colonna, a long standing foe of papal power.

Pope John's successor, Benedict XII (1334-1342), was favorably disposed toward Louis's cause, but he was pressured by King Philip of France to withhold a settlement unless additional German lands were ceded to the French. At the Diet of Rhens, held in July of 1338, the great lords of the Empire, excepting only King John of Bohemia, responded that "when anyone has been elected king of the Romans, he does not need the nomination, approbation, confirmation, assent, or authority of the pope to assume the administration of the Empire or the royal title." One month later, Louis added that "the imperial dignity and power have always proceeded from God alone, and the emperor is made emperor solely by the election of those who have the right to elect him. The election does not need the confirmation or approbation of any other person." The pope was not convinced.

As time wore on without a settlement, opposition to Louis grew, supported by the new pope, Clement VI (1342-1352). In 1346, Louis's opponents chose the Luxemburger candidate, Charles of Moravia, as king, but the greater part of Germany retained its allegiance to Louis. The issue was settled, however, when Louis died of a stroke in 1347.

With the succession of Charles IV (1347-1378), attempts by the emperor to strengthen the monarchy came to a virtual end. Dynastic and territorial interests had grown ever more important to the German rulers since the death of Frederick II in 1250. The king, shorn more and more of effective royal authority, pursued the same ends as the other princes of the Empire. He had become in effect one of them. All this was formalized in the reign of Charles IV by the so-called Golden Bull.

B. THE GOLDEN BULL

Selected king on July 11, 1346, Charles IV soon proved himself a master of dynastic aggrandizement. He widened his Luxemburg family lands in and around Bohemia and even went so far as to learn Czech, the language of the majority of Bohemians. Charles maintained excellent relations with Pope

Clement VI, even accepting clerics nominated by the pope to German bishoprics. He obtained the pope's approval to cross the Alps in 1354 for the purpose of securing his imperial coronation in Rome. Charles was interested only in the prestige the crown would win him in Germany, and he made promises to the pope and the other powers in Italy not to interfere in that peninsula. Charles's actions were instrumental in the subsequent separation of Germany and Italy.

Through Charles's four politically beneficial marriages, he gained additional support in the Rhineland and in the towns of the southwest, in the portion of Silesia that he still lacked, and, most significantly, Pomerania and Poland. He was equally successful in marrying off his children well.

By far Charles's most important act was his convocation of a Diet at Nuremburg that, in 1356, promulgated the so-called Golden Bull. This document, sealed and thus authenticated by a golden seal (a *bulla* in Latin), regulated the election of the emperor by continuing the traditional practice of the Germanic tribes of old.

Election had continued to provide emperors throughout the middle ages; the problem was who had the right to vote. The answer had been unclear. What was clear was that the imperial electors had the right to vote. But who those electors were was not certain. They were, of course, those with the right to vote. This confused and confusing tradition was clarified by the Golden Bull, which codified the fourteenth-century practice.

The Golden Bull fixed the number of electors at seven. Of those, four were lay princes: the king of Bohemia, the count palatine of the Rhine, the duke of Saxony, and the margrave of Brandenburg. Three electors were ecclesiastical princes: the archbishops of Trier, Mainz, and Cologne. Of the electors, four came from the western part of the empire, along the rivers Rhine and Mosel. Three electors possessed lands in the East, territories that had once been on the frontier.

At the death of a king, the electors were to gather at Frankfurt on the Main, and each elector was to "swear on the holy Gospels and by the faith I owe to God and the holy Roman Empire to cast my vote in this election of the king of the Romans and future emperor for the one person best suited to rule the Christian people." The man whom the majority selected was to be declared the choice of all. No mention was made of any papal role in the election. To prevent a multiplication of electoral votes, division of the electoral territories was forbidden.

The Golden Bull wrote into law what had been increasingly the reality since 1250. Every dynastic change had diminished the power of the monarchy. The rulers of the stronger territories were now independent, joined only by a weak confederation chaired, but not ruled, by the emperor.

Charles was a realist. He used the prestige of his imperial position to enlarge his territorial power and strengthen his dynasty. To his eldest son

Wenzel, he granted Luxemburg, Silesia, and the kingdom of Bohemia–the last bringing with it the status of elector. Another son, Sigismund, received the margravate of Brandenburg, and so also assumed the status and role of an elector. Still another son, John Henry, was given the newly created duchy of Görlitz. Moravia was divided between two nephews, Jobst and Procopius.

Charles's last years were given over in large part to securing Wenzel's succession as king of the Romans, and this he accomplished in 1376. Charles died in 1378 in Prague, the capital of his beloved kingdom of Bohemia and the site of his prized foundation, the first university in German lands.

C. CONTINUING DECENTRALIZATION

Not all the rulers whose reigns followed that of Charles IV were unsuccessful, but their fortunes depended on their family possessions, not their imperial office. The German kings continued to use their office chiefly as a source of prestige and as a means of aggrandizing their houses.

Charles's son Wenzel (or Wenceslaus) peacefully succeeded his father in 1378. Wenzel did not seek an imperial coronation in Rome; his only Italian venture was to sell the position of imperial vicar and the title "duke" to Milan's ruler Giangaleazzo Visconti.

Wenzel's reign began in the same year, 1378, that saw the election of two competing popes. One, Clement VII, was a Frenchman elected by French cardinals, who took up his residence in Avignon, across the Rhone River from France. The other newly-elected pope was Urban VI, an Italian who remained in Rome. Germany was divided in its allegiance, a reflection of the political fragmentation of that land. Wenzel favored the Roman pope, but his efforts to bring unity on the question by calling a Diet met with failure.

Virtually everything Wenzel touched ended in failure. Conflicts within cities and between cities and the nobles were left unresolved. Despite Wenzel's love for Bohemia and continued residence there after 1389, he angered his subjects by attempts to extract revenue from them through arbitrary fines, by quarreling with Archbishop John II of Prague, and by murdering the bishop's closest advisor–later venerated as Saint John Nepomuk. These and many other failures led the imperial electors to summon Wenzel before them in August 1400. When Wenzel ignored the summons, the electors declared him deposed. He died in Prague on August 16, 1419.

Meanwhile, in 1400, the electors had chosen as emperor Rupert, the Elector Palatine, whose capital was Heidelberg. From there Rupert set out for Rome, in 1402, to receive the imperial crown from the pope. A coalition, led by the duke of Milan, blocked Rupert's way; his allies deserted him; and Rupert was forced to abandon the venture. Rupert failed as well in his efforts to bring peace to Germany. His power base was simply too small to make effective his well-intentioned efforts to bring order to the empire. On September 14, 1405, a group of cities and territorial rulers formed the Marbech League under the leadership of the elector and archbishop of Mainz. As Rupert and the archbishop were preparing to do battle in 1410, Rupert died. By all accounts he was a learned and benevolent ruler of his small electoral territory, but he was considered incapable of ruling the Empire.

At Rupert's death, the electors chose as his successor Sigismund, the second son of the emperor Charles IV and younger brother to King Wenzel. Sigismund had great plans to restore the power and prosperity of the Empire and the unity of the Church. To accomplish the latter he called for a great Church Council to meet in the south German town of Constance. This grand assembly had a triple purpose: to end the Schism in the papacy, to reform the Church, and to combat heresy. Only the first of these aims was seriously pursued and successfully achieved. The contesting popes were deposed and a new pope, Martin V, elected.

In dealing with heresy, the Council's sole "success" was the execution of the Bohemian reformer, John Hus. Hus had denounced the vices of the clergy in his homeland–also the most important of Sigismund's lands. Hus had come to Constance protected–he thought–by a safe-conduct issued to him by Sigismund. This availed him not at all. The Council members found him guilty of heresy and had him burned at the stake. The execution preceded Sigismund's arrival at Constance, but news of Hus's death aroused the ire of the Bohemians, and ultimately cost Sigismund his kingdom.

Sigismund's reign was marked by an era of unfulfilled plans. His troubles in Bohemia led the electors to oppose his plans for royal reforms: they refused to assemble when he called them together, and they claimed the status of co-rulers with the king. Sigismund's plans and efforts to reform imperial politics left him so destitute financially that he was forced to grant the margravate of Brandenburg–and hence an electoral vote–to Frederick of Hohenzollern, the burgrave (city-count) of Nuremberg. Another electoral princedom, Saxony, was granted to the Wettin family.

In 1437, as Sigismund lay dying, his overriding concern was that his son-in-law, Albrecht of Habsburg, duke of Austria, should succeed him as king and emperor-elect. When the imperial electors met, they supported Sigismund's last wishes by choosing Albrecht.

Albrecht II was a Habsburg who had been chosen king of Hungary in 1437, and then, a year later, king of the Romans and emperor-elect. With his election Albrecht's duchy of Austria was joined to the German, Bohemian, and Hungarian crowns. Hungary was Albrecht's chief concern. That land was threatened by the Ottoman Turks, who were advancing through the Balkans after having recently conquered Serbia. In 1439, Albrecht flung back the Turkish attack in Hungary. But while waiting for reinforcements, he contracted dysentery and died at the age of forty-two on the way back to Vienna.

Albrecht's very short reign was followed by the very long reign of Frederick III (1440-1493). At his election this Habsburg prince was the undisputed ruler only in Styria. In the other Austrian lands he was viewed as a foreigner whose wardship of Albrecht's son Ladislaus was greeted with deep-seated distrust.

Frederick's virtually only ally was a Sienese scholar, Aeneas Silvius Piccolomini, later elected as Pope Pius II. Frederick hired Aeneas as his secretary. In 1446, Frederick recognized the superiority of the pope over fractious Church councils, and Aeneas worked with his ruler to persuade the German princes to follow his lead. In 1452, Frederick set out for Rome to reap his reward: imperial coronation.

No sooner was Frederick back home than he was besieged by an Austrian League, joined by a coalition of Hungarians and Bohemians and their southern German allies. The emperor bought off those enemies by surrendering his ward Ladislaus, the posthumous son of Albrecht II. Ladislaus was crowned king in both Hungary and Bohemia but died of the plague in 1457. The ties of both lands to Austria were broken by the election in both countries of heroes of Turkish campaigns.

Frederick's only response was to secrete himself almost entirely in his dynastic Austrian lands. During that period of twenty-seven years, the emperor ignored the chaos in Germany caused by wars between territorial princes, between town leagues and princes, and the continued fragmentation of political territories. In 1486, the ineffective Frederick was superseded as king though he retained the title. The Electors chose as ruler his son Maximilian and, on his father's death in 1493, elected him king.

Years before, in 1477, Frederick had scored a resounding success in an otherwise dismal reign by arranging the marriage of his son Maximilian to Mary, the daughter of Charles the Bold, the powerful duke of Burgundy. With Mary came lands stretching from the Netherlands in the North, through Luxemburg and Lotharingia, to both the duchy and county of Burgundy. When these were added to Maxmilian's recovered dynastic possessions in the upper Rhine, the eastern Alps, and along the Danube River, the house of Habsburg became incomparably stronger than any other German princely family.

Maximilian's ambitious plans for Germany met little success. In 1495, he issued a *Perpetual Peace of the Land*, proclaiming that

> no one, no matter of what rank or position, shall carry on a feud against another, or make war on him or rob, seize, attack, or besiege him, or aid anyone else to do so. And no one shall attack, seize, burn, or in any other way damage any castle, city, market town, fortress, village, farmhouse, or group of

homes, or in any way aid others to do such things. All such matters must hereafter come before the supreme court.

Maximilian did indeed establish a supreme court, but its existence was virtually ignored by the powerful, and that left those with little power unprotected. The attacks of the Turks that brought misery to both high and low in eastern Europe were also the object of Maximilian's deep concern, but he accomplished little beyond local successes within his Austrian possessions.

In 1494, King Charles VIII of France invaded Italy, nominally still part of the Empire. Maximilian joined forces with Pope Alexander VI and the cities of Milan and Venice in an effort to drive the French out of the Italian peninsula. The emperor played little part in the league's ensuing victory, chiefly because of lack of support from within the Empire. Charles's successor, Louis XII, was the next French king to invade Italy, and in 1499 he succeeded in conquering Milan. In a treaty of 1504, Maximilian ceded Milan and its sizable possessions to the French.

In 1508, Maximilian returned to Italy to be crowned by the pope. This venture was supported by an irritatingly modest monetary and military grant from the Imperial Diet. This time it was the Venetians who frustrated his plans. Their opposition led Maximilian to join France, Spain, and the pope in an effort to dismember the far-flung Venetian domains in the Mediterranean. In this effort, as well as in the subsequent "Holy League" sponsored by the war-like Pope Julius II, Maximilian provided much advice, but little material assistance. Maximilian's final effort to take Italy came in 1515. Francis I, the new French king, annexed Milan. To counter this, Maximilian went into debt and hired more troops than he could pay for. Deprived of wages, his small army mutinied, and Maximilian fled back to Germany, where he recognized the French claim to Milan. Maximilian's Italian expeditions succeeded only in bringing him a new wife; his first wife Mary having died in 1482. Maximilian's sole Italian conquest was Bianca Maria Sforza, the niece of Ludovico il Moro, formerly his regent in Italy.

D. TERRITORIALISM

By the end of the fourteenth century–perhaps earlier–the basic political unit in north central Europe was no longer the empire, no longer Germany, surely not the old Ottonian and Salian duchies, but the consolidated princely territory. The size of these princedoms was diverse, the smallest of them miniscule, typified by the castles above the Rhine gorge, often within sight of three or four neighboring castles. The westernmost territories were larger than these but still very small, thus affording the French king the opportunity for intervention and annexation.

The largest of the German territories lay in the East, most of them in what had been sparsely populated frontier lands. By the fourteenth and fifteenth centuries, they were by far the most powerful German territories. Brandenburg and Saxony, begun as frontier marches, were now governed by electors. Bohemia had not changed in size, but had grown in population. Its inhabitants had been almost exclusively Slavic, specifically Czech, in 1000, but were now mixed German and Czech. The higher nobility of Bohemia was also partly German and partly Slavic. Meetings of nobles served as a sort of supreme court that had the right to elect the Bohemian king.

All of the German territories, even the largest, were subject to division between brothers, sometimes cousins. As a result the Habsburg lands in southeastern Germany at one time comprised seven independent duchies. Bavaria was divided into two, sometimes four, duchies. Each of the seven electorates was theoretically indivisible, but in Saxony fraternal quarrels resulted in splitting that land into one duchy and one electorate. The increasing number of territorial rulers in the later middle ages brought with it severe economic consequences. The multiplication of princely castles, courts, and households placed an increasingly heavy burden on Germany's economic resources.

Farther east, in the lands south of the Baltic, there had been colonies of German merchants scattered throughout Prussia and what became Lithuania, Latvia, and Estonia. Unity was brought to the Baltic lands by the Order of the Hospital of Our Lady of the German House in Jerusalem. As that name indicates, this "Teutonic" Order originated in the East. The knights of the Order took vows of chastity and obedience and had been devoted to protecting pilgrims in the Holy Land. In the thirteenth century, at the urgent request of both pope and emperor, the knights shifted their focus to the Baltic where most of the natives were still pagan. Commanderies were set up to protect and organize the Baltic peoples; bishoprics were established to convert the natives and serve their spiritual needs. By the fourteenth century, there were many houses of the Order in Germany and its headquarters had been moved from Acre in the Holy Land to Venice, and then to Marienburg in Prussia. The Grand Master of the Order, elected by the knights, had become a prince of the Empire.

In 1410, however, the Order was defeated by the recently united Poles and Lithuanians at the battle of Tannenberg. By the end of the fifteenth century, Prussia had been reduced to the status of dependency on the Polish crown. This story of the rise and fall of the Teutonic Knights is hardly typical of late medieval German territorialism.

Atypical too is the story of the beginnings of Switzerland. In August of 1290, three forest districts or cantons, neighboring one another in the shadow of the Alps, entered into a treaty of mutual defense. They agreed that it is a good thing if communities agree to preserve order and peace. Therefore, let all know that the men of the Uri valley, the community of the valley of Schwyz, and the commune of those living in Unterwalden promise to assist each other with aid, counsel, and support against all who may try to molest, harm, or injure any of us.

This was not a declaration of independence from their king, Rudolf of Habsburg, for "each man shall be bound to obey his lord and to serve him well." Rudolf was far too intent on defending his new crown and acquiring the Austrian territories to interfere in what was to become Switzerland. Over the next century the Forest Cantons were joined by alliance with the cities of Zürich and Bern, and with the cantons of Glarus and Zug. When the Habsburgers later objected to Luzern's adherence to the confederation, the Swiss roundly defeated them in 1386 at the battle of Sempach. During the fifteenth century several more towns and cantons joined the original alliance.

Switzerland was not a country but a confederation. Indeed, in the Empire there were few political entities that could be counted as countries in the same sense that England and France were. The Habsburg lands were many, and the family was powerful, but none of the components of the family's possessions could even begin to match the size and power of the countries to their West.

Chapter Sixteen

The Late Medieval Laity

Medieval society was divided into laity and clergy, the latter to be considered in a later chapter. Layfolk belonged to one of three classes: the upper that included the military and governing classes, the middle class of townsfolk, and the farmers–the last by far the most numerous.

A. THE GOVERNING AND MILITARY CLASSES

The upper class consisted of the nobility, who possessed various titles that had originally indicated specific functions. In the tenth century, a duke was the leader (*dux* in Latin) of a tribe, a large group of kindred people: Bavarians, Saxons, Franks, or Swabians, for example. The count (Latin *comes*, German *Graf*) had been designated in the eighth century by Charles the Great to serve as a local administrator within the empire. By the later middle ages, the titles duke, count, and such derivative titles as *Markgraf* (march count or margrave) and *Pfalzgraf* (castle count)–no longer indicated superiority or inferiority. Power had become the key to noble status, although princely rank was, generally speaking, reserved to those rulers who swore fidelity directly to the emperor. That oath and relationship, however, meant little in the late medieval struggle for power. The minimum requirement for independence from other nobles in that struggle was the possession of a castle, a combination of fortress and residence. In 1300, there were perhaps as many as 10,000 castles in Germany.

The lesser nobility were simple knights–most of whom were attached to the households of the high nobility. These knights also served their lords as well-armed and armored cavalrymen. The armor worn by knights had originally been chain mail, a flexible suit of interlocking metal rings. After the late twelfth century, chain mail was increasingly replaced with armor made of intricately coordinated and overlaying steel plates. Plate armor offered better protection to the knight, but also was heavier and much more expensive. To support each well-equipped knight required more than fifteen men, from squires to men-at-arms, from archers to variously armed footmen, from cooks to carriers of supplies.

Knights continued to be important in the warfare of the late middle ages, but several factors made cavalry less and less crucial to victory. The use of gunpowder, first in siege operations, then in field artillery, and finally in hand held weapons of all sorts, reduced the effectiveness of the knight. Cavalry was increasingly replaced by highly trained and coordinated infantry. Even so, the commanders and lesser leaders of the evolving armies of the period were still men of the nobility or knightly classes.

The late medieval upper classes faced constantly increasing demands on their economic resources. Highly organized armies and expensive siege and field weapons were financial drains on increasing numbers of territorial governments. These expenses were compounded by the adoption by almost all of the nobility of ever more expensive life styles. The longing to imitate the armor, clothing, furniture, jewelry, and other items of those in still wealthier circumstances was well-nigh universal.

B. MERCHANTS, MANUFACTURERS, AND TRADESMEN

The members of the middle class were primarily manufacturers and distributers of those goods necessary for the maintenance and the enrichment of medieval life. The agricultural revolution of the Early Middle Ages and the warm weather prevailing down to the fourteenth century had provided a food surplus that made it possible to feed ever larger numbers of these manufacturers and merchants.

Within most towns, tradesmen grouped themselves into guilds. The guild was an economic and social organization that included all those working in a particular trade or industry: the goldsmiths, the bakers, the fine cloth makers, the shoe makers, for example. The guild protected its members and their customers by guaranteeing fair prices and high standards of workmanship. Members could compete with one another only by increasing the quality of their product.

Training in the guild's craft was given through an apprenticeship system. For two to five years a boy served a master craftsman without pay. In return the master took the boy into his home and cared for his professional, social, and religious education. After completing his apprenticeship, the young man became a journeyman, now paid by the day. He often wandered from place to place working and learning the techniques of masters in other cities and countries. There was no social gap between the master and the journeyman, between employer and employee. Wages were set by the guild at a level that permitted a reasonable standard of living, hours of work were limited, and there was no work on Saturday afternoons, Sundays, and the many holidays that the town celebrated. To qualify as a master, the journeyman presented the masters of his guild with a custom-made piece of work that demonstrated his skill. If the work met the standards of the guild, it was acknowledged a "masterpiece," and the young man attained full membership in the guild as a master.

The guild was not merely an association of merchants or craftsmen. Its members provided for the religious and social needs of one another. If a member were sick, other guild members sat with him, and the guild paid his doctor bills. If he were disabled, a guild fund supported him. If he died, the guild members supported his widow and children. The guild hall often included a chapel with its own chaplain. Frequently, the guild contributed a window to the town's cathedral or principal church and sponsored scenes in the religious plays that the town presented on great feast days. The guild also sponsored dances and banquets to enliven the lives of its members. In the thirteenth century each guild was represented in the town council that legislated for all its citizens. Later on many town councilors represented only the most economically important guilds.

Not all towns were the same. Some were hardly larger than villages that made available the goods that manors and individual farmers of the area could not provide themselves, like salt and metals, for example. Some towns were part of a wider economic nexus. Towns threatened by acquisitive territorial rulers also formed associations.

At the end of the thirteenth century, many towns that had formed various economic and political associations entered into one vast league, the German *Hanse*. The Hanseatic League embraced eighty cities, from Ravel in present-day Estonia to Amsterdam in the Netherlands, from Cologne in the West to Breslau and Cracow in the East. There were permanent trading posts in Bergen, Norway; in Novgorod, Russia; in Bruges in present day Belgium; and in London. The Swedish towns of Wisby and Stockholm were founded by Hanseatic traders. Furs and cloth, herring and beer, wheat and wax, lumber and honey were conveyed from town to town all along the Baltic and North Seas and up the broad rivers that emptied into them, in large hulled ships called *kogge*.

The power of the Hansa was demonstrated when, in 1367, a Hanseatic Diet or parliament held at Cologne declared war on the kingdoms of Denmark and Norway, which had cut off trade with the Hansa. The League won that war and reopened trade with those Nordic lands, establishing garrisons in the fortresses they erected on the territory of their erstwhile adversaries. The power of the League waned, however, at the close of the fifteenth century. The growing strength of the Scandinavian kingdoms and the emergence of Russia as a Baltic power threatened Hanseatic trade routes. The shift of international commerce to the south, to and from the New World and India, hastened the Hansa's decline.

C. THE FARMERS' LIFE

No single description is adequate in speaking of late medieval farmers. There were farm families who lived in one-room cabins; there were farm families who lived in four story half-timbered houses. The chief problem challenging farmers in long-populated areas, most notably in the western and southern parts of Germany, was the ever-increasing number of sons who laid claim to the farm lands of their fathers. The farm fields of medieval villages were divided into long strips to minimize the number of turns needed by farmers who worked with their large, heavy plows and teams of horses. When these strips were divided equally among sons again and again over the years, the land belonging to each farmer could easily have pushed the profits of succeeding generations of farmers below the subsistence level.

This did not happen. The response to this potential problem was to send farmers' sons off to work frontier land. An internal frontier also beckoned many of those seeking to avoid overpopulation. Forests abounded in Germany. "Freedom of the forest" was a German principle with a long history. Clearing forest for farm land or harvesting trees for the lumber-trade supported many families.

Migration to towns was another popular means of attaining prosperity. Young men who sought work in the flourishing towns of the time were often accepted as apprentice blacksmiths, bakers, butchers, and tradesmen. Young men who sought to serve their neighbors as priests could enter the ecclesiastical equivalent of apprenticeship. The apprentice would live with the priest in his house and learn Latin and the rituals of the Church from him. Priests at this time were often married, openly or surreptitiously; they usually tilled a garden to help feed their families. In short, their life style was much like that of the people they served.

The major destination of medieval German migrants was the lands to the East, which now included territory extending along the Baltic Sea to Russia. In these under-populated lands there were lords happy to offer much better financial arrangements than those available in the West. Often the villagers in the East were obliged only to pay an annual rent and were otherwise virtually self-governing.

Still another source of employment–and adventure–for the farm boy was enlistment in the infantry of some armed force–large or small. Even a single knight required some fifteen armed retainers, as we have seen. The armies of territorial princes required hundreds, sometimes thousands, of infantrymen.

Archers, crossbowmen, and pikemen were joined by those wielding halberds, long-shafted weapons ending in a spear point, with an axe-like cutting blade and a hook used to unseat cavalrymen. Increasingly, infantrymen carried unwieldy but effective guns. As time went on, cannon that initially were fixed in place and therefore used only against castle or town walls in siege operations, became light enough to be transported on sledges or, eventually, wheels. All these weapons required experienced and well-paid men to operate them.

D. PANDEMIC AND PERSECUTION

In the fourteenth century, Europe suffered from a plague that probably originated in central Asia. Europeans first observed it exercising its deadly effects somewhere on the shore of the Caspian Sea. The pandemic spread westward, reaching Italy in 1347. By 1348 it spread to France, Spain, the British Isles, and Scandinavia. The disease also reached Germany and Eastern Europe. Throughout Europe as a whole, it is possible that, between 1347 and 1350, one out of every four or five persons lost their lives. The mortality rate was still higher in densely settled areas like western Germany. Whole towns were wiped out or abandoned because of the plague. Settlement in eastern Germany and in central Europe was less dense, and the mortality rate was less devastating, though often still serious. Bohemia and eastern Franconia seem to have enjoyed almost complete immunity.

We now know that the plague had its source from bacteria infesting the gut of fleas whose bites then infected humans. The invading organisms found their way into the lymph nodes of their human hosts which swelled, creating *bubos*–and gave the mortal illness the name Bubonic Plague.

We know the cause, but the people of fourteenth-century Europe did not, and the horror of the pandemic caused them to search for solutions, some of which seem absurd today. For example the School of Medicine at the University of Paris attributed the disease to the planetary alignment of Jupiter, Saturn, and Mars.

The most popular explanation for the outbreak of the plague was that wells had been somehow poisoned. Along the Rhine River in hard-hit cities and towns, it was sometimes believed, especially by the lower classes, that Jews had poisoned the community's drinking water. This despite the sensible declaration of Pope Clement VI that Jews would hardly poison the water that they themselves drank. In Strassburg, for example, a contemporary chronicler recorded that sixteen thousand people died. A mob of tradesmen called on the town council to deal with Jews who, they claimed, were the cause of the deaths. The town councilmen refused to punish their Jewish citizens, so the mob deposed them and elected a council that proceeded to burn some one thousand Jews–another thousand saving themselves by accepting baptism.

It was clearly a different world than the one in which Bernard of Clairvaux had forbidden the townsmen of twelfth-century Cologne to persecute, slay, or exile their Jewish neighbors. Bernard also forbade attempts to convert Jews. Germany was indeed a different land in the fourteenth-century than it had been in the twelfth.

Chapter Seventeen

Thirteenth-Century Friars and Holy Women

By the early thirteenth century, Cistercians and Praemonstratensians had become successful, at least in terms of numbers of houses and in the economic security of individual houses. However, Cistercian monks no longer worked in the fields; Cistercian lands were now farmed by sharecroppers. Twelfth-century monastic authors sought their inspiration from prayerful meditation on Scripture and the spiritual works of Christian antiquity. Increasingly, monks and canons spent their time in scholarly pursuits, a life prepared by study at universities. Neither the Cistercian nor the Praemonstratensian orders were corrupt, but with institutional middle age came a measure of relaxation in the wholehearted commitment that many young women and men sought.

As a result, the thirteenth century saw a new movement of reform, a movement based on a new idea of how the Christian life could be led. This movement produced a new form of religious life, the friar (from *frater*, the Latin word for "brother"). Many different orders of friars (Franciscans, Dominicans, Carmelites, Augustinians, and others) followed the varying inspiration of their founders, but all were committed to a life of apostolic service in the world. They even took the message of Christianity outside Europe, to North Africa and the Middle East, and traveled across Asia to bring that message to China. Friars felt a special call to minister to the needs of the growing and increasingly prosperous middle class in medieval cities. They hoped by the example of the simplicity in which they lived to lead people away from undue preoccupation with material things.

A. BLACKFRIARS

Despite the fact that the founder of the Dominican order was a Spaniard, the thirteenth century saw significant leadership roles assumed by German friars. In the thirteenth, fourteenth, and fifteenth centuries many Dominicans were major contributors to the spirituality of the times.

Dominic Guzmán was born about 1170 in a rugged, mountainous region of Spain only newly won back from the Moors. He was recruited by the prior of the cathedral chapter of Osma, and later, as subprior, he accompanied his bishop on an embassy to Denmark. The story goes that, during an overnight stay at the southern French city of Toulouse, he persuaded the landlord to give up his Albigensian faith and become a Christian. Albigensianism was a religion brought from the East. It taught that there were two gods, an evil one who had created matter, that was all and always evil, and another god who had created spirit that was good. The ultimate act of perfection for an Albigensian was, therefore, suicide. Despite these teachings, Dominic resolved to spend his life in the service of these people. However, he disapproved of the techniques of the Cistercian missionaries sent by the pope, rejecting parades of richly garbed prelates in favor of simple dress, and traveling on foot instead of on horseback.

Dominic was soon joined by scores of young men whose outer garb was a black cloak and were thus called "Blackfriars." The Order of Preachers, is what they called themselves. Dominicans sought to serve their neighbors through their preaching–preaching by word and example. Whatever ideas or institutions they saw might serve them in their task, they eagerly embraced. The Order did accept donations of churches and houses, though the individual friars remained without personal possessions. Their houses were not only residences but schools for continuing education in theology. In each house the friars elected a prior, and in each house resided a lecturer in theology and a director of studies. As preachers and missionaries the Dominicans had to be well educated, and so very early they began to establish regional schools, as well as sending their young men to the newly emerging universities.

1. Jordanus of Saxony

Dominic's choice of a successor as Master (in the sense of teacher) General was a German, Jordanus of Saxony. He had been a professor at the University of Paris and had been in the Order for only two years when elected Master in 1222.

The May 1233 letter of Jordanus of Saxony to all the men of the Order captures admirably the spirit which enlivened Dominican life. This letter vibrates with the energy and enthusiasm permeating the Order. Jordanus began, as was often the case in medieval exhortations, with descriptions of negative models:

> There are those living among us, those who hide under a bushel basket whatever grace of preaching or counsel they receive from the Lord. They are not, therefore, following their father Dominic's rule of love. There is another kind of carelessness widespread in our days: many superiors are not concerned about study and frequently divert from that study their spiritual sons who have talent and intellectual ability. In some places theology teachers are half-hearted about their calling. They give lectures so reluctantly and infrequently that it is no wonder students become even more unenthusiastic than their unenthusiastic teachers.

Even when the teachers are doing their work properly, Jordanus wrote, there is another problem. The brothers are all too often "uninterested in their study and stupid in debates." Some of them "do not want to be distracted from their unintelligent religious devotions." Thus, said Jordanus, "they deprive many people of the opportunity for salvation, when they could have helped them on their way to eternal life if only they had studied properly."

The time set aside for communal and private prayer in Dominican life was much shorter than that in monasteries. Dominicans who "seek perfection," Jordanus concluded, "work hard at their preaching and are zealous in study. Their hearts catch fire in their prayer and meditations, and keep the Lord always before them, looking to him as the one who will judge and reward them." Preaching, teaching, prayer, and lifelong study were the hallmarks of Dominican life. It is little wonder that the Order attracted many university students and some of the most renowned scholars of their age.

2. Albert the Great

One of these great scholars was Albert, called by posterity "the Great." He was born in Lauingen, a small town on the Danube River near Ulm. He came from knightly stock, but opted for a life of scholarship. As a young man he visited Italy and studied at Padua where he gained an introduction to Aristotle's philosophy. It was at Padua that he was received into the Order of Preachers, a relatively mature recruit then in his thirties. Jordanus of Saxony sent him to the Dominican house of study at Cologne in 1229 or early 1230. Shortly thereafter he was appointed reader (lecturer) in theology at the Dominican house at Hildesheim. From there he was sent to Freiburg, Regensberg, and Strassburg. Paris was his next post, where he lectured on theology. Meanwhile he was studying for and earning (in 1233) his degree of Master (we would say Doctor) of Theology.

Albert reveled in the intellectual world of Paris. In Albert's work *On Creatures*, written at this time, he demonstrated his mastery of most of Aristotle's works, as well as a wide range of Arabic commentaries on that ancient Greek philosopher's thought. Albert taught at Paris until 1248, when he was sent back to Cologne to preside over the Dominican *studium generale*, an institution of higher education. Accompanying Albert on his return to Germany was his student Thomas Aquinas, who was later to return to Paris to teach and write in theology.

In 1254, Albert was elected provincial, leader of the Dominicans in Germany. This kept him on the road (literally: he always walked) until his assignment to the papal court in 1257. In 1260, the canons of the bishopric of Regensburg were unable to settle on a new bishop, so the pope appointed Albert, who reluctantly assumed the post. During his busy tenure as bishop, Albert wrote a commentary on the book on geometry of the ancient Greek mathematician, Euclid, and a massive work *On Animals*. Albert then persuaded a new pope to accept his resignation as bishop.

Though now in his seventies, Albert found no rest. Among other tasks, he was sent to the Second Council of Lyons in 1274, where he spoke on behalf of Rudolf of Habsburg's candidacy for the imperial throne. Albert also conducted a spirited defense of Thomas Aquinas, whose works had been attacked by other Parisian professors in 1277. In the same year Albert finally retired from teaching and, on the fifteenth of November in 1280, he died in the Dominican house at Cologne.

The range of Albert's intellectual interests was astonishingly wide. He wrote treatises on animals, plants, and minerals. To gather material for the last, he visited working mines on paths that did not take him too far from his next preaching assignment. When questioned why a theologian should concern himself with scientific questions, he replied: "The whole world is theology for us." As to zoology, he remarked: "God, as the cause of all causes, creates the animals and gives them shape. So when that cause is known, it will be the cause of great delight. That is why we ought to look at the forms of animals and rejoice in him who is their maker, because the artistry of the maker is revealed in the way that he works."

Albert took great delight in "field" sciences, to be sure, but he was equally at home in the laboratory, as we see in reading his small treatise on the *Transmigration of Metals*, what we might call alchemy. In this work Albert tells his readers that he has "laboriously traveled to many regions and numerous provinces as well as to cities and castles, in the interest of this science. I have consulted the books learned men have used concerning this science, but I found them worthless." Albert did not despair, however: "I persevered in studying, reflecting, and laboring over works on this subject until I finally found what I was seeking, not by own knowledge, but by the grace given by the Holy Spirit."

Some of Albert's scientific conclusions are no longer of interest, but his discussion of the virtues and vices of scientists is still relevant. "I have observed some scientists," Alfred began, "who have made a good beginning, but who, because of excessive drinking or other stupid practices, were unable to carry on their work." He had observed others "who have made a good beginning but, because their task was long and tedious, have left it uncompleted." Alfred pointed out that some scientists pursuing their goal have failed due to defective equipment; some incapable of patience in pursuing that goal have lost faith in their efforts. Although a deeply religious man, Albert was quite aware of the practical necessities in this as in any enterprise. He wrote: "I have seen many who were carrying forward their work with diligence and yet in the end have failed because they did not have the necessary means of support. One must have enough money to cover expenses for at least two years." There is no record of Albert's success or failure in transmuting metals, but his method of pursuing scientific inquiry was surely down to earth.

In Albert's work *On Plants*, he described his scientific approach to German flora. "What I have to say," he wrote, "is partly proven by experience and partly taken from the reports of those, who, I have discovered, do not make statements not proven by experience."

Albert wrote some thirty-six commentaries on the works of Aristotle. He did not always agree with the Greek philosopher: "If you acknowledge that Aristotle was a man, then no doubt he could make mistakes like the rest of us." Nevertheless, Albert wrote: "You cannot be a complete philosopher without knowing the thought of both Aristotle and Plato."

However, Albert's professional role was as a theologian. He summarized his teachings in his commentary, written over the period of 1246 to 1249, on the basic text on that subject, *The Sentences* of Peter Lombard. At the end of his life Albert continued to work on his theological writings. That time saw him devoting himself especially to commentaries on the books of the Bible. One of Albert's students tells of his last days:

> He prayed fervently, and freely proclaimed the word of God to the people. He gave good advice and useful counsel both pleasantly and with affection to people who asked for it. He studied, dictated, wrote, prayed, and sang the psalms. He was honored and venerated by everyone, old and young, small and great.

B. HOLY WOMEN

In addition to his many other duties, Albert was the spiritual advisor to many Cistercian nuns in Germany. One of his students at Cologne, Thomas of Cantimpré was also a spiritual advisor to the nuns at the Cistercian monastery at Aywières in present-day Belgium. It was in the capacity of spiritual advisor to that community that he met a nun named Liutgard whose biography he wrote after her death.

1. Liutgard of Aywières

At the age of twelve, Liutgard entered the Monastery of Saint Catherine at Trond, also in present-day Belgium. She did not become a novice, but lived rather informally and received friends–including a young man who was her admirer. It was on the occasion of one of this young man's visits that the first of Liutgard's many visions occurred. Jesus suddenly appeared to her and revealed the wound in his side, saying: "Seek no more the pleasure of this unbecoming affection. Behold, here, forever, what you should love. Here in this wound I promise you the purest of delights." Understandably, this vision had a noticeable effect on Liutgard's life. She not only cut off ties with her gentlemen admirers, but she also imposed on herself a regimen which cut her off from the ways of her sisters, and from their comfort and sympathy as well. She wanted to be left alone for God, and her sisters did indeed leave her alone.

Liutgard's asceticism became severe. She undertook many penances, fasting beyond the measure of the rest, and spending much of the night in prayer. After nine years of this, Liutgard had apparently excited the admiration of her sisters, for they elected her prioress. Liutgard was not flattered or pleased; she took the election as a disaster. So Liutgard left Saint Trond for the Cistercian community at Aywières. Since the nuns there spoke French, which was a foreign tongue to her, she thought herself safe from any more disastrous elections.

Liutgard's penances continued apace, however. She undertook a seven-year fast–on bread and beer–followed by another, and then still another–the last interrupted by her death in 1246. Indeed, it was during one of her fasts that a rationale for Liutgard's penances emerged, a rationale that was new to medieval spirituality. For Liutgard undertook her fasts in order to suffer, suffering in reparation for the sins of the world. Liutgard saw a vision–indeed a series of visions–in which she found justification for her practice. These visions occurred almost daily and usually took place at Mass. She would see Jesus standing before the face of the Father, showing him his wounds, which had the appearance of having been freshly opened and were full of blood. Turning to Liutgard, Jesus would say: "Do you not see how I offer myself entirely to my Father for my sinners? In the same way, I would have you offer yourself entirely to me for my sinners and avert the anger which has been kindled against them in retribution for sin."

To deny oneself food–or anything else for that matter–for the sake of suffering was foreign to the medieval monastic tradition. In that tradition the quest for wholeness and holiness may have involved self-discipline, but that action was a means to an end, not an end in itself. Still less was the notion of suffering to atone for another's sins part of the monastic heritage. But Liutgard had had her vision, and that was enough for her.

Liutgard was forever having visions, and in these visions she talked to Jesus in ways which might seem presumptuous. She freely expressed her likes and dislikes to her Lord. Having been granted a "power of healing" in which her very touch had the effect of instantly curing the little sicknesses of those who came to her, Liutgard found herself beginning to be overly busy with those who appealed to her to cure them. She complained to Jesus of this, assuring him that it interfered with her prayer: "Why did you go and give me such a grace, Lord? Now I hardly have time to be alone with you! Take it away, please!" And then she added: "Only give me another grace; give me something better!"

Jesus asked in reply: "What grace do you want me to give you then in its place?" Liutgard thought it would be a good thing if she were granted a miraculous understanding of Latin, so that she could comprehend what she was reciting in choir–not a word of which had any meaning for her. Jesus, Thomas tells us, gave her what she asked for, but she did not like that either. Understanding seemed to interfere with her devotion rather than nourishing it.

So Jesus asked her: "What then, do you want?" "Lord," she told him, "I want your heart." "What do you mean: 'You want my heart,'" said Jesus. "I want your heart," Liutgard replied, "let me take it, dear Lord. But take it in such a way that your heart's love may be so mingled and united with my own heart that I may possess my heart in you, and may it ever remain there secure in your protection."

Liutgard's friend and advisor, Thomas of Cantimpré, had to confess that he did not understand much about her visions, and he thought that other people would not either. But the sort of mysticism she represented–one never ending series of visions and conversations with Jesus and Mary, saints from heaven and sinners from purgatory, angels and devils–became an increasingly popular way of expressing closeness to God, a way that continued to be a strong, but not exclusive, element in modern Catholicism.

2. Hedwig of Brabant

Liutgard left us no written work. We know of her only through Thomas of Cantimpré's biography. Hedwig of Brabant, on the other hand, was a prolific author of poems, letters, and a series of "visions" narrating her encounters with God. We know almost nothing of her life, not even the dates of her birth, life, and death. She very probably lived in the mid-thirteenth century, but even that is merely a learned guess. Unlike Liutgard, Hedwig was not a nun. She was rather a Beguine, having embraced a new form of religious life.

Beguines lived in simplicity, engaged in meditation, and prayed the hours–the recitation of psalms, hymns, and readings from the spiritual authors of Christian antiquity and the middle ages. Unlike nuns, they did not take vows or live in monasteries. They chose to engage in manual labor, study, teaching, or caring for the sick. At first, individual Beguines lived in their own or their parents' homes, but gradually they formed groups, living together and supporting each other. They also chose one of their members to be a "mistress," who provided leadership and governance. The Beguine movement grew rapidly, soon numbering hundreds of women. In 1216, Pope Honorius III authorized the Beguines to live a life in common, exhorting them to support each others' effort to live a holy life.

Hedwig, like Liutgard, was a visionary, sometimes called a mystic. Hedwig's mysticism, however, went far beyond Liutgard's homey conversations with Jesus. Hedwig's works show her as a woman of considerable sophistication, as well as profound spirituality. She surely knew French and Latin, but wrote in her native German dialect, a language now called Flemish.

The central motif in Hedwig's writing is love, often personified as a woman, since love (*minne*) is feminine in her native tongue: "Love's deepest abyss is her most beautiful form." Hedwig counseled her reader: "See to it that you make haste to virtue and serve those who love, that they may help you know the ways that belong to sublime Love."

The path to God, Hedwig insisted, is the path that Jesus trod: "We all wish to be with God. God knows, however, there are few enough of us who desire to live as men and women following Jesus' humanity." Following him includes carrying his cross. Hedwig recognized that the path to union with God is often a painful one, so one should "embrace with a burning heart" the suffering that is sometimes the human lot. Perseverance in the often burdensome yet noble service of God and one's fellow human beings can lead Love "to burst her dikes and so touch us with herself that we are one spirit and one being with herself and in her." The God who is Love, Hedwig knows from her own experience of him, will unite herself to him in this life and in the next.

3. Beatrice of Nazareth

Beatrice of Nazareth's ascent to God is recorded in her autobiographical *Seven Degrees of Love*. Like Hedwig, Beatrice wrote in Flemish, her native tongue. Born in 1200, she came from a devout family. Her mother, Gertrud, was renowned for her holiness, but died when Beatrice was only seven years old. Her father, Bartholomew, entrusted Beatrice and two sisters to schools run by Beguines. She completed her classical education at the monastery of Bloemendael, and there she and her two sisters were clothed in Cistercian habits. Around 1250, she transferred to Our Lady of Nazareth, a Cistercian house near Antwerp, where she lived as prioress until her death in 1268.

Beatrice's first degree of love consists of longing to regain the purity, freedom, and nobility in which the human race was created:

> The soul seeks God in his majesty. She so burns with desire for him that she cannot pay heed to any saints or sinners, any angels or creatures, except with that all-comprehending love of him by whom she loves all things. She desires to see God, to possess and to enjoy him with all the longing of her heart, and with all the strength of her soul.

In the second degree of love the soul strives for a totally disinterested state of loving service to her Lord. The third level is the experience of the "torture" of the soul that cannot satisfy her desire for loving service because of the limits of the human condition. The fourth degree Beatrice describes as an "abyss" of love into which the soul is immersed and absorbed. The final three degrees of love build on the idea of the abyss. The fifth describes the excitement, indeed frenzy, of the soul "in his sweet embrace of love." In the sixth degree of love Beatrice sees the soul as "the bride of the Lord." Here she experiences the power, purity, sweetness, and freedom of that marital state. The seventh and final state of love is a summary describing the state of the soul drawn into the experience of God:

> She is drawn into the eternity of love and the incomprehensibility, vastness, inaccessible sublimity, and the deep abyss of the Godhead that is all in all things and remains incomprehensible in all things and that is immutable, all-existent, all-capable, all comprehending, and all-working.

In this final state the soul will be united with her Bridegroom and will become one spirit with him in inseparable faithfulness and eternal love.

4. Mechthild of Magdeburg

All of the women discussed so far in this chapter came from the westernmost parts of the Empire. That the spirituality of thirteenth-century women was much more widespread is demonstrated by the life and thought of the next three women, all nuns of the Cistercian monastery of Helfta, located in the eastern part of Germany, in a land that was once on the frontier.

Mechthild of Magdeburg was born somewhere within the diocese of Magdeburg, sometime between 1207 and 1212. In 1230, she left her home for the city of Magdeburg where she joined a community of Beguines. Of this period we know virtually nothing except that, during the next forty years or so, she wrote, in her north German dialect, the first six books of her spiritual masterpiece, *The Flowing Light of the Godhead*. About 1270, she entered the Cistercian monastery of Helfta, for reasons unknown. Helfta was a flourishing center of learning, and it was at Helfta that she finished Book Seven of her remarkable work. It was there too that, in 1282, she died.

Mechthild's work was a splendid exposition of a form of spirituality called *Brautmystic* (bridal mysticism), the loving union of Christ as Bridegroom with the soul as bride. In Mechthild's version of the dialogue between the two, she has Christ declaring: "It is my nature that makes me love you often, for I am love itself. It is my longing that makes me love you intensely, for I yearn to love you intensely, as I yearn to be loved from the heart. It is my eternity that makes me love you long, for I have no end."

The precondition for the lovers' consummation of their love is "setting aside all fear, all shame, all outward things." The Lord then embraces the soul, saying: "You are by your very nature already mine. Nothing can come between us. Your endless desire I shall evermore fulfill." The soul responds: "Lord, now I am a naked soul, and you a God most glorious! Our twofold intercourse is love eternal which can never die." Surely there are traditional components drawn here from both Bernard of Clairvaux's *Sermons on the Song of Songs* and the German love poets, the *Minnesänger*.

5. Mechthild of Hackeborn

Mechthild of Hackeborn was a nun of Helfta whose abbess was her older sister Gertrud. The nuns of Helfta enjoyed the fruits of Abbess Gertrud's embrace of classical learning. She had amassed a large and well-read collection of patristic authors and the writings of the twelfth-century Cistercian fathers. These were made accessible to the nuns to support their understanding of the Old and New Testaments. Helfta also provided a good classical education which aided the younger nuns in their growing mastery of classical literature, the Bible, and the texts of the liturgy which occupied much of their time.

All of this fostered the spiritual growth and maturity of Gertrud's younger sister, who was charged with directing the choir. The beauty of her own voice led to her pseudonym "God's nightingale." Like Gertrud and Mechthild of Magdeburg, Mechthild of Hackeborn was a spiritual counselor to novices, nuns, and to many from outside the monastery.

It was only in 1291, some seven or eight years before her death, that Mechthild of Hackeborn confided to two nuns the content of her spiritual revelations. The nuns wrote Mechthild's words down in Latin in a seven part *Liber spiritualis gratiae, A Book of Spiritual Grace*. She tells of a month-long suffering from pain. During this time the Lord revealed to her

> his marvelous secrets. She rejoiced so much in the delights of his presence that she could not now hide it, although she had kept his visits hidden for many

years. She displayed her joy even to guests and strangers. Because of this, many people committed to her petitions that they hoped she would bring before God. In return she revealed to them, as God had revealed to her, the desires of their hearts. Then they too gave thanks to God.

Like many thirteenth-century spiritually gifted women, Mechthild was a visionary who left vivid descriptions of her experiences:

> The King of Glory once appeared with indescribable splendor in the fullness of his joy. He was wearing a golden robe embroidered with doves. This garment was open on its two sides to indicate that the soul has free access to God. The King was also covered by a red cloak that symbolized his Passion. The doves represented the simplicity of his divine heart, whose dispositions are unchangeable even though his people so often fail in fidelity to him.

Mechthild's reference to Jesus' heart signifies simply her lover's will, not his physical heart as had been the case with Liutgard.

6. Gertrud the Great

Gertrud, sometimes called "the Great," was the third of the Helfta nuns whose writing powerfully influenced her contemporaries and subsequent spirituality. About 1261, Gertrud's parents left her at Helfta when she was only four years old–whether out of poverty or for some other reason, we do not know. Gertrud was given the outstanding education given all the nuns at Helfta so that her Latin was fluent. She probably served her sisters as a scribe, copying the works of classical antiquity and of patristic and medieval authors. Gertrud was much sought after as a counselor by her sisters, as well as by lay folk who were welcomed to the monastery.

Gertrud's literary legacy is contained in *The Herald of God's Lovingkindness*, preserved in four books. Only the second of these books is from Gertrud's own hand, but the others lay credible claim to reflecting her teachings. Works known as *Spiritual Exercises* and *Gertrud's Prayers* have also come down to us from the hands of anonymous sources.

Chapter Twenty-three of Book 2 of Gertrud's book on loving-kindness is devoted to thanksgiving. Its form is a prayer to the "Lord God, my Creator." She first asks that her soul might bless God. "Bless" here is used in the sense of acknowledging and thanking her "most delightful lover" for the "unbounded loving-kindness with which God has so overwhelmingly surrounded" her.

She acknowledged that all her life, all her childhood and youth, until she was almost twenty-five, she spent in a state of what she calls "blinded madness." "Nevertheless," she wrote, "you [God] choose to prepare for yourself some from among your most devoted friends dining in the banquet hall of the life of a nun."

Gertrud's meditations on the scriptural texts describing Christ's life were clearly extensive and intense. For example she wrote: "To make up for all my acts of negligence, I offered to God the Father the suffering in the Babe's wailing on hay in a manger, through the needs of infancy, the weaknesses of childhood, the trials of adolescence, right up to the moment when, on the cross, with bowed head he yielded up his spirit with a great cry."

Gertrud's response to her reflections was to "plunge in thanksgiving into the deepest abyss of humility." She offered praise and adoration at God's "surpassingly excellent mercy." She worshiped "that delightful goodness that prompted God, the Father of all mercies, to bear toward me thoughts of peace and not affliction." Gertrud acknowledged that God had given her "access to knowledge and love" of him. As a culmination of God's gifts, Gertrud asserted that, already in this life, "God initiated a relationship with me in supernatural and hidden ways so that, from then on, like friend with friend or, rather, like husband with wife, he was able to take constant pleasure in my soul."

Gertrud, like the other nuns at Helfta, was able to take advantage of an atmosphere deeply permeated with classical learning, an uplifting liturgy, and the deep friendship of her community. Through the proliferation of her works, and the writings about her, Gertrud exerted a profound influence on the spirituality of succeeding generations.

Chapter Eighteen

Fourteenth-Century Spiritual Leaders

A. MEISTER ECKHART

John Eckhart was born into the lower German aristocracy not long before 1260, at Tambach, a town in Thuringia. In the late 1270s, he left home to join the Order of Preachers, the Dominicans. After his training in the local novitiate, Eckhart was sent to Cologne in the last years of Albert the Great's tenure at the house of "general studies" there. In 1293, he was sent to Paris, acknowledged as the preeminent university in the field of theology. There he lectured on the basic compendium in that discipline, the *Sentences* of Peter Lombard (d. 1160). In the fall of 1291, the Order called Eckhart back to Germany as prior of the Dominican house at Erfurt. Then in 1302, Eckhart, now a Master (*Meister* in German), was sent back to Paris to take up one of the professorships in theology assigned to the Order.

After only a year at Paris, Eckhart was recalled to Germany, to take up the post of prior of the newly created province of Saxony, stretching from the Netherlands to Bohemia. Eckhart's responsibilities included supervision of and service to forty-seven houses of men and nine of women. In 1311, the General Chapter, the highest legislative body in the Order, posted him back to Paris as a professor. Two assignments to Paris was a rare privilege, Thomas Aquinas being the only other Dominican so honored. Eckhart spent the next two years at Paris, from the fall of 1311 to the summer of 1313. He was then well over fifty years old.

Eckhart's next assignment was at Strassburg where he spent the years 1319 to 1323 as a special vicar to the Dominican Master General. Much of his time he spent traveling up and down the Rhine valley engaged in pastoral care and spiritual counsel. He devoted himself especially to preaching to communities of Beguines and houses of Dominican nuns, now numbering seventy-four. He spent his waning years at the Dominican house of studies at Cologne. There his teaching was investigated and condemned by the archbishop. The case ended up at the papal court in Avignon, where excerpts from his writings were condemned. He died in 1327 on his way back to Cologne.

Eckhart's whole life was spent alternating between the pastoral life of an itinerant preacher and the demanding academic regimen of lengthy classroom lectures and public disputations. He devoted many hours to composing treatises and sermons in both Latin and German.

Unlike most other theologians, Eckhart asserted that God's essence, that which makes God what he is, is Intellect rather than Being. Eckhart put it in this way: "God is Intellect that lives in the knowledge of itself alone." He reasoned that, because God as Creator is the cause of all being, God must therefore transcend being. In God there is neither being nor existence.

Humans are made in God's image and God's essence is intellect. It follows that intellect must be what makes humans human. The uniquely rational nature of human beings is not only God-given, it is a participation in the Divine Nature itself. For Eckhart, the human intellect is not merely the capacity to know about things, it is consciousness itself. The source of that consciousness is God who is the "ground" of the soul.

Since the ground of God and the ground of the soul are the same ground, it is incumbent on each person to enter into his or her soul through moderate ascetic practices that will facilitate union with God. Asceticism should be a means but never become an end, otherwise it would be a distraction from one's true end, which is God. Union with God requires utter disinterestedness in, or detachment from, all things temporal. The highest goal of the human person is the total stillness of silence, for God is utterly still and silent, and likes attract likes.

Believing all this, how should one act? Eckhart answered: one must retreat from the world and its images to the inner space that is the intellect. There, human consciousness is one with the Divine Intellect. Indeed, one's intellect has no existence apart from its inherence in the Word of God. The end result, Eckhart taught, is "the birth of God in the soul."

Eckhart did not speak of visionary experiences in this union. In true contemplation, the soul is one with the Godhead, the incomprehensible essence of God, the essence that is above and beyond the God of whom we can shape an image that we are able to comprehend.

Eckhart's positions are both profound and difficult. It is surely no wonder that his teaching was misunderstood. A warning of what was to come was the caution issued by the Dominican Chapter General meeting in the spring of 1325, directed at "friars in Germany who say things in their sermons that can easily lead simple and uneducated people into error." There is no evidence, however, that Eckhart's superiors passed this caution along. Significantly, in the troubles that were shortly to beset Eckhart, his Dominican brethren remained supportive and even accompanied him on his trek to the papal court at Avignon to defend himself against the accusations leveled at him there.

Those accusations resulted from an investigation authorized by Henry II of Vieneburg, the archbishop of Cologne from 1309 to 1332, a strong ally of Pope John XXII in his struggle with the emperor Louis the Bavarian. In 1326, two lists of excerpts from Eckhart's works were laid before the archbishop–lists prepared by two renegade Dominican friars. Called before an archdiocesan commission, Eckhart declared: "I am able to be in error, but I cannot be a heretic, because the source of error is the intellect, our ability to know, but heresy has its source in the will, our ability to choose." Admitting that his works sometimes contained rhetorical overstatements, Eckhart appealed to the good intentions behind some questioned passages. He publicly proclaimed he was willing to retract any and all errors, thus, according to church law, forestalling any attempt to declare him a heretic. Nevertheless, the archbishop condemned him.

Eckhart responded that, as a master of theology at Paris, he and his teaching could only be judged by that university. Then too, as a Dominican, whose order was exempt from any bishop's jurisdiction, his case could only be judged by the pope. As a canon lawyer, Pope John XXII knew full well he could not refuse Eckhart's appeal. The pope was no theologian, however, so he appointed a commission to consider the case and found himself virtually forced to accept that commission's condemnation of sentences and phrases drawn out of context from Eckhart's works. John XXII's bull of condemnation was issued on March 27, 1327. Eckhart had already left Avignon for home. He died on the way.

B. JOHN TAULER

Like Eckhart, Tauler was a Dominican, and their life spans were closely parallel. Eckhart lived from the late 1250s to 1327; Tauler's life spanned the period from c. 1300 to 1361. Both spent much of their time preaching in the Rhineland, especially to lay folk and at Dominican houses of women. There the similarity ceased, for Eckhart, as we have seen, was sent twice to Paris and there took his doctorate in theology. Tauler, on the other hand, received only the basic training in liberal arts and theology that all Dominicans were given. There is no evidence that Tauler was sent to the house of general studies at Cologne, whereas Eckhart not only studied but spent his waning years as a professor there. Tauler, however, never attracted the hostility of the archbishop of Cologne or the condemnation of the pope. Tauler, in fact, often expressed his skepticism about the purely intellectual life. "The professors at Paris," he wrote, "read large tomes and busily turn over the leaves of their books. That is all very well, but those who meditate on Scriptures read the living book in which everything lives."

The perfection of the human person, Tauler taught, requires that one knows what a person is. The human problem, he asserted, is not that we are trapped in a body, but that our souls are disordered. Not unlike Eckhart, he would not have his hearers tame their flesh by keeping long vigils or wearing hair-shirts, for he believed that all human components, including the body, are by their nature good:

> The human person is quite correctly described as if it were three people, and yet it is one person. The first is the outer, animal person, who knows the world through the senses. The second is the rational person with powers of the intellect. The third person is the highest part of the soul, its basic orientation.

The transformation of the person "into a God-like form, uniting the created spirit with the uncreated God," cannot be accomplished by human beings. Their role is to yield themselves to the transforming gift of God's grace. By the action of grace, the outer person is purified through a life of virtue, and the rational person is transformed by growth in understanding and intention. God sets afire the highest part of humans with his divine love. For this last transformation no human effort is necessary or possible. Embraced by God's mighty love, "the human spirit falls away from itself, losing itself in its Beloved like a drop of water in a deep ocean. This state must be experienced; about it no words are adequate."

However much one so transformed rejoices in the contemplation of God, "he or she should go forth into outward activity." As a Dominican, Tauler's activity was preaching. But, Tauler said of the true preacher, "in the depths of his soul he is immersed in God."

C. HENRY SUSO

The third of the fourteenth-century Dominican friars who greatly influenced their contemporaries was Henry Suso. That he was born on March 21, we know. The year is less certain, but was probably 1295. The place was Constance, a town situated in southern Germany on the lake of the same name, to which his noble family had moved from the countryside.

At the age of thirteen, Henry's parents took him to the local Dominican house. Church law dictated that a lad must be fifteen to enter a religious order, and Henry was long tormented by the thought that his parents had committed the sin of simony by paying for his acceptance into the Order. It was his older confrère, Meister Eckhart, who convinced Henry that his fears were unreasonable.

For some five years after entering the Dominican order, Henry's attitude toward his new life was less than enthusiastic. Then he underwent a conversion experience that led him to embrace wholeheartedly the life of a friar. That life included a rigorous education, beginning with the perfection of his command of the Latin used in the community prayer, in the reading of the Bible, and in studying the works of eminent spiritual authors of early and medieval Christianity. That education was followed by some five or six years spent mastering the logic, metaphysics, and ethics of Aristotle, as well as mathematics and the physical sciences. Theology was the subject studied for the next two or three years. The Bible and the *Sentences* of the twelfth-century theologian Peter Lombard, as well as the works of Thomas Aquinas were the fundamental texts.

Henry proved to be an outstanding student, and so was sent to the house of advanced studies in Cologne. The goal of this stage of Dominican education was to prepare professors of philosophy and theology for the friaries of the German provinces of the Order. Henry returned to Constance where, in 1326 or 1327, he was made the director of studies and, eventually, prior. After serving in these posts, he happily embraced the life of a preacher in the towns and countryside along the Rhine River in southwest Germany. By now based in Ulm, he visited the many Dominican houses of women in the area, making himself available as spiritual advisor to the nuns. Local communities of Beguines also benefitted from his counsel.

All the while Henry was counseling others, he was struggling with his own inner demon, scrupulosity. In his semi-autobiographical book, *The Exemplar*, he spoke of the guilt he felt at the slightest stirring of sexual feelings:

> In his youth he was very [sexually] sensitive, and this he found bitter and difficult. He sought all sorts of remedies and practiced rigorous penances to subject his flesh. For a long time he wore a hair shirt and a chain made with iron points. These caused him to bleed like a fountain so that he had to give up these garments.

He tried an array of other instruments of self-torture "until a vision appeared to him in which a heavenly gathering announced that God no longer desired this of him. He then gave up the use of those tools of self-torture and threw them all into a river."

In a passage in his *Little Book of Eternal Wisdom*, Henry turned his attention to the sorry state of the contemporary Church, describing it as "a town in ruins." He was especially harsh in his description of the clergy:

> The moats surrounding that town have begun to cave in, and the walls have started to collapse. Eager obedience, voluntary poverty, and holy simplicity are beginning to disappear. Most of the town's inhabitants have driven God out of their own hearts by their frivolous preoccupation with fleeting concerns.

Henry's response to this sad state of affairs was to seek to serve by his counsel those whose "good will and good beginnings" in the spiritual life "have been perverted by the advice and example of others."

In an effort to serve a wider audience than his advisees, Henry collected and edited his works in a volume that included his *Life, The Little Book of Eternal Wisdom, The Little Book of Truth*, and *The Little Book of Letters*. This collection and two of Henry's sermons survived him in hundreds of manuscripts, testifying to his great popularity in the subsequent centuries of later medieval Europe.

D. JOHN RUUSBROEC

John Ruusbroec, unlike Eckhart, Tauler, and Suso, was not a Dominican. Born in 1293 in the village of Ruusbroec, he was sent at the age of eleven to the flourishing city of Brussels, only some five miles away from home. There he completed his education while living with an uncle who was a canon serving the church of Saint Gudula (now the cathedral). Ruusbroec was ordained priest in 1317 and served at that church until 1343.

By that time he had become thoroughly disillusioned by what he regarded as the sorry state of the Church's leadership. Most of the popes, bishops, and priests of times past had lived exemplary lives, but, thought Ruusbrouc, "today the situation is quite the opposite." Today the leaders of the Church

> have turned completely to worldly concerns. They pray with their lips, but their hearts do not savor the meaning of their prayers. Often they seek to eat and drink well and to enjoy bodily comfort–and would to God they were chaste of body.

Dismayed at the low standards prevailing among the clergy in the city, Ruusbroec, his uncle, and another priest left Brussels for Groenendaal, the "green valley" in the nearby forest of Soignes. Attracted by the life at Groenendaal, a number of others joined the small community. In 1345, they adopted the *Rule* of Saint Augustine.

Groenendaal became a celebrated pilgrimage center. Many people came to see Ruusbroec for spiritual counsel and were cheerfully received. He also wrote treatises on the spiritual life, and these works reached a wide audience.

In Ruusbroec's treatise *The Spiritual Espousals*, he spoke of God as above being, eternity, and all other human concepts. He is "a simple unity, without any mode of being, beyond time and space, without any before or after, without desire or possession, without light or darkness. He is the perpetual now, the bottomless abyss, the darkness of silence, the desert wilderness."

The human soul comes forth from God the Creator and possesses three faculties or powers: intellect, memory, and will. Human beings, have lost the unity of these faculties, and they can return to God only by passing through three stages of life. The first of these is the active life, marked at its beginning by a moral conversion. The second stage is the interior life, in which Christ enters into the soul, ultimately into its very essence. Contemplative life, the third stage, raises the human person above reason and intelligence and that person is united to God in one simple life and spirit. In that condition, "beyond all activities and virtues, one looks with a simple and inward gaze of blissful love. There one meets God without any intermediary."

Ruusbroec, his contemporaries thought, was a matchless guide on the spiritual journey, and they flocked to Groenendaal to seek his counsel. Before he died in 1381, one of the last of those who approached him for help was Gert Groote, commonly considered the father of the Devotio Moderna.

E. GERT GROOTE AND THE DEVOTIO MODERNA

Gert Groote was born at Deventer (now in the Netherlands) in 1340. His father, a wealthy merchant, died of the plague when Gert was only ten. Only five years later, in 1355, the wealthy orphan went to the University of Paris where he received the degree Master of Arts. Returning to his homeland he spent a few years in a monastery as a brother, without taking vows but occupied with useful labor and in reading the works of the great spiritual authors. He gradually came to realize that his path to God included active service in the world. "It would be wrong," he wrote, "to disregard what cannot be done by another for the good of your neighbor, even at the cost of your contemplative prayer, devotion, and righteousness."

In 1374, Gert gave up the clerical incomes he had amassed and made his house over to a group of women who were leading a quasi-monastic life. That was only the first of a large number of communities called the Sisters of the Common Life. Many foundations of Brothers of the Common Life soon followed. Gert died of the plague in 1384, but his foundations continued to flourish and spread over the Low Countries, western Germany, and northern France.

Members of these communities did not take vows, but they prayed and worked together at some trade; copying manuscripts was a popular means of support. Although the Brothers did not ordinarily found schools, they did offer schoolboys classes in religious education as well as food and lodging. Those who were considering entering the priesthood or a religious order could also stay at the Brothers' house where lectures and discussions on the spiritual life formed a regular part of their day. They could join the community in meditations, Scripture studies, prayers, and work. By this means they were introduced into what Gert called "the imitation of the humanity of Christ."

The classical expression of this ideal was contained in a small book immensely popular in the later middle ages. The book, *The Imitation of Christ*, is sometimes ascribed to Gert Groote, sometimes to Thomas Hemerken of Kempen (or à Kempis).

Book I of this classic treatise aims to assist the reader in attaining humility and inner peace. There is a strongly anti-intellectual component of this advice:

> What good does it do me to speak learnedly about the high, secret mysteries of the Trinity while by lacking humility I displease the Trinity? I would rather feel contrition for my sins than know the definition of contrition. What would it profit me to know by heart all the books of the Bible and all the sayings of all the philosophers without living in God's grace and love.

Book II teaches that one should embrace the tribulations of this life as Jesus embraced his suffering and death. Books III and IV consist of a conversation between Christ and a "Faithful Soul" that exhorts readers to forsake their own will in imitation of Christ and so bear the Cross with him. In Book IV the reader is also urged to prepare properly before receiving Communion and to receive it frequently, confident that "God walks with simple people, shows himself to humble people, opens wisdom to pure, clean minds, but hides his grace from the curious and proud."

Chapter Nineteen

The Failure of the Institutional Church

A. THE LATE MEDIEVAL PAPACY

In the Late Middle Ages, the spirit of reform that had been central to high medieval culture no longer drove the Church. After Pope Innocent III's death in 1215, all the popes of the thirteenth century were canon lawyers–save one who reigned for less than a year. Each claimed universal and supreme jurisdiction over the Church as its administrative, judicial, and legislative head. But the considerable prestige gained for the papacy through its earlier leadership of reform movements was largely squandered in attempts to secure expansion of the Papal States and extend political influence in the Italian peninsula. There were popes who deposed monarchs and saw to it that their heirs were eliminated. At one point, a pope presumed to offer the crown of Sicily to the highest bidder. To many contemporaries, including the saintly king of France, Louis IX (who reigned from 1226 to 1270), the popes' use of spiritual authority to achieve political ends seemed a gross abuse of power. As the Late Middle Ages went on, more and more people saw the popes as much more concerned with worldly power than spiritual ministry, and the result was a loss of the moral prestige of the papacy.

B. THE BABYLONIAN CAPTIVITY

In 1294, Benedetto Gaetani was elevated to the Roman See as Boniface VIII. His predecessor, Celestine V, had been a saintly hermit. The cardinals, however, under the leadership of Gaetani, had found saintliness an inadequate preparation for the administrative role demanded of a thoroughly politicized papacy. Gaetani played a principal role in urging, if not forcing, Celestine's resignation. As Boniface VIII, Gaetani proved himself an able administrator, a forceful defender of papal prerogatives, and a generous patron of his own family's fortunes.

This resulted in a protracted quarrel with the king of France, Philip IV the Fair, over the king's taxation of the Church to support his wars. This dispute led to Boniface's downfall: Philip sent a force to Italy that attacked the octogenarian pope, and Boniface died three weeks later. After Boniface's death, his successor, Benedict XI, lived for only eight months.

In 1305, the cardinals elected as pope the archbishop of the French city of Bordeaux, who took the name Clement V. Clement was a weak and vacillating man whose advisors were often in the pay of the French king. Clement was made pope in France in the presence of Philip the Fair, who browbeat Clement into remaining in France and appointing French cardinals. The pope took up residence in Avignon, a French speaking city, where he and his successors built a huge fortress/palace and appointed an overwhelmingly French college of cardinals, who in turn elected Frenchmen as popes.

The Avignon papacy suffered from a state of chronic fiscal crisis. Its revenues were never sufficient to support the horde of papal officials, dignitaries, pensioners, and relatives. Much resentment was aroused by the financial policies of the Avignon papacy, which resorted to many new and ingenious devices to raise the ever larger revenues needed to support the elaborate bureaucracy that now developed. Although the Avignon popes were not wicked men, they seemed far more concerned with levying more and more burdensome taxes on the clergy than with the spiritual welfare of the Christian flock.

We have seen that one of Clement's successors, John XXII, had, in 1323, declared that it was he alone who had the right to determine who was the rightful emperor. When Louis of Wittelsbach (the Bavarian) protested, the pope excommunicated him. This was the beginning of a protracted period of controversy that was settled only with Louis's death in 1347. Widespread resentment at the pope's perceived highhandedness joined with the German bishops' increasing resistance to ever higher papal taxes. Both bishops and lay lords resisted the popes' attempts to appoint their subservient candidates to vacant bishoprics.

Everyone but the French wished that the pope would return to Rome. In 1377, Pope Gregory XI did go back to Italy. Once there, however, he was dismayed by the anarchy that prevailed and was about to return to Avignon when he suddenly died. The Roman populace then set up a clamor for the election of a native of their city as bishop of Rome. The cardinals chose a compromise candidate who was an Italian though not a Roman. The new pope took the name Urban VI and surprised everyone by being bent on sweeping reform of the church, starting with the cardinals at the papal court. This was too much for the French cardinals, who fled Rome and elected another pope, who took the name Clement VII. Clement established himself and his court back at Avignon. There were exchanges of anathemas and mutual excommunications, and for some forty years there were at least two lines of claimants to the chair of Peter.

It is difficult for us to imagine the confusion wrought by this great division or schism. So tangled were the conflicting claims that no one could be certain who the legitimate pope was. For most countries allegiance was governed by political considerations. France, obviously, acknowledged the pope in Avignon, while England, at war with France, chose Rome. The princes of the Empire, both lay and ecclesiastical, were divided in their allegiance, a reflection of the political fragmentation of Germany.

In March of 1409, twenty-four cardinals–fourteen "Roman" and ten "Avignonese"–accompanied by some three hundred leading clergymen, held a meeting at Pisa. They voted to depose both popes and elected Alexander V in their stead. However, both the Roman and Avignon popes refused to abdicate, and instead of two contending popes there were now three. These events gave rise to the view, called conciliarism, that a general or ecumenical council was not subject to the pope, but was reflective of the will of the whole Church. It was, then, an ecumenical council that was to be responsible for the healing and reform of the Church.

Impressed by the popularity of this position, the Emperor Sigismund issued a call for an ecumenical council that would meet in Germany. That appeal was widely heeded, and, during the course of the year 1414, representatives from all parts of western Christendom and all three papal camps–all together more than 1,200 Church officials and laymen–streamed toward the little south German town of Constance. This great assembly had a triple purpose: to end the schism, to reform the Church, and to oppose an increasing number of heresies. Only the first of these was seriously pursued and successfully achieved. Reform was found too complex for so large a body. The council's sole "success" in dealing with heresy was to imprison and then burn John Hus, a Bohemian priest and reform advocate, who had come to Constance protected, he mistakenly thought, by Emperor Sigismund's safe-conduct.

Although no great reform of the Church had resulted, the schism had been ended, and the popes had resumed their residence in Rome. The Council of Constance had elected Martin V in 1417, and the new pope received widespread support. However, he and his successor, Eugenius IV, devoted their pontificates not to eliminating corruption but to fighting the stubborn remnants of conciliarism. By 1455, the popes were free from any important check on their authority by other clergymen. By this time, however, the papacy was almost completely powerless outside its central Italian territory. In most countries of Europe, kings had assumed far-reaching authority over the Church in their lands. This was not the case in the empire.

C. THE GERMAN CHURCH: THE BISHOPS

Though nominally responsible to the Emperor, the princes of the late medieval Empire were in effect independent rulers of relatively large territories. Most of the German bishoprics were also principalities, and most of the bishops who ruled them were sons of noble families. Bishops and the abbots of major monasteries were able to behave like lay princes who ruled layfolk: local lords, knights, and farmers alike. The desires, ambitions, and behavior of most of the higher clergy were similar, if not identical, to the lay rulers who were their princely relatives.

Some bishops were successful rulers; others were not. Some bishops were faithful shepherds of their flocks. Some ignored their spiritual responsibilities, appointed vicars as substitutes, and lived off revenue from episcopal and family lands

An example of a bishop considered successful by his peers was Baldwin of Luxemburg. Baldwin had been a student at Paris and the head of the cathedral chapter at Mainz when elected its archbishop in 1307. The chapter was, in theory, the clergy–called canons–serving the Mainz cathedral. Their duties, however, were carried out by substitutes paid far less than the income attached to their posts. Most of the canons came from noble families of lesser importance than that of their Luxemburger archbishop.

Baldwin, now archbishop of Mainz at the age of twenty-two, was also one of the seven electors of the Empire. In 1308, Baldwin helped elect his brother Henry, count of Luxemburg, to the imperial throne. Henry repaid the favor by granting Baldwin large sums of money.

Baldwin was hugely successful both monetarily and politically. By 1340, he had acquired 103 castles, managed by paid officials, not by knights who might forget their allegiance to him. Baldwin divided this greatly expanded territory into administrative districts–a political structure that endured until 1794. By the end of his life in 1354, Baldwin had nearly doubled his territory and made himself very, very rich. Not all the bishops in the late middle ages could claim the sort of "success" that Baldwin obtained, as we shall see in a later chapter.

D. THE GERMAN CHURCH: PARISH LIFE

Unlike the friars–Dominicans and the like–the priests who served the churches in towns and villages were not highly educated. They did attend a Latin school to learn the language of the liturgy, some of them residing in a house belonging to the Brethren of the Common Life. Beyond that they had to serve an apprenticeship with a priest in a parish. Ordinarily ordination by their bishop required no special examination. Ulrich of Strassburg wrote in his *Treatise on the Good*:

> A priest must have enough grammar to be able to pronounce the words of the Mass correctly and to understand at least the literal sense of what he reads. He must know at least the basic doctrine of faith that leads to love. He must be able to distinguish between what is sin and what is not, and between one kind of sin and another.

This is a low standard indeed, and some parish priests did not rise above it, which is not to say that their behavior when virtuous did not serve as an edifying example to their parishioners.

Because the Mass was in Latin, even the biblical readings, the vast majority of the lay folk could not participate effectively in the solemn service. The liturgy in cathedrals, monasteries, and the largest of the town churches became a performance, beautiful but unintelligible to lay folk. Even the vision of the liturgical drama being ceremoniously enacted at the altar was in some churches hidden by a screen shutting off the people. The elaborate music in these larger churches was no longer sung by the congregation but by professionals.

Because the liturgical use of the Latin language cut off the faithful from participation, Christian teachings were very largely conveyed through sermons. Preaching in the vernacular took place on Sundays and at weekday liturgical feasts, during or before Mass. Before or after the sermon, prayers for the community and for needy individuals were made. These were the minimal liturgical duties of priests, but the complaints of local, regional, or even national meetings of clergy indicate that the minimum was sometimes ignored by parish priests or shunted off on poorly paid vicars. It is no wonder that the itinerant preachers, like the Dominicans, drew such large crowds whether preaching from church pulpits, in town squares, or at rural meeting places.

E. POPULAR PIETY

The peace and order, the security and justice that in the High Middle Ages had been provided by the cooperative efforts of Church and State, were, in the Late Middle Ages, only a memory. The Black Death had carried off thousands and induced despair in those that survived. Then too, Late Middle Europe experienced the beginning of a cooling period called the "Little Ice Age," which made agricultural production fall off so severely that many areas formerly under cultivation were abandoned.

Despite the widespread failure of the institutional Church, most late medieval people did not reject Christianity or the Church, but found new ways of expressing their religious devotion. They followed their high medieval forbears in taking the humanity of Jesus seriously. But the aspect of that humanity that meant the most to often hungry and plague-ridden people was the physical suffering of Christ. The instruments of Jesus' torture–hammers and nails, crowns of thorns, scourges, and his wounded and bleeding body hung on a cross (now become a crucifix)–became the focus of depictions of Christ in sculpture and painting.

The belief that Jesus was really present in the eucharistic bread distributed at Mass had led high medieval churchmen to encourage frequent reception of communion. In the Late Middle Ages, however, the very presence of Christ in the Sacrament led to widespread avoidance of communion. A people burdened by pessimism about human nature, and fearful for the consequences of their sins, sought to avoid Saint Paul's threatened condemnation of those who communicated unworthily. However, they seized the opportunity of viewing the communion wafer whenever possible. The practice grew rapidly of installing a eucharistic wafer in a monstrance, a splendidly decorated altar vessel with a transparent center. It was widely believed that viewing the "Sacrament"–even by those in a state of sin–somehow conferred saving power. Nicholas of Cusa, the fifteenth-century cardinal and reformer, complained that the Eucharist "was instituted as food, not as something to be gawked at." No one listened.

The fear and awe aroused by Jesus' presence in the Eucharist was enhanced by a radically increased emphasis on Jesus' role in the Last Judgement. He was the one who would reward the virtuous and condemn sinners to Hell. Late medieval people sensed a pressing need for an advocate to represent them before Jesus the fearsome judge.

Who better to turn to than Jesus' mother, Mary? Those who came before Jesus' awesome seat of justice could plead with his mother for the protection she could provide. In the twelfth century, Mary had been viewed primarily as a model of humility and loving obedience. In the thirteenth century, she was increasingly seen as an intercessor. By the Late Middle Ages, Mary had become the Queen of Heaven. A frequent depiction of her coronation as queen was a statue or painting showing Mary as the central figure on a cross. God the Father occupied the left crossbar while Jesus, from his position on the right crossbar, joined his Father in placing a crown on the Queen's head. Above fluttered a dove, representing the Holy Spirit.

Lay people in the Late Middle Ages filled many of their religious needs by joining pious confraternities devoted to the veneration of one of a host of saints to whom they assigned a special sphere of competence. Artists prayed to Saint Luke; the athletically inclined attended masses at altars dedicated to Saint Sebastian. Bakers had Saint Elizabeth of Hungary as their patroness; bankers relied on the intercession of Saint Mark. Every occupation had its favorite saint: musicians looked to Saint Cecilia, dancers to Saint Vitus.

The bones and scraps of clothing thought to belong to these saints were credited with miraculous power and venerated with fervor. This led to a traffic in relics that resulted in many aberrations. There were perhaps as many as seven right arms of John the Baptist circulating in late medieval Europe. The crown of thorns and pieces of the Ten Commandment tablets that Moses broke, were available for veneration. The cathedral at Aachen boasted–as did many other churches–of its possession of the swaddling clothes in which Mary wrapped her son Jesus. The cathedral at Cologne served as a pilgrimage site for those who wished to be blessed through viewing the gifts of the Three Magi. Cologne also possessed a vial of the Virgin's milk, as did several other churches. Perhaps the most powerful of all relics was that of the Holy Foreskin, which, it was said, had survived Jesus' circumcision.

F. INDULGENCES

Nervous sinners also sought other ways of mitigating the effects of their sins, among them recourse to indulgences. Indulgences had begun as an innocent practice in the twelfth century. At that time, they were merely a statement by an ecclesiastical authority that a specified pious activity, from helping install a new church roof to enrolling in a crusading pilgrimage, was a meritorious act. That action, if done in a spirit of genuine repentance and preceded by confession of guilt, would make up for the evil brought into the world by one's sin.

Indulgences were to become a central part of religious life in the Late Middle Ages. The fourth of the Avignon popes, Clement VI (reigned 1342-1352) contributed the classic description and justification of indulgences in a decree of 1343. Ironically, the central image around which Clement structured his decree was a treasure chest–ironic because Clement was one of the most politically active and financially rapacious popes of his century. According to Clement, through the "precious blood" of Jesus that he "shed as an innocent victim on the altar of the cross," God the Father "acquired a great treasure for the Church." Although it was "an infinite treasure, the merits of the Blessed Mother of God and of all the elect are known to have supplied their increment." The agent who portioned out this infinite treasure was the pope–and he alone, for he, as the sole successor of Peter, was "the bearer of heaven's keys." The recipients of this largess were those "truly penitent," those who had confessed, those who had performed some meritorious act of reparation. The meritorious act that soon eclipsed all others was the contribution of money to a financially strapped papacy.

Some contemporary theologians were puzzled. If the acts of reparation done by Christians were truly meritorious, why did they need the treasury? If it were the treasury that made their acts meritorious, did this not deny freedom of the will–a freedom considered necessary to good works? And if the will's choice were crucial in determining the goodness or merit of an act, why did Christian folk need the pope's authority to gain access to God's mercy?

In 1476, Pope Sixtus IV compounded these misgivings. He decreed that indulgences were henceforth applicable to souls suffering in Purgatory. By this action, the jurisdiction claimed by popes over the Church Militant–the people struggling in this world to attain a blissful next world–was extended to papal control over life after death in the Church Suffering. Still more disturbing to many theologians was Sixtus's assertion that buyers of indulgences for their dead relatives and friends need not themselves be repentant for their sins or confess them. This seemed to make money, not merit, the means to the release of souls from Purgatory and their entrance into Heaven.

What seemed to be magic to many theologians was embraced with enthusiasm by most late medieval lay people. They were told that, when their coins clinked into the money box of the papal indulgence peddlers, the souls of their dear relatives would fly away to Heaven. They eagerly contributed.

Chapter Twenty

The Cusanus

Nicholas of Cusa was both an outstanding thinker and a most prolific writer in fifteenth-century Germany. He combined the roles of canon lawyer, theologian, philosopher, and churchman. Nicholas' philosophy was based on sophisticated mathematical insights that arouse interest even in today's philosophical world. His tireless classical scholarship also led him to discover manuscripts of hitherto lost Latin literature. He spent much time and energy promoting peace between church and state and union between the eastern and western churches. Above all he was a reformer.

A. YOUTH AND EDUCATION

Nicholas Krebs was born in 1401 at Kues, a town on the Mosel River. He is often referred to today as "the Cusanus" from the Latin form of the town's name. He was the son of a fairly well-to-do boatman and merchant, Johan Cryfftz (or Krebs), engaged in transport on the Mosel River which flowed past the impressive house run by Nicholas' mother, Katherina Roemer.

In 1416, at the age of fifteen, he entered the university at Heidelberg, where he graduated as Bachelor of Arts the following year. That same year he took up the study of canon law at Padua in northern Italy. While there he gained the friendship of several Italian students of classical literature, and also studied mathematics, physics, and astronomy. In 1423, he was awarded the degree Doctor of Canon Law. Back home in Germany in 1425, he lectured on canon law at Cologne while studying theology.

Nicholas' talents became well-known to several German princes. In 1426, he was called on to testify before the archbishop of Cologne and Louis the Count Palatine in a case involving the duke of Cleves. In 1432, Duke

William of Bavaria sent Nicholas as his matrimonial agent to the same duke of Cleves, whose daughter William wished to wed.

In 1430, Ulrich of Manderschied enlisted Nicholas as his personal advisor, secretary, and agent at the Council of Basel. There Nicholas represented his patron's disputed claim to the archbishopric of Trier.

B. THE COUNCIL OF BASEL

In 1417, the Council of Constance had come to its unsuccessful end. The Churchmen there assembled had issued a decree calling for "frequent" holding of ecumenical or church-wide councils. In accordance with this decree and despite the opposition of Pope Eugenius IV, those churchmen advocating reform met in 1431 at the Swiss town of Basel. Although Nicholas's efforts on behalf of his patron were unsuccessful, he so impressed the Council delegates that he was assigned to the Commission on Matters of Faith. He was delegated by that Commission to negotiate the return of the followers of John Hus to unity with the Church. The issue led to Nicholas's treatise *On Communion Under Both Species*, which proposed that unity with the Hussites was more important than whether or not the laity should receive the chalice as well as the bread as was the Hussite practice.

Unity was the continuing motif in Nicholas' efforts at the Council of Basel, a meeting that was facing the continuing opposition of Pope Eugenius IV. In 1440, Nicholas offered his alternate solution to the claims of superiority made by both Council and pope. In his *Catholic Concordance*, Nicholas defined the Church as the extension of Christ in time and eternity. He asserted, furthermore, that the Church must be an expression of the fundamental freedom that every individual possesses by nature. It followed, he wrote, that the pope does not have the power to legislate independently of the Church. However, the pope, as the "captain of the ship of Saint Peter," must participate in–but not dictate–all decisions affecting the whole Church. The power of bishops, however, does not derive from the pope, since all the apostles were commissioned by Christ to be equal in authority.

In his *Catholic Concordance* Nicholas also presented his position that all government, ecclesiastical as well as temporal, arises from the consent of the people. The presidential authority of the emperor derives from the election by the people through the Seven Imperial Electors, not by papal mandate. In temporal matters, the Church is subject to the state, as the state is subject to the Church in spiritual matters. Nicholas also declared that in the state the Imperial Diet (or parliament) performs the function of representing the people, just as an ecumenical council represents them in ecclesiastical matters.

The Council of Basel went farther than Nicholas, however, in asserting its supremacy in the Church and its intention to direct a thoroughgoing reform of the Church, starting with the papacy. But government by committee proved inadequate to the task.

C. THE MISSION TO CONSTANTINOPLE

Dismayed at the disorder prevailing at Basel and fearing continuing schism between pope and council, Nicholas asserted his loyalty to Rome. In 1437, Pope Eugenius had called a general council loyal to himself, thus fulfilling Nicholas' views on both pope and council and the relationship between them. This council opened its first session at Ferrara on January 8, 1438, and Nicholas became one of its leading advocates.

The most important task facing the pope and this council was reunion between the churches of the Greek East and the Latin West. The Byzantine emperor was faced with a massive threat from the Turks, and so he turned to the pope in the hope of enlisting the help of Latin Christians. Pope Eugenius sent Nicholas and two bishops to Constantinople to help secure Greek approval for a joint East-West council to be held in Italy. Eugenius' choice of Nicholas as ambassador was surely due at least in part to the latter's reconciliation with Rome, but may well have reflected a widespread confidence in Nicholas' knowledge of Greek. One contemporary wrote:

> At last we have someone well acquainted with the Greek language, in other respects is very learned, and has universal talent. He is a discoverer of innumerable manuscripts and, above all, owner of Greek works, among them some with Latin definitions of words and grammatical explanations.

Among the sources Nicholas brought back from Constantinople were manuscripts containing the minutes of the sixth through eighth ecumenical councils, invaluable in the attempt to reconcile the theological divisions between East and West. The Council of Ferrara, then transferred to Florence, accomplished a fragile and temporary union of the churches, but Nicholas was not at either location. The pope had sent him back to Germany burdened with many tasks.

D. THE PAPAL LEGATE

During 1438 and 1439, Nicholas' first task was to represent the pope at the meetings of the Imperial Diet. In June of 1438, he argued before the Diet against a representative of the Council of Basel that continued to deny the authority of Pope Eugenius IV. Nicholas refuted the Council's claim to superiority over the Church by pointing to those delegates who were more and more deserting it. Nicholas also cited the fact that the Greek Church had recognized the primacy of Rome and had thus healed the centuries-old schism with the West.

In January 1440, Nicholas served as papal legate to the meeting of the imperial electors at Frankfurt, called to choose a successor to the emperor Albrecht. As we have seen, the electors chose as Albrecht's successor, the long-lived but ineffectual Frederick III.

E. THE REFORMING CARDINAL

In 1448, Pope Nicholas V rewarded Nicholas of Cusa with the red hat of a cardinal in recognition of his tireless efforts on behalf of church unity. The Jubilee Year of 1450 drew innumerable pilgrims to Rome, but for Nicholas it was a year of rest and reflection, his first for many years. He saw, however, that the settlement of the Schism between Council and pope and between the Greek and Western churches were but steps toward the healing of Church and society. Reform would remain superficial if the corrupt practices of churchmen were not rooted out and the lax moral standards of clergy and layfolk were not raised.

The pope responded enthusiastically to Nicholas' petition to be appointed legate charged with the reform of the German church. To that end the pope granted Nichols extensive powers and complete freedom of action in dealing with other ecclesiastical officials. He could punish with penance, excommunication, or interdict whenever the situation demanded. Nicholas did indeed employ these powers in his more than year-long travels in German lands: banning clerical concubinage, forbidding money payments for church offices, and attempting to restore monastic life to its former standards. He forbad trade in, and veneration of, fraudulent relics, and he attempted–unsuccessfully as we have seen–to eliminate the display and veneration of consecrated Eucharistic bread. In an attempt to increase the laity's knowledge of their faith, he encouraged parish priests to hang banners in their churches displaying the Lord's Prayer, the Hail Mary, the Apostles' Creed, and the Ten Commandments.

F. THE BISHOP OF BRIXEN

In 1450, the pope selected Nicholas as bishop of Brixen, a city in the Tyrolean Alps. Conflict arose immediately because the count of Tyrol had pressured the canons of the cathedral to elect Leonard Wismayer as bishop. After an intense struggle, a papal bull nullified Wismayer's claim, and in 1451 the emperor, Fredrick III, recognized Nicholas' claim.

Nicholas' journey from Rome to Brixen followed a roundabout route along which he preached reform in much of Germany. It was not until 1452 that he entered Brixen as its new bishop. Once there he held annual diocesan meetings on pastoral topics, one of which urged lay-folk to receive communion frequently. He also set aside diocesan funds to assist local parishes and charities. His attempts to bring monasteries up to traditional standards were sometimes met with resistance, particularly from the nuns of Sonnenberg, who held out for some seven years. Opposition to his reforms also came from Duke Sigismund of Austria, a conflict marked by the threats, ambush, and attempted murder that won Sigismund a papal condemnation.

Nicholas was diverted from his struggles to reform his diocese of Brixen by his friend Pope Pius II. Pius had left Rome in order to promote another crusade against the Turks. In 1459, Pius appointed Nicholas vicar-general in Rome with power over the papal territories in central Italy. Nicholas' attempts to reform the clergy stationed at the papal churches of Saint Peter, Saint John Lateran, and Saint Mary Major were only partially successful. During his brief stay at Rome he submitted, at the pope's request, a proposal for the reform of the whole church.

At the beginning of 1460, Nicholas returned to Brixen, only to find the troops of Duke Sigismund patrolling the streets. Nicholas fled to his castle at Andraz that the duke then successfully besieged. Nicholas was forced to surrender and submit to a humiliating treaty. When released he fled to Rome. Shortly thereafter, both ill and frustrated with the failure of the pope and the curia–the papal administration–to reform, he wrote to Pius: "I like nothing that goes on in this curia. Everything is corrupt. Neither you nor the cardinals have any care for the Church. All are bent on ambition and avarice. When I speak to the cardinals about reform I am laughed at. I am an old man, and I need to rest." Pius dissuaded him from retiring and continued to impose burdensome tasks on him. One of them involved a trip to Ancona, which was to prove his last.

G. THE WIDE RANGE OF INTELLECTUAL CONCERNS

Nicholas' overwhelming interest lay in spirituality, reflection on growth toward union with God. The proper study of spirituality necessitated, he thought, the mastery of theology, which is the study of the contents and implications of God's revelation. That study, in turn, required the vocabulary and study of philosophy, the application of logic to the observed world. Since Nicholas was convinced that the natural world is numerically structured, mathematics is necessary to philosophical pursuit. Because of his belief that the whole of creation is structured in this way, it is often difficult to tell whether a work by Nicholas belongs to one or many disciplines, and, if many, which ones. This difficulty is compounded by the volume of Nicholas' writings: well over fifty treatises and hundreds of sermons. Properly mathematical were surely Nicholas' treatises *On the Transmutations of Geometry* (1450), *On the Fulfillment of Mathematics* (1453), and *On Mathematical Perfection* (1458).

How close mathematics and theology were in Nicholas' mind is shown by the title of Book I, Chapter 2 of his *On Learned Ignorance* (1440): "That Mathematics Greatly Helps Us To Apprehend Various Divine Truths." In Book III, Chapter 11 of the same treatise, Nicholas wrote:

> Our forbears all agreed that faith is the beginning of understanding. It is of course necessary for everyone who aspires to ascend to knowledge of the truth to believe those things without which that ascent is impossible. As Isaiah says, "If you do not believe, you will not understand." Therefore, faith enfolds in itself everything understandable, and understanding is the unfolding of faith. Here, the intellect is directed by faith, and faith is extended still further through the intellect.

For Nicholas, however, the highest sort of knowing is the realization of the extent of one's ignorance, of one's learned ignorance, as he put it. On the other hand, Nicholas asserted in his treatise *On the Beryl* (1458) that one can learn much about reality through the study of that mineral, a relatively insignificant part of nature.

H. THE LAST DAYS

In 1464, responding to Pope Pius II's wishes, we remember, Nicholas set out for Ancona to deliver a final version of a document citing King Podiebrod of Bohemia to appear before the papal court. On July 16, Nicholas became seriously ill at Todi in Umbria. On August 6, he made his last will, and he died on August 11.

As part of his testamentary document, Nicholas left the vineyard he inherited from his father to a hospital that he had built in his birthplace at Kues. Thirty-three poor old men were to find a home at this institution. The chapel, cloister, and refectory are still open to visitors. Nicholas' extensive library and collection of astronomical instruments are also housed in the same complex, testimonies to the broad range of his interests.

Chapter Twenty-One

The Death of the Eagle

A. TWO GERMAN REFORMERS

The Reformation, both Protestant and Catholic, accelerated the many forces leading to the splintering of the Empire. The several issues that led to the schism in the western Christian Church were, and are, complex. An examination of the thought of two theological giants of the sixteenth century, Martin Luther and Desiderius Erasmus, will illuminate the fundamental theological issue separating Protestant and Catholic.

Martin Luther was born in 1483, the son of Hans and Margaret Luther, who had expectations their son would become a lawyer. They sent him off to the university at Erfurt where he earned his Bachelor of Arts degree in 1502 and the degree Master of Arts in 1505. Much to his father's dismay, young Martin entered the house of Augustinian friars at Erfurt, the result of an overwhelming religious experience. Transferred to the Wittenberg house of that Order in 1512, he earned the degree Doctor of Theology and became a Scripture professor at the young university there. He remained at this post until his death in 1546.

Desiderius Erasmus was born in 1469, probably at Rotterdam, a town in the province of Holland. His mother enrolled him in the school at Deventer run by the Brethren of the Common Life, and there he obtained an outstanding education in Latin literature. After the death of his parents, Erasmus entered the monastery of Augustinian canons at Steyn, near Gouda. There he continued his reading of classical and patristic Latin literature–the latter the works of early Christian authors. Because of his outstanding literary ability and his pleasant personality, the bishop of Cambrai invited him to serve as his secretary. In 1492, he was ordained a priest.

Through the continuing patronage of the bishop of Cambrai, Erasmus began his higher studies at Paris. There he met an Englishman, Lord Montjay, who invited him to England for the first of his six or more visits. Between 1498 and 1514, he lived in Paris, Oxford, and Italy. He taught for two years at Cambridge, then settled in the south German town of Basel. When Basel accepted Protestantism, he moved to the nearby town of Freiburg im Breisgau where he remained until 1535. He then returned to Basel, and he died there only one year later.

B. THE INDULGENCE CONTROVERSY

Both Luther and Erasmus devoted their lives to reform of the Church. Both saw the corruption of Christianity through practices that cheated Christians of their birthright as baptized members of the Church.

The practice that initiated Luther's reform efforts was the thriving trade in indulgences. It was not, however, the indulgences themselves which disturbed Luther's conscience; it was the sale of them that aroused his ire. On October 31, 1517, Professor Luther posted ninety-five theses on the door of the local castle church at Wittenberg. The door was covered with such notices, for it served as the university's bulletin board, and discussions of theses on all sorts of topics were a standard means of instruction at a medieval university.

Luther's theses were posted, as he put it, "with the aim of elucidating the truth" about indulgences through a disputation among fellow theologians at Wittenberg. The theses were posted in Latin, clearly not intended for popular consumption. Luther's purpose was threefold: to clarify the Church's teaching on indulgences; to expose and reform the shoddy salesmanship of indulgence preachers; and–perhaps surprising to us–to affirm the authority of the Church and encourage a revival of respect for that authority. For Luther, indulgences are "by no means to be despised," since they are "a declaration of divine remission" of the punishment due to sin. But the practice of those who were preaching–and selling–indulgences Luther attacked vehemently: "To think that papal indulgences have such power that they could absolve a man's sin even if he had violated the Mother of God is madness!"

The reaction to Luther's theses was mixed. The bishop of Brandenburg, Luther's bishop, approved of the theses. Bishop Adolf of the nearby diocese of Merseburg was enthusiastic. He urged that Luther's theses "be posted in many places" to warn the poor against the indulgence preachers' "humbuggery and hoaxes." The troop of indulgence preachers were, of course, furious, but Pope Leo X's response was bored indifference to what he termed "a monks' quarrel."

In 1518, Luther attempted to calm the waters by writing to the pope, addressing him as "Holy Father." This "Holy Father," Leo X, had attained his office through the liberal use of money and the influence of his father, Lorenzo "the Magnificent" de' Medici, the *de facto* ruler of Florence. Once elected pope, Leo distinguished himself by his lavish life-style. His favorite activities were hunting and the theater, so, to support his life of pleasure, Leo was willing to traffic in indulgences. He also saw in the indulgence trade a way out of the enormous expense entailed by the building of a new and grander Saint Peter's Basilica in Rome. Leo had no training in theology, and his response to Luther's widely-read treatises was to condemn Luther as a heretic. To theologians all over Europe Leo's decree was a source of profound embarrassment, for Leo's list of Luther's heresies included a condemnation of historically accurate statements, of universally accepted Catholic beliefs, and of positions Luther had never held.

Luther's stance was hardened by the papal excommunication that followed. Reform of the Church, he proclaimed, was impossible unless the pope's temporal power was abolished along with the corrupt practices associated with papal pardons, dispensations, and indulgences. All these and other corrupt practices must be rejected, he thundered, to make possible the moral reform of the people of God.

C. BIBLICAL EDITIONS AND TRANSLATIONS

To assist in this reform, Luther translated the New Testament into German, a translation that was published in 1522. By 1534, his translation of the entire Bible was in print. These were not the first translations of the Bible into German, but Luther's version displayed a literary superiority that led to its widespread acceptance. It also formed the basis of biblical translations into other European tongues, including English.

Erasmus likewise called for a revitalized Church based on a scripturally informed faith. To this end, he issued the critical edition of the New Testament that served as the basis from which vernacular translations, including Luther's, were made. Erasmus was convinced that all Christians should have access to the Bible in their native tongue. The preface to Erasmus' edition contains an affirmation that all men and women, "even Turks and Saracens," should have access to the Scriptures, so that

> the plowman would sing a text of Scripture with his plowing, that the weaver with her singing would drive away the tediousness of her time at the loom. I would have the wayfaring man assuage the weariness of his journey with this practice. To put it briefly, I wish that all Christians be conversant with the Scriptures.

The other side of Erasmus' reform effort was his composition of sometimes hilarious satirical essays on the corruption in the Church. In their vehemence these exceeded Luther's calls for reform. One of Erasmus' works for example, was entitled *Julius Excluded*. This featured a dialogue between Pope Julius II and his predecessor Saint Peter. At his death, Julius begs to be allowed entrance into heaven. Peter, the guardian of the gates, reviews Julius' life and his nearly exclusive concern with political and military matters, and concludes that Julius had not served his people who are the Church. Pope Julius must be left outside heaven.

D. GRACE AND FREE CHOICE

What brought about the break between Luther and Rome was not, as he wrote, "irrelevant points about popery, purgatory, indulgences, and other similar baubles." Addressing Desiderius Erasmus in 1525, Luther continued: "You, and you alone, have seen what is the great hinge upon which the whole matter turned. And therefore you attacked the vital concern at once. For this I thank you with all my heart." These words come at the beginning of Luther's fundamental and monumental work, the very title of which indicates this "hinge": *On the Bondage of the Will*. Luther wrote:

> The human will is, so to speak, a beast. If God sits on it, it wills and goes where God wills it to go. But if Satan sits on the beast, it wills and goes where Satan wills it to go. It is not within the beast's power to choose either rider.

With this Luther denied the possibility of free choice. The human will is not free; it is in bondage. "As for myself," he wrote, "I openly confess that I should not wish to be given free choice–even if that were possible. I should not wish to have control over anything that pertains to my own salvation." Freedom, Luther asserted, is a serious threat to our psychological security. "Even if there were no dangers, conflicts, or devils" to threaten him, Luther wrote, "if I possessed freedom I should be compelled to labor under a continual uncertainty; for whatever I would do there would remain doubts about whether my action pleased God or whether he demanded still more." Luther had learned from many years' experience the extreme psychological stress of a scrupulous conscience, and so he concluded: "By the power of free choice, no one at all could be saved, and all would perish forever."

As a biblical scholar, Erasmus began his treatise *On the Freedom of Choice* with a consideration of what Scripture seems to say about the human will. The Gospel's account of the prodigal son (Luke 15:11-32) Erasmus found especially instructive: "How could the prodigal son have wasted his inheritance if it had not been his to do with as he pleased?" His affirmation of free choice was balanced by an affirmation that this power, this grace, is

God's gift. He added: "We too must remember that all our natural powers are gifts of God."

Erasmus' theology of grace provides a three-step explanation of salvation. God creates human beings and gives them a will that possesses freedom of choice. God motivates humans to choose the good by a gift or grace: the freedom to choose the good or reject it. If the good is chosen, God then provides the power to accomplish that good. Erasmus thought that, through his approach, "free will can be preserved at the same time that we avoid flagrant overconfidence in our own merits and the other dangers seen by Luther." This is the fundamental theological dispute that was to separate Catholic from Protestant.

E. THE CHURCHES SPLIT

Few sixteenth-century people were aware of the theological niceties at the heart of the Protestant-Catholic schism. For most of those who opted for the "reformed" as opposed to the "old" Church, clerical corruption was a major factor in their decision. In the grander political arena of kings and princes, religious reasons often seemed secondary in the choice of church affiliation. Some rulers profited from becoming Protestants through their acquisition of neighboring lands formerly ruled by bishops. Both Catholic and Protestant princes–as well as many city governments–could and did gain control of the Church within their domains. Economics also played a role in defining the denominational map of Germany. Many German princes and the moneyed citizens of many German cities resented the outflow of cash to Rome–not all accepted Protestantism, but they stood up to clerical domination, including that of Rome.

F. THE THIRTY YEARS' WAR

In 1618, the "Defenestration of Prague" took place. Those "defenestrated"–pitched out the window at the Hradčany palace in the Bohemian (now Czech) capital of Prague–were the agents of the new king of Bohemia, the emperor Ferdinand II. The "defenestrators" were the leaders of the Protestant resistance to local Catholic authorities. The rebels had chosen a fellow Protestant, the elector Frederick, as king of Bohemia. In the Bohemian phase (1618-1623) of the ensuing Thirty Years' War, powerful Lutheran states refused to help Frederick, contending that the Bohemian brand of Protestantism was less than Christian. Frederick's reign lasted but a year–hence his sobriquet "the Winter King." He was defeated resoundingly at the battle of White Mountain, not far from his erstwhile capital of Prague.

The next phase of the Thirty Years' War exhibited the same confusing sort of rivalries between Christians. This phase, which lasted from 1624 to 1629, began when the Lutheran King Christian IV of Denmark took up the Protestant cause. Yet, the most powerful Lutheran state in Germany, Brandenberg-Prussia, fought on the side of the Catholic emperor against the Danes. It seems the Lutheran faith of the Danes was not sufficiently orthodox, as it did not adhere fully to Luther's teaching on the Eucharist. It is just barely possible that Danish ambitions to acquire territories in northern Germany clashed with the expansionist policies of Brandenberg.

On the Catholic side there were two armies in the field. One, under the command of Count Tilly, defeated the Danes in 1626. Tilly served not the emperor but the Catholic League that had been formed by a party of German Catholic princes to oppose the political ambitions of the Catholic emperor. The other, the emperor's army, served under the leadership of a colorful mercenary, Count Albert Wallenstein. At the point of seeming victory over the Protestant army, Emperor Ferdinand dismissed Wallenstein, who had urged a peace settlement that ignored denominational differences. Once more religion and politics were enmeshed in confusing and often contradictory ways.

On July 6, 1630, King Gustavus II Adolphus of Sweden marched into Germany to rescue the Protestant cause. The Protestant princes of Germany refused to accept his leadership, however, until forced to do so by Gustavus Adolphus. Thus reinforced, the Swedes beat Tilly in 1631. They overcame Wallenstein as well, in 1632, but Gustavus Adolphus lost his life in the battle, and two years later the imperial army defeated the Swedes.

The chief diplomatic and financial supporter of Sweden had been His Eminence Cardinal Armand Jean de Plessis de Richelieu, the chief minister and real power in King Louis XIII's Catholic France. With the Swedish defeat, Richelieu decided that France must enter the war–on the Protestant side. The French phase of the Thirty Years' War (1635-1648) saw the Swedes defeating the imperial forces and the French victorious over their Catholic co-religionists, the Spanish allies of the emperor. Religion, in the end, was ignored, and political power proved to be the only interest of the Roman Cardinal Richelieu.

The Peace of Westphalia that followed showed the true colors of France and all the other states. The Holy Roman Empire of the German Nation, as the Empire was now known, was virtually destroyed–which had been the French goal all along. The mighty medieval Empire was reduced to three hundred independent states–by 1800, over 1,200–most of them postage-stamp-sized principalities ready to be licked by France. France and Sweden took large chunks of German territory, and still more church lands were taken over by secular states. The pope's protests were ignored. In fact, he was not even invited to take part in the deliberations. To none of the international treaty conferences that concluded the wars of the seventeenth and eighteenth centuries was a pope invited. Everywhere he was treated as a foreign potentate–by Catholic as well as Protestant states. The primary goal of the rulers of those states was terrestrial power, not celestial bliss, and they treated the churches in their realms as state departments for religion. The popes, who had once served as the moral arbiters of Europe, had been reduced to being a fourth-rate power. This reduced status exactly mirrored the popes' almost exclusive concern with their central Italian principality.

In Germany, the medieval roles of Church and State had disappeared. A unified Empire was nothing but a memory. The effect of the Thirty Years' War on the German people was devastating. The war reduced the population by thirty-five to forty percent, from 18 million to 12 million by some accounts, from 21 million to about 16 million according to others. The Swedish Royal Archives yield the information that that nation's armies alone destroyed 1,976 castles, 1,629 towns, and 2,041 villages. By the Peace of Westphalia of 1648, medieval Germany had ceased to exist.

Genealogical Tables

THE SAXON AND SALIAN KINGS OF GERMANY

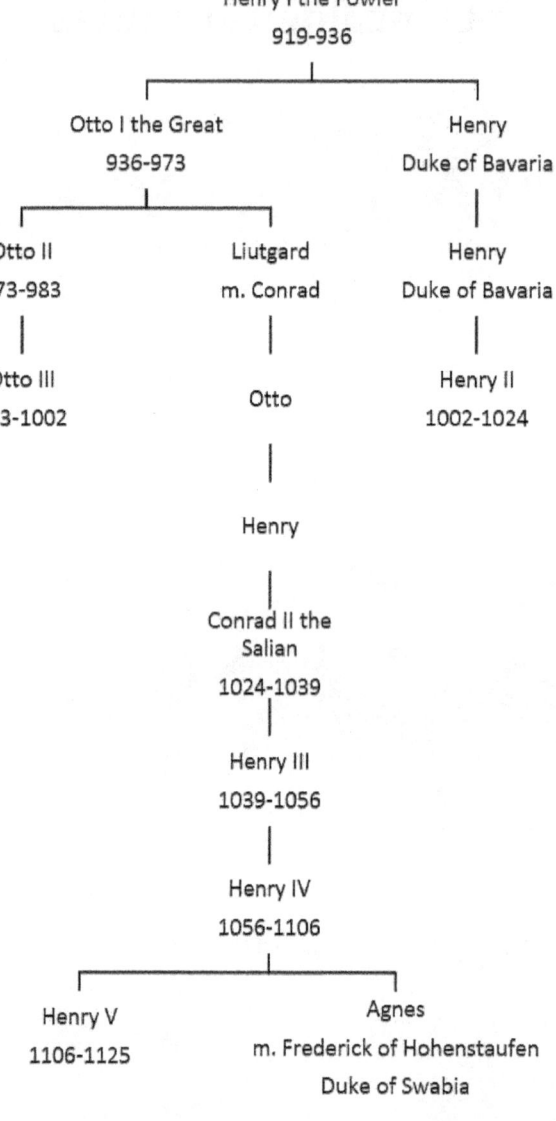

THE HOHENSTAUFEN AND THEIR RIVALS

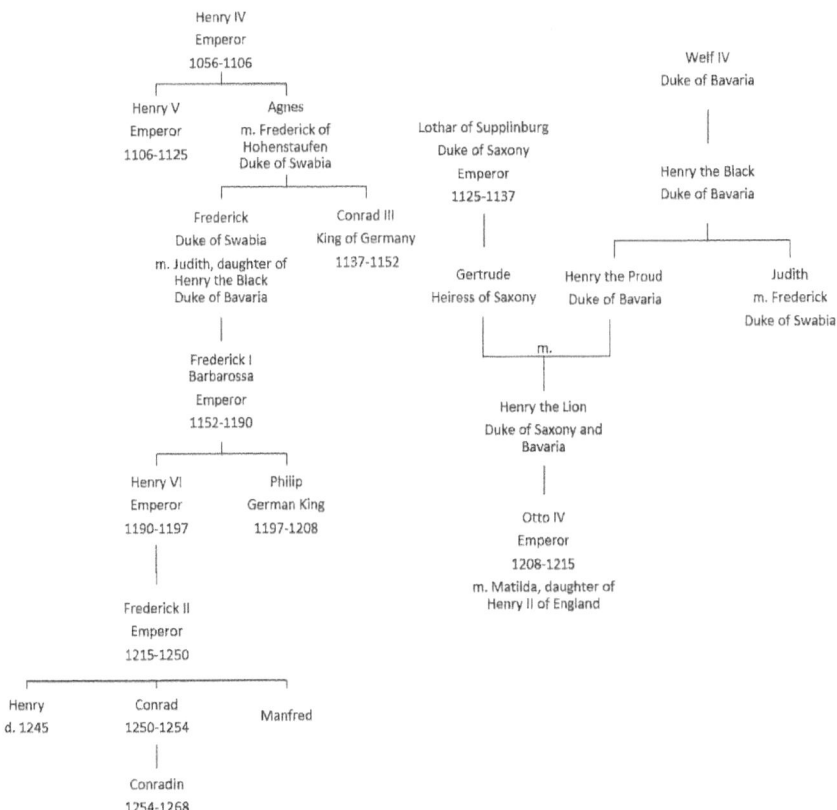

THE LUXEMBURG, HAPSBURG, AND WITTELSBACH RULERS

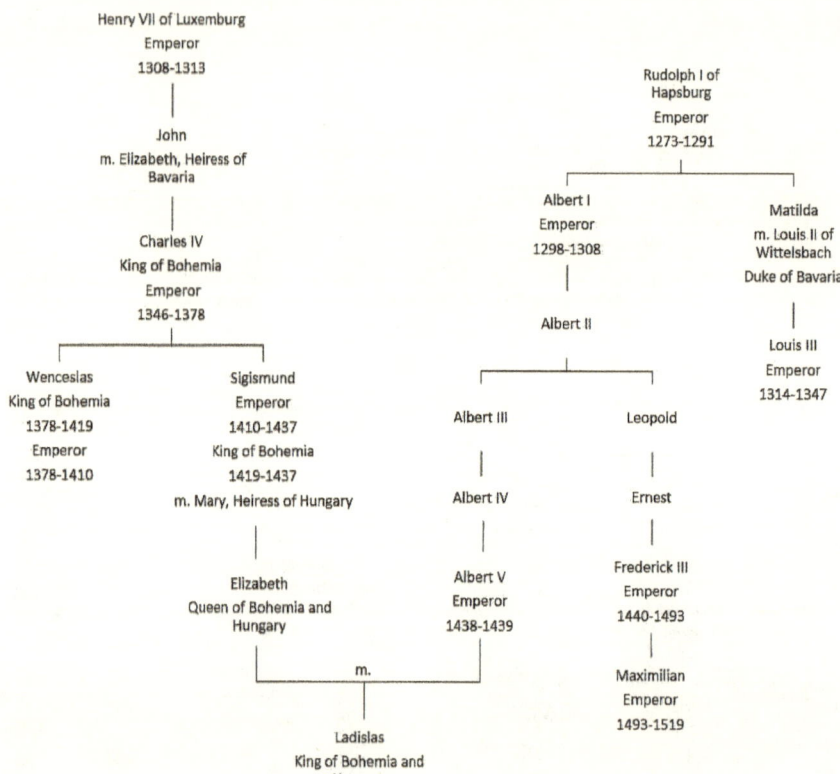

Index I: Most Important Persons

Adelbert, bishop of Prague, 33
Adelbert, bishop of Hamburg, then archbishop of Hamburg-Bremen, 57, 60, 65
Adolf of Nassau, king and emperor elect, 128
Aeneus Silvius Piccolomini, 134
Agnes of Poitiers, empress, 57, 64–65
Alberic II of Spoleto, 16
Albert the Great, 147–149, 157
Albrecht of Habsburg, king and emperor, 128–129
Albrecht II of Habsburg, duke of Austria, king of Hungary, king of the Romans, and emperor elect, 133–134
Alexander III, pope, 104–105, 106
Anacletus II, antipope, 82–83
Anselm of Havelberg, 89–91
Aquinas, Thomas. *See* Thomas Aquinas
Arnulf, duke and emperor, 7
Augustine of Hippo, 2, 3, 19, 89, 162

Baldwin of Luxemburg, archbishop of Mainz, 168
Beatrice of Nazareth, 152–153
Beatrix of Burgundy, queen and empress, 99, 101, 105, 114, 119
Benedict IX, pope, 60

Bernard of Clairvaux, abbot, 2, 82–83, 83–84, 86–87, 89, 92, 93, 98, 110, 144, 154
Boleslav the Bold, king of Poland, 33
Boleslav I Chobry, duke of Poland, 43, 50
Boniface VIII, pope, 129, 165, 166
Bratislav, duke of Bohemia, 58
Bruno, archbishop of Cologne, 14, 17–18, 20
Bruno, bishop of Toul. *See* Leo IX, pope
Bruno of Carinthia. *See* Gregory V, pope

Callixtus II, pope, 73, 77, 78
Celestine III, pope, 119, 121, 122
Celestine V, pope, 165
Charlemagne. *See* Charles the Great, king and emperor
Charles the Great, king and emperor, 1–4, 6, 7, 8, 9–10, 27, 31, 32, 36, 46, 52, 55, 72, 104, 112, 139
Charles of Anjou, king of Sicily, 125, 127
Charles IV of Moravia, king and emperor, 130–131, 131–132, 133
Chrétien de Troyes, 115
Clement II, pope, 60, 61
Clement VI, pope, 130, 131, 143
Clement V, pope, 166
Clement VI of Avignon, pope, 171
Clement VII, pope, 132, 166

191

Conrad, duke of Franconia, king and emperor, 7–9
Conrad II, king and emperor, 45–48, 48–53, 55, 56, 61, 64
Conrad III of Hohenstaufen, king and emperor, 79, 80, 82, 83–84, 85–86, 93, 97
Conrad, duke of Zähringen, 80, 82
Constance of Sicily, queen and empress, 107, 119, 120, 122

Dominic Guzmán, 146–147

Eckhart. *See* Meister Eckhart
Einhard, 1–3
Eleanor of Aquitaine, queen of England, 91
Erasmus, Desiderius, 179, 180, 181, 182–184
Ernst, duke of Swabia, 47, 48
Eskil, archbishop of Lund, 102
Eugenius III, pope, 44, 81, 84, 85, 86, 90, 92, 93, 95, 96, 98, 101

Ferdinand II, king of Bohemia, 183, 184
Frederick of Hohenzollern, burgrave of Nuremberg, then margrave of Brandenburg, 133
Frederick I Barbarossa, king and emperor, 92, 93, 94, 95, 97–98, 98–99, 101–105, 106–109, 111, 112, 113, 114, 119, 120
Frederick II, king and emperor, king of Sicily, 121, 122, 123–124, 127, 128, 130
Frederick III, king and emperor, 134

Gaetani, Benedetto. *See* Boniface VIII, pope
Gelasius II, pope, 76, 77
Gerard, archbishop of Florence. *See* Nicholas II, pope
Gerbert of Aurillac. *See* Sylvester II, pope
Gert Groote, 163, 164
Gertrud, abbess of Helfta, 154
Gertrud the Great, 155–156
Godfrey the Bearded, duke of Lotharingia, 148, 149
Gregory I, the Great, pope, 34
Gregory V, pope, 31, 32, 34

Gregory VII, pope, 66–67, 67–68, 69–70, 73, 74
Gustavus II Adolphus, king of Sweden, 184
Guy, archbishop of Vienne. *See* Callixtus II, pope

Hadrian IV, pope, 101–102, 104
Hartmann von Aue, poet, 115, 116
Hedwig of Brabant, 151–152
Henry I, duke of Saxony and king, 9, 17, 37
Henry II, king and emperor, 37, 38, 39–41, 42–44, 45, 49, 50, 53, 55, 58, 61
Henry III, king and emperor, 46, 49, 52, 53, 55, 56–57, 58, 59, 60–61, 63, 65
Henry IV, king and emperor, 64–65, 66–68, 68–69, 71, 73, 74, 81, 89, 93
Henry V, king and emperor, 69, 71–73, 74, 76–77, 79, 81, 93
Henry VI, king and emperor; king of Sicily, 119–121, 122, 123, 168
Henry VII of Luxemburg, king and emperor, 129
Henry II, king of England, 92, 104, 108, 114
Henry III, king of England, 127
Henry Jasomirgott, duke of Austria, 100
Henry the Lion, duke of Saxony and Bavaria, 99, 100, 107–108, 109, 111, 114, 122
Henry the Quarrelsome, duke of Bavaria, 27, 31, 37
Henry Suso, 160–162
Hildebrand, monk. *See* Gregory VII, pope
Hildegard of Bingen, 91, 92–93
Hrotswitha of Gandersheim, 19–20
Hugh, abbot of Cluny, 60, 64
Hugh, monk of Fleury, 74
Hus, John, 133, 167, 174

Innocent III, pope, 121–122, 122–123, 165
Ivo of Chartres, 76

Jesus Christ, 27, 33, 35, 37, 41, 46, 56, 67, 68, 75, 98, 115, 116, 121, 150, 151, 152, 154, 155, 163, 164, 170–171, 174
John, bishop of Sabina. *See* Sylvester III, pope

Index I: Most Important Persons

John XII, pope, 15, 16–17
John XXII, pope, 130, 159, 166
John Comnenus, Eastern Emperor, 85
John Hus. *See* Hus, John
John, Meister Eckhart. *See* Meister Eckhart
John Ruusbroec. *See* Ruusbroec, John
John Tauler. *See* Tauler, John
Jordanus of Saxony, 146–147
Julius II, pope, 135, 182
Justinian, ancient Roman emperor, 51, 103, 111

Karl der Grosse. *See* Charles the Great, king and emperor
Knut, king of England and Denmark, 53

Ladislaus, king of Hungary and Bohemia, 134
Leo VIII, pope, 17
Leo IX, pope, 57, 61
Liudprand of Cremona, bishop, 30
Liutgard of Arwières, 150–151, 152, 155
Lothar of Supplinberg, duke of Saxony, king and emperor, 79–80, 82–83, 90
Lotario dei Conti. *See* Innocent III, pope
Louis of Bavaria, king and emperor, 129–130, 159, 166
Louis the Pious, emperor, 3, 72
Louis IV, king of France, 10
Louis VII, king of France, 84, 104
Louis XII, king of France, 135
Luther, Martin, 2, 179, 180–183, 184

Manegold of Lautenbach, 75, 76
Martin V, pope, 133, 167
Mary, mother of Jesus, 39, 151, 170, 171, 176
Mary of Burgandy, queen, 134
Mathilda, countess of Tuscany, 68, 71, 106
Maximilian, king and emperor elect, 134–135
Mechthild of Hackeborn, 154–155
Mechthild of Magdeburg, 153–154
Medici, Lorenzo d', 98
Meister Eckhart, 157–159, 160

Nicolas II, pope, 63, 64
Nicholas of Cusa, 173–178
Norbert of Xanten, 89, 90

Otto I, king and emperor, 9, 10–11, 12–13, 14–16, 17, 18, 19, 20–21, 24, 26, 29, 31, 33, 78, 80
Otto II, king and emperor, 26–29, 30, 31, 32
Otto III, king and emperor, 28, 31–35, 36, 37, 53
Otto of Braunschweig, king and emperor, 122, 123
Otto of Freising, bishop, 93–96, 97, 111, 112

Paschal II, pope, 69, 71–73, 74, 76
Paschal III, antipope, 104, 105
Paul, apostle, 77, 87, 101, 110, 170
Peter, apostle, 33, 34, 40, 59, 60, 67, 68, 74, 77, 85, 101, 106, 171, 177
Peter Damian, hermit, 61
Peter Lombard, 149, 157, 161
Philip of Swabia, king of the Romans, 122, 123
Philip IV the Fair, king of France, 128, 166
Pius II, pope. *See* Aeneus Silvius Piccolomini

Rahewin, historian, 102, 103, 112
Reginald of Dassel, archbishop of Cologne, 102, 104
Richard I Lionheart, king of England, 108, 119–120, 122
Richelieu, Armand Jean de, cardinal, 184
Robert Guiscard, king of Sicily, 64, 69
Roger II, king of Sicily, 83, 85, 100, 107
Rolando Bandenelli. *See* Alexander III, pope
Rudolf of Habichsburg (Habsburg), king and emperor elect, 127–128, 137, 148
Rudolf, king of Burgundy, 42, 49, 53
Rupert, elector Palatine, king and emperor elect, 132, 133
Rupert of Deutz, 90
Ruusbroec, John, 162–163

Saladin, king of Saracens, 108
Sigismund, margrave of Brandenburg, king and emperor elect, 132, 133, 167
Sigebert of Gembloux, 18
Stephen, king of Hungary, 33
Suso, Henry. *See* Henry Suso

Sylvester II, pope, 29, 32, 34
Sylvester III, pope, 60

Tancred of Lerra, king of Sicily, 119–120
Tauler, John, 159–160, 162
Theophano, empress, 27, 28, 30, 31, 35
Thietmar of Merseburg, 21, 28, 42
Thomas Aquinas, 148, 157, 161
Thomas Becket, archbishop of Canterbury, 92
Thomas of Cantimpré, 149, 151
Thomas Hemerken of Kempen (Thomas à Kempis), 164
Tilly, count, 184

Ulrich of Strassburg, 169

Wajk, king of Hungary. *See* Stephen, king of Hungary
Wallenstein, Albert, count, 184
Walther von der Vogelweide, 114
Welf, duke of Bavaria and Saxony, 83, 84, 85
Wenceslaus, duke of Bohemia, 10
Wenzel, king and emperor, 132, 133
Wernher the Gardiner, 116, 117
Widukind of Corvey, 9, 10, 11, 20–21
William I, king of Sicily, 101, 105
William II, king of Sicily, 107, 119
Wipo, historian, 45, 46, 47, 49, 51, 52–53
Wolfram von Eschenbach, 115

Index II:
Lands, Peoples, and Their Languages

Africa, African(s), 5, 28, 120, 145
Alsace, Alsatian(s), 8, 15, 26, 111, 127
Arab(s), Arabic, 27, 28, 30, 148
Asia, Asian(s), 5, 85, 109, 143, 145
Austria, Austrian(s), 14, 27, 58, 93, 100, 128, 133–134, 135, 137

Bavaria, Bavarian(s), 7, 8, 9, 11, 12, 16, 26, 27, 28, 37, 43, 46, 47, 55, 58, 65, 79, 83, 84, 85, 93, 98, 100, 107, 108, 109, 136, 139
Bohemia, Bohemian(s), 9, 10, 11, 33, 43, 49, 55, 58, 128, 129, 130, 131, 132, 133, 134, 136, 143, 157, 167, 183
Brandenburg, 28, 131, 132, 133, 136, 180
Braunschweig, 108, 111, 122
Bulgaria, Bulgarian(s), 20, 108
Burgundy, Burgundian(s), 16, 38, 42, 43, 47, 49–50, 51, 52, 53, 55, 57, 59, 60, 65, 73, 77, 78, 99, 101, 114, 120, 128, 134
Byzantium, Byzantine(s), 16, 20, 27, 28, 30, 35, 44, 85, 100, 105, 107, 109, 120, 175

Carinthia, 34, 47, 58, 65, 128

Denmark, Dane(s), 5, 9, 20, 27, 53, 57, 85, 102, 141, 146, 184

Eastern Roman Empire. *See* Byzantium, Byzantine(s)
England, English, 5, 29, 38, 40, 53, 85, 86, 127, 137, 167, 180, 181

Flanders, Flemish, 42, 86, 152
France, French, 1, 5, 6, 7, 8, 10, 11, 13, 14, 16, 18, 26, 32, 38, 40, 42, 44, 61, 74, 76, 85, 86, 89, 104, 114–115, 116, 125, 127, 128, 129, 130, 132, 135, 137, 143, 146, 150, 152, 163, 165, 166, 167, 184
Franconia, Franconian(s), 7, 8, 9, 11, 39, 40, 43, 46, 84, 85, 95, 143
Frankland, Frank(s), Frankish, 1, 8, 9, 10, 11, 26, 46, 139
Frisia, Frisian(s), 8, 53, 57, 86

Greek(s), 2, 16, 18, 28, 31, 35, 44, 90, 101, 109, 111, 148, 149, 175, 176

Habsburg, Habsburger, 127, 128, 129, 133, 134, 136, 137
Holland, 80, 179
Holy Land, 3, 81, 84, 87, 108, 110, 119, 120, 136
Hungary, Hungarian(s), 11, 20, 33, 34, 37, 58, 85, 108, 133, 134

Italy, Italian(s), 1, 5, 6, 13, 14, 15, 16–17, 20, 27, 28, 31, 32, 34, 35, 39, 43–44, 49, 50–51, 52, 53, 56, 59, 60, 61, 64, 68, 71, 73, 76, 77, 78, 83, 86, 97, 100, 101, 102–103, 105, 106, 107, 109, 111, 116, 119, 120, 122, 123, 125, 129, 131, 132, 135, 143, 147, 165, 166, 167, 173, 175, 177, 180, 185

Jew(s), Jewish, 28, 49, 87, 109, 110–111, 114, 143, 144

Latin, 2, 18, 19, 28, 31, 35, 38, 46, 48, 89, 91, 93, 94, 111, 113, 115, 121, 131, 139, 142, 145, 151, 152, 154, 155, 158, 161, 168, 169, 173, 175, 179, 180
Lombardy, Lombard(s), 3, 43, 51, 57, 100, 102, 104, 105, 106, 107
Lotharingia, Lotharingian(s), 8, 9, 10, 12, 15, 18, 26, 27, 30, 38, 42, 43, 46, 47, 52, 55, 57, 65, 134
Luxemburg, Luxemburger(s), 129, 130, 132, 134, 168, 190

Magyar(s), 5, 7, 8, 9, 11, 20. *See also* Hungary, Hungarian(s)

Netherlands, 1, 134, 141, 157, 163
Norman(s), 64, 69, 71, 83, 85, 100, 101, 105, 120
Northmen. *See* Vikings
Norway, 5, 81, 105, 141

Papal States. *See* States of the Church
Poland, Pole(s), Polish, 14, 20, 33, 38, 43, 50, 55, 58, 131, 136
Prussia, Prussian, 33, 136

Rhineland, Rhenish, 87, 89, 91, 127, 131, 159
Rus, Russia, 5, 15, 20, 141, 142

Saracen(s), 5, 6, 16, 20, 28, 108, 109, 181
Saxony, Saxon(s), 4, 7, 8, 9, 10, 11, 13, 15, 26, 28, 43, 46, 50, 55, 56, 65, 68, 71, 73, 79, 83, 98, 99, 100, 107, 108, 109, 133, 136, 139, 157, 188
Sicily, 5, 16, 27, 28, 64, 83, 85, 100, 101, 105, 106, 119–120, 121, 122, 123, 124, 125, 127, 165
Slav, Slavic, 15, 20, 28, 29, 33, 39, 43, 50, 55, 80, 86, 100, 136
Spain, Spanish, 5, 85, 86, 105, 125, 135, 143, 146, 184
States of the Church, 16, 17, 165
Swabia, Swabian(s), 7, 8, 9, 11, 15, 16, 26, 27, 28, 43, 46, 47, 48, 55, 58, 65, 79, 80, 83, 85, 95, 98, 99, 108, 109, 139
Sweden, Swedish, Swede(s), 5, 141, 184–185
Switzerland, Swiss, 127, 136, 137, 174

Thuringia, Thuringian(s), 7, 8, 9, 71, 79, 83, 157
Turkey, Turk(s), 83, 85, 133, 134, 135, 175, 177, 181
Tuscany, Tuscan, 44, 65, 68, 106, 107, 125
Tyrol, Tyrolean, 101, 176

Viking(s), 5, 6, 7

Wends, Wendish, 10, 86
Wittelsbach(s), 108, 166

Index III: Major Cities and Towns

Aachen, 9, 26, 27, 31, 32, 33, 36, 42, 46, 55, 98, 104, 119, 129, 171
Augsburg, 11, 43, 47, 55
Ancona, 105, 177, 178
Avignon, 129, 130, 132, 158, 159, 166–167, 171

Bamberg, 39, 40, 44, 47, 60
Basel, 174, 175, 180
Besançon, 59, 99, 100, 101, 102, 104
Bologna, 111, 121, 122, 129
Bremen, 29, 61
Brixen, 61, 84, 176–177
Byzantium. *See* Constantinople

Cambrai, 56, 179, 180
Cologne, 14, 18, 31, 65, 73, 86, 87, 90, 96, 98, 102, 104, 107, 108, 110, 122, 127, 128, 129, 131, 141, 144, 147, 148, 149, 157, 158, 159, 161, 171, 173
Constance, 58, 100, 101, 106, 107, 133, 160, 161, 167, 174
Constantinople, 27, 30, 61, 85, 90, 109, 120, 175
Cremona, 30, 104

Erfurt, 157, 179

Florence, 44, 61, 106, 129, 175, 181

Frankfurt, 40, 98, 128, 131, 176
Freiburg, 80, 147, 180
Freising, 46, 55, 93

Goslar, 56, 58, 64, 107

Hamburg, 28, 29
Havelberg, 28, 89

Jerusalem, 86, 108, 123, 136

Kiev, 5, 15, 50

Magdeburg, 15, 20, 29, 49, 153
Mainz, 6, 7, 9, 14, 39, 43, 45, 46, 61, 68, 69, 73, 79, 83, 85, 108, 129, 131, 133, 168
Milan, 50, 51, 94, 100, 101, 103, 104, 105, 107, 119, 132, 135

Nuremberg, 85, 133

Paris, 10, 27, 74, 93, 121, 122, 147–148, 157, 159, 168, 180
Pavia, 16, 28, 43, 53, 60
Pisa, 111, 120, 129, 167
Prague, 33, 132, 183

Ravenna, 29, 31, 32

Rheims, 10, 29, 32, 40, 61
Rome, 3, 8, 16, 17, 27, 28, 32, 34, 35, 36, 40, 43, 53, 59, 60–61, 63–64, 66, 68, 69, 71, 72, 74, 77, 81, 82–83, 85, 86, 90, 97, 98, 100, 101, 102, 105, 119, 121, 122, 125, 129, 130, 131, 132, 134, 166, 167, 175, 176–177, 181, 182, 183
Roncaglia, 99, 102, 103, 104, 111

Salerno, 69, 116
Speyer, 53, 55, 84
Sutri, 60

Trier, 7, 8, 14, 18, 42, 83, 129, 131, 174

Utrecht, 17, 53, 57

Venice, 104, 106, 135, 136
Vienna, 85, 134
Vienne, 59

Wittemberg, 179, 180
Worms, 77, 78, 81, 99, 110, 111

Xanten, 89

www.ingramcontent.com/pod-product-compliance
Lightning Source LLC
Chambersburg PA
CBHW022012300426
44117CB00005B/153